Lies That Bind

Lies That Bind

Chinese Truth, Other Truths

Susan D. Blum

ROWMAN & LITTLEFIELD PUBLISHERS, INC.
Lanham • Boulder • New York • Toronto • Plymouth, UK

ROWMAN & LITTLEFIELD PUBLISHERS, INC.

Published in the United States of America
by Rowman & Littlefield Publishers, Inc.
A wholly owned subsidiary of The Rowman & Littlefield Publishing Group, Inc.
4501 Forbes Boulevard, Suite 200, Lanham, Maryland 20706
www.rowmanlittlefield.com

Estover Road, Plymouth PL6 7PY, United Kingdom

British Library Cataloguing in Publication Information Available

Library of Congress Cataloging-in-Publication Data
Blum, Susan Debra.
 Lies that bind : Chinese truth, other truths / Susan D. Blum.
    p. cm.
 Includes bibliographical references and index.
 ISBN-13: 978-0-7425-5404-7 (cloth : alk. paper)
 ISBN-10: 0-7425-5404-X (cloth : alk. paper)
 ISBN-13: 978-0-7425-5405-4 (pbk. : alk. paper)
 ISBN-10: 0-7425-5405-8 (pbk. : alk. paper)
 1. Truthfulness and falsehood—China. 2. Social values—China. I. Title.
 BJ1421.A45B58 2007
 177'.30951—dc22

                                                                    2006018473

Printed in the United States of America

∞™ The paper used in this publication meets the minimum requirements of
American National Standard for Information Sciences—Permanence of Paper for
Printed Library Materials, ANSI/NISO Z39.48-1992.

For Hannah and Elena

Truly

Contents

Part IV: Humanity and Language

Preface

Tell all the Truth but tell it slant—
Success in Circuit lies
Too bright for our infirm Delight
The Truth's superb surprise

As Lightning to the Children eased
With explanation kind
The Truth must dazzle gradually
Or every man be blind—

—Emily Dickinson 1993

Let me tell you a story. Once upon a time there was a society where people always told the truth. Whatever they thought, they said. People went around saying things like "Gee your hair looks silly like that" or "This food is terrible. I wish I hadn't agreed to come over for dinner." One day a devil came and whispered into a person's ear. Let's call this person Face Giver. Face Giver recoiled but the devil persevered. The next day, Face Giver was invited to her friend Favor Asker's house. Favor Asker said, "I would like you to come over for tea so that you will owe me something and then next month you'll be able to help me carry books when I move." Face Giver said, "I'd be happy to help you carry books anyway; you don't have to invite me first." Favor Asker: "Do you really mean that? You always hated carrying books before. Thanks!"

Face Giver paused. She debated and debated and finally said, "It works! I met the devil who told me I could make people happy by saying things they want to hear, even if I didn't mean them. I didn't believe the devil, but his words had wisdom. Just now I said I was happy to carry books even though you knew I wasn't—but because I said it, you believed me and were happy. If people did this all the time, imagine what a friendly world we'd have!"

Imagine, indeed.

In this book I will show some of the ways this devil's bargain functions in everyday life in contemporary China and elsewhere. I will argue that a richly developed schema of anticipating hearers' reactions contributes to an abundance of apparent violations of truth and sincerity in speaking. These are notions that touch on profoundest morality. At first it may seem that in China people place weight on relationships and consequences, while in the U.S. people place weight on truth. But we also recognize ourselves in China, and recognize all humankind in each society, as each struggles to find a balance between purity and truth—an ideal shared in some form by all societies—and the many ways language can be manipulated.

I am naïve. I never expect that people will be plotting moves three steps in advance; I'm always blindsided when colleagues show up at department meetings and say that they have gone door to door to lobby for their position. I tend to believe praise and to give it only when I mean it. I'm completely persuaded that other-directed attention is motivated by genuine interest.

I'm also blunt—sometimes. One of my worst traits is that I blurt out what I think without considering how people will react. "No, it won't work that way because the administration has shown lack of support for the project in the past." "No, I don't know who Cosmo is on *Seinfeld*; I never watch TV."

Add to that that I am very sensitive to people's feelings and reactions (but don't think it's honest to prepare in advance), and you have a person who is somewhat at odds with the society around her, at least in terms of interactional style. This lays the ground perfectly for an intellectually inclined person on the margins of society to become an anthropologist.

I was drawn to the study of other cultures and of anthropology because it seemed to show the arbitrariness of my own cultural norms and practices. If in the United States families are somewhat dispersed and remote, in China and Russia families are everything. If in the United States the focus on material acquisition is ubiquitous, among the !Kung hunter gatherers of southern Africa, accumulation is abhorred because it hinders free movement. If in the United States people believe that every individual makes choices in utter liberty—despite clear evidence of great conformity—in Japan there is in some contexts a premium placed on fitting in with the group. Ultimately my study focused on China, on its culture and language and ethnicity and psychology and nationalism, and in many domains I was fascinated by the contrasts with my own society. At the same time, I began to learn how thoroughly American my attitudes are, despite my youthful fancy that I was unbounded by cultural norms and was a free-floating child of the universe.

As an academic, I do not apologize for interest in matters unconnected to a researcher's own life or to practicalities. I believe that there is a place for the deep study and comprehension of human practices. One of life's greatest pleasures is in contemplating initially outlandish, implausible, odd, and disturbing ideas. Using one's brain to think hard is excellent exercise.

But sometimes the connection of the intellectual and the personal is so obvious that it must be explored. This book does just that.

My intellectual interest in China was accompanied by my personal reactions to experiences I had while doing research in China. As a blunt, naïve person, I was frankly shocked by some of what I experienced. Presumably people more savvy than I, including others from the United States, would not be so surprised. First I reacted as anyone would, without examining reasons or consequences, by automatically judging the people around me according to my own values. But as my anthropological education proceeded, I began to see that there were important issues to understand. These issues were moral, ethical, philosophical, practical, political, religious, psychological, national, historical, and cultural. My motive for understanding was part curiosity, part moral imperative: I had to find out how people in China—and ultimately elsewhere as well—came to interactions with expectations about honesty, bluntness, sincerity, self-protection, and so forth. This question became quite urgent. I felt I had to delve deeply into Chinese society—present and past—to assess what many Chinese believe to be a crisis of public life and also to understand the nature of language in general. How is it that we lie? What do we use language for? How do mutual understandings get worked out in the course of interaction?

I wanted to start with a thorough, concrete case and move from there wherever the inquiry led, finally sharing my findings with a public that is genuinely concerned about matters of interpersonal trust and social lubrication. This material is too fascinating to keep within the sphere of academic readership. Of course it is built on an academic foundation, and there are details that help construct the picture I'm painting of linguistic resources used for a variety of purposes, but I have not assumed that my readers are experts on China or on anthropology. I explain everything that needs to be under-stood to get the gist of the argument.

In a nutshell, the argument is this: In some ways, one could observe a tendency for deception in public interactions in China, where people in the United States would expect truthfulness. (Note that I try not to say "Chinese culture is X and U.S. culture is Y." These are merely prevalent tendencies. See Wierzbicka 2003, xiii–xviii.) In private, people may also be calculating about how they choose to use speech. These tendencies are evaluated morally within Chinese society using values different from those that Americans might use. (Chinese tend to emphasize the consequences of the speech, Americans the absolute truthfulness.) Chinese tend to consider language a kind of action like other action, and Americans view language/speech as separate from other action. There are some long-standing values in Chinese history that lead to this tendency, such as the awareness of the effects of speech, while other factors are more recent and political, such as the government's control over expression (itself an outgrowth of earlier factors).

But it is essential to note that not only Chinese society has such tendencies. As I suggested above, many people in the United States also excel in manipulation of language, but there is a simultaneous moral absolutism opposed to lying in any form. Other societies similarly struggle to control the possibilities of lying but celebrate cleverness, which might lead to manipulation of apparent truth. Finally, I conclude that deception and lying are part and parcel of what it is to be a human being with language. Truth telling is in some ways ideal but in other ways impossible.

So what does naïve Susan do with this conclusion? In some ways I struggle even more than I used to, because I understand even more about the potential for manipulative speech, but I am even clearer about my own impulses toward misplaced honesty. I see the possibilities for deceit daily; I am less trusting of people's praise. But I am even more fascinated, because all this is made possible by our wily, deft, subtle nature as social beings with language. Every day brings something to notice—to deplore, to celebrate—because every time humans interact they choose how to present themselves to others. In this dilemma, Chinese, Americans, and all the rest of humankind share the pleasures of spinning tales, heaping flattery, protecting themselves from danger, and telling the simple truth. We are all the same in some ways, but in the proportion of our solutions, we differ importantly.

I feel about China as I do about the United States and about my family: love, deep familiarity, and frustration. The flaws jump out at me because my hopes are so high. But I write as an American. Many Chinese would prefer to keep China's flaws private; my American, academic self believes in frankly airing them. But I also air the flaws of the United States and in fact see the American tendency to tout truthfulness while society is pervaded by lying as greatly hypocritical and self-deluded.

So this book is about China, but only partly. It is thoroughly anthropological; the subject touches everything about what it is to be human, past and present, here and there. Our species is flawed and fascinating—roses and thorns—with different fragrances grown in different soils. To see the culture within which the roses grow adds dimension to our self-understanding. Quest for self-knowledge is a primary human trait.

I have lived with the ideas for this book since my first eye-opening stay in China as an English teacher at the Jiangsu Educational Institute in Nanjing in 1982. I am grateful to numerous institutions and individuals for direct and indirect support, and sometimes even for obstacles through which I learned.

Research for my first book, carried out during the 1990–91 academic year, was supported by the Committee on Scholarly Communication with the People's Republic of China, and has provided the foundation for all my subsequent work, including the present book. My host institution in China was Yunnan University, Kunming, where I was assisted by Professor Li Zhaotong and Professor Lin Chaomin of the departments of Chinese and history, respectively. *Lies that Bind* received support from a number of institutions and foundations: The University of Pennsylvania provided a grant, though I was unable to take advantage of it. A small grant from the American Philosophical Society allowed me to travel to China for a month during 1996–97. Writing time was provided by a summer stipend from the College of Liberal Arts and Sciences, University of Colorado at Denver, and by a Junior Faculty Development Grant, University of Colorado at Denver. The University of Colorado at Denver provided summer funding for further involvement in the project, and just prior to my move to Notre Dame awarded me funds to conduct another month of research. Notre Dame graciously took up this support.

At an international conference on Rusing and Its Reasons (La Ruse et ses raisons) held in March 2001 in Louvain, Belgium, I was enriched by the opportunity to present my latest thoughts on this topic to a broad group of scholars. My travel to Louvain was generously supported by the Laboratoire d'Anthropologie Prospective at the Catholic University of Louvain, under the direction of Professors P-J Laurent and Olivier Servais, and by the Institute for Scholarship in the Liberal Arts at Notre Dame, under the direction of Julia Douthwaite; Beth Bland took care of details. ISLA also provided support for the book cover.

All in all, I lived with these questions for around a decade, finally bringing the book to the light of day thanks to a perfectly timed grant from the National Endowment for the Humanities, which permitted me to spend the 2002–2003 academic year immersed in these thoughts. Ken Garcia, Alicia Knoedler, and Cindy Bergeman of the Institute for Scholarship in the Liberal Arts at Notre Dame helped with the grant writing and other aspects of scholarly production. Mark Roche, dean of the College of Arts and Letters, and Greg Sterling, associate dean, provided a supportive intellectual atmosphere. Patrick Gaffney, Jim McKenna, and Mark Schurr steered the Department of Anthropology and cheered the leaves of colleagues. Diane Pribbernow, Kathy Johndrow, and Suzette Vandewalle kept everything flowing, especially printers and paperwork. The Center for Asian Studies at Notre Dame provided a hospitable context in which to think about these issues.

I have had the fortune of presenting aspects of this work to an assortment of audiences over the past decade or so. Various incarnations, becoming ever more complicated, have been presented to the Department of Asian Studies, University of Texas at Austin; the Department of East Asian Studies, University of Pennsylvania; the Teaching English to Speakers of East Asian Languages (TESEAL) seminar (departments of Linguistics and East Asian Languages and Literatures) at the University of Colorado at Boulder; the Department of Anthropology, University of Colorado at Denver; and the Department of Anthropology, University of Notre Dame.

I have benefited from conversations (some of them electronic) with and help from Fran Benson, Martin Bloomer, Anne Bower, Don Brenneis, Bruce Brooks, Penelope Brown, Tim Cheek, Danny Chen, Meredith Chesson, Roberto DaMatta, Norma Diamond, Greg Downey, Alessandro Duranti, Lizzie Fagen, Ted Fox, Rabbi Michael Friedland, Patrick Gaffney, Leon Liangyan Ge, Teresa Ghilarducci, Howard Goldblatt, Jiansheng Guo, Craig Janes, Lionel Jensen, Jiang Xinnan, Satsuki Kawano, Webb Keane, Ian Kuijt, Robin Lakoff, Sylvia Li-chün Lin, John Lucy, Ma Jing, Ma Ruoyu, Cynthia Mahmood, Victor Mair, Bruce Mannheim, Brian McVeigh, Lise Menn, Don Munro, Dian Murray, Hindy Najman, Carolyn Nordstrom, William O'Rourke, Pu Fengying, Karen Richman, Sonia Ryang, Haun Saussy, Michael Schoenhals, Janet Shibamoto Smith, Tammy Stone, Cindi SturtzStreetharan, John Temple, David Tracer, Greg Urban, Margaret Baptiste Wan, Wang Shujen, Wang Xiaoqing, Sydney White, Yang Ping, Yang Xiaoshan, and Zhao Zhengmin. Some interactions were fleeting—perhaps a chat about the title for half an hour—and others have persisted over many years, but I am grateful to all for what I have learned.

Susan McEachern, editor extraordinaire, once again was a pleasure to work with. Her sensible guidance, along with her courage at embracing a potentially controversial book, have been immensely reassuring. The editorial and production team at Rowman and Littlefield—Drew Bryan, Bridgette Moore, Jessica Gribble—provided efficient expertise in bringing the book into the world. The cover art was suggested by the talented Hal Aqua of Aqua Studio, an old friend who happens to be a professional designer as well.

My parents, Joyce and George Blum, introduced me to the complex world of valuing honesty while preserving one's own interests and caring for others' sensibilities. They still find me naïve. But we are bound together with genuine respect and sometimes fascination at how different people can be despite having intertwined lives and biographies.

Lionel Jensen, my eternal companion, has cheered me on, watched out for my well-being in countless ways, reminded me of incidents that slipped my mind, helped with the historical chapters, taken care of business, and basically been an engaged partner whenever I asked—and even when I didn't. Our intellectual partnership is only overshadowed by our emotional bond.

This book is dedicated to my daughters, Hannah Neora Blum Jensen and Elena Oriana Blum Jensen, who have taught me everything about the complex, sometimes contradictory, and always interesting challenges of learning—and, terrifyingly, trying to teach—to be a good, loving, responsible person. They are both insight-filled, observant, articulate, and forceful. After I'd worked on the book steadily for about eight months, Hannah said, "Why don't you just finish it already!" Good advice. I am truly blessed to be able to learn from my children. They have enriched my life beyond my wildest dreams.

PART I

DECEPTION AND TRUTH

CHAPTER ONE

Truth, Lying, and Deception: Blum's Maxims for China

"Truth" is linked in a circular relation with systems of power which produce and sustain it, and to effects of power which it induces and which extend it. A "régime" of truth. This régime is not merely ideological or superstructural; it was a condition of the formation and development of capitalism. And it's this same régime which, subject to certain modifications, operates in the socialist countries (I leave open here the question of China, about which I know little).

—Michel Foucault 1980

. . . the vast majority of both metalinguistic and metacommunicative messages remain implicit.

—Gregory Bateson 1972

If you ask most people, they will take for granted that we know what "truth," "lying," and "deception" are, and that they are opposed in straightforward ways. If someone tells the truth, she does not lie; if she tells a lie, she intends to deceive. Deception and lying are ways of fooling people. And they are bad. Too much deception, especially self-deception, can ruin a marriage. Lying will eat away at the liar's inner being and can be cured only with therapy. Telling the truth will give people a clean conscience, friends, love of God, and a kind of sunny, simple approach to life that is enviable to those who are forced by circumstances or temperament to be duplicitous. Not only that, the conventional wisdom continues, but truth is in the nature of science and the universe, so one way or another, truth will out. Science and mathematics are concerned with truth; philosophy is consumed by how one knows the true and the real. Religions proclaim their own truths; politicians accuse their opponents of lies, mistakes, and deliberate misstatements.

I think most of these ways of thinking about what is true and what is false, what is genuine and what is fake, are too simple. I have come to see that in our everyday actions we juggle a huge number of considerations every time we speak or act, even if we claim outright that we are mostly guided by matters of truth. This is the case in the United States as well as in China and elsewhere, only it is more commonly acknowledged in China than in the United States. Some differences stem from our different histories and from different social organizations; some stem from different moral systems and from what anthropologists call "culture."

This book is concerned with the question of deception, its cousins lying and cheating, and its opposites truth and sincerity. It is anthropological in the broadest possible sense, which is to say it asks about—if it does not definitively answer—what it is to be human in the context of our animal and non-animal selves. Sometimes readers will have the impression that I am saying something specific about Chinese people's practices in order to single them out, to say that only *they* do it. This is not my point. My point is that all humans do it—all societies have instances of deception and lying—but that the details differ and the values and expectations placed on these practices differ. This is in part how anthropologists ask our big questions: we collect a lot of little pieces of information and put them together. If all people do similar things, we might be able to conclude that there is a universal principle operating. If most people do similar things, we might conclude that there is a general tendency in force. If some people do one thing and others a very different thing, we might conclude that there is a lot of permitted variation and that this has influences from some direction.

Before we can discuss causes, however, we need fairly good descriptions. That's why anthropologists travel to faraway places and spend long periods of time living among people different from themselves. We believe that familiarity breeds lack of observation, and that only by seeing things that are not comfortable and familiar can we really *see*. This, of course, biases us toward highlighting the different and ignoring the similar. No anthropological works begin with the observation that the people being studied eat, sleep, reproduce like mammals, etc. They might show how the eating, sleeping, and reproducing are done with specific beliefs and practices that differ from those of the anthropologist's own culture, observations with roots in the anthropologist's surprise, which then turns into familiarity once the other culture's rules and expectations are explained. Then in a final twist the anthropologist often finds that her own society's norms have become odd and somehow unfamiliar. This book aims to do some of that as well.

At the same time, personal experience—ethnography—is not the only way to understand the workings of human society. Anthropologists who study literate societies with long recorded histories have an overwhelming amount of written material to consult. It seems foolish to ignore all this in pursuit of an ideal—participant-observation fieldwork—that arose in the context of small-scale, non-literate, technologically simple societies (which were also wrongly conceived of as self-contained entities, without history or context). So I connect my own firsthand experience with written contemporary and historical sources on China.

I began to wonder about truth when I did my first fieldwork (see Blum 2001). I was investigating the ways ethnic minorities were regarded in southwest China, in a place of great ethnic diversity and in a society in which the government is very involved in matters relating to ethnicity. The Chinese state helps shape the school curriculum that features ethnic minorities, and it commissions television documentaries about the fifty-five minorities and their defining characteristics. The features of ethnicity in China are quite different from those in the United States, since they include subsistence patterns, marriage, religious systems, language, and much more.

As in the United States, however, in China the ethnic minorities are often regarded with prejudice and condescension, if not outright horror. I was interested in the social stereotypes that people carried around with them, looking to see if there were patterns in those stereotypes. One aspect of minorities that was often mentioned was that they were *laoshi*, simple and honest. This was said not with admiration, but rather with a slight—and sometimes blatant—tone of contempt. I found this puzzling. In contrast to the simplicity and straightforwardness of the minorities—traits they shared with peasants, children, and some foreigners—the Han Chinese (urban Han) were almost universally said to be *congming*, clever.

One night in my apartment, after everyone else had gone, a student I'll call Ma Qing who was half Han (majority) Chinese and half Chinese-speaking Muslim (Hui), told me sadly, "My parents taught me to lie." We had a long talk about what this meant. She explained that children had to be taught to conceal their true feelings and even to cover up facts about their lives. This required much rehearsing on the part of their parents, who monitored very closely what their children said in front of whom. Within the family people could be frank, but outside, *zai shehui*, in society, concealment was the guiding principle. Again, this did not make much sense to me, coming as I did from the United States, where we sing the praises of truthfulness at every turn. "Honesty is the best policy." Isn't it?

In various parts of China over a period of two decades, I, along with many other people, have been victim and beneficiary of deception. I have pretended to be a student when in fact I was a teacher, combating what I felt were unjust price differences. (Foreign students paid the low Chinese price, while foreign teachers paid the foreign price, often ten times higher.) I have had people buy tickets for me on who knows what pretext. I have been denied goods and services that were plainly visible in front of me. I have been complimented beyond my merit and I have been insulted unknowingly. My children have been threatened and promised things that the adults never intended to provide. I have seen merchants cheat buyers, and I have seen buyers try to outsmart merchants. I have seen administrators invent rules on the spot, and I have seen feigning of ignorance of rules by those same administrators. I have bought things that were claimed to be genuine and later turned out to be anything but, and I have bought things admittedly fake. In conversation with people I have been told that lying is deplorable but inevitable, and I have been told that children must be taught both to lie and to detect others' lies. I have been told that dying people must never be told the truth about the severity of their illness. I have been told that all ethnic minorities and peasants are more honest and simple than the majority ethnic group and than urban dwellers, and even though honesty is explicitly valued it is genuinely laughed at.

My first reaction, then, was to conclude that "people in China lie a lot!" But this can hardly be an adequate analysis. My second reaction was that "we think people in China lie a lot but they are actually doing something else." My third reaction was that "everybody everywhere lies a lot."

Ultimately I hope to convince you that people in many societies lie but they lie in differing circumstances and hold differing judgments of that lying and deception. Whether deception, ruses, cons, lies, are for protection or for gain, whether they are primarily done by the powerless or by the powerful, whether these are seen as morally wrong or merely necessary, such are the ways we find variation in the human condition. In the final analysis, any theory of language and culture must include an account of the range of possible uses of language and of goals for that use. Many general accounts of language imply that the transparent exchange of information is the basic function of language. That is, we shall see, far too naïve and thus a wrong view.

I attribute some of what I've observed in China to a view of language as, to use Levi-Strauss's distinction, cultural rather than natural. Language is hard to learn; it must be taught like any other skill. There is no automatic transparent kind of language that bubbles innocently from the font of feeling harbored in all individuals; it is artistry that shapes and drives the use of language. Country bumpkins and ethnic minorities have more "natural" lives and more "natural" uses of language, but there is nothing good about this—at least from the perspective of the urban Han majority. In a society where untouched landscapes are inferior to shaped gardens, the hard work of cultural and social learning is valued profoundly over the mereness of the natural. Pure, simple, honest, heartfelt language is not as good as the complex, subtle language inculcated through training. Well-raised children submit to this training until it is thoroughly internalized.

Puzzling over the negative connotations of *laoshi* and Ma Qing's report about being taught to lie, I began to recall other moments of being confused about what was going on. You'll read more about these in the following chapters, but there were cases when people pronounced what seemed like outright lies with no remorse. Why would this happen? And even more difficult to understand, why was this not regarded as offensive or wrong? Clearly, different principles were operating here than the ones I'd grown up with. Yet it would be too easy just to say, "In China people lie." As an anthropologist, I had to get the nuances right. This book is my attempt to do just that.

Since that day in 1991 when Ma Qing confided to me about her torn loyalties—to Han and self-preservation, to Hui and honesty—I have read widely on the topics of truth, deception, lying, forgery, corruption, sincerity, and politeness, in China and elsewhere. I've kept track of all the movies with *liar* or *lies* in the titles. I've collected magazines such as the issue of *Time Magazine* with a cover story: "Lying: Everybody's Doin' It (Honestly)" (October 5, 1992), and the *Utne Reader* with its "The Whole Truth About Lying (Trust Us)" (November/December 1992); *Success Magazine* had a cover story on "The Art of Deceit: Outsmart the Competition" (March 1994), and in January 2002, *Oprah* magazine advertised revolutionary benefits if only one were truthful: "Truth: Embracing it, denying it, spinning it, and (brave move) telling it like it is" and "How to spot a lie," featuring testimonials about people's encounters with hard truths and an article about lie detection that includes a box about psychologist Paul Ekman's research on genuine and imitation smiles.

Books dealing with truth and deception are plentiful. The Notre Dame library catalogue lists 803 items concerning "truth," 116 concerning "deception" (interestingly only nine concerning "lying"). On Amazon.com there are 4,271 book titles containing the word *truth*, 808 that contain *deception*, and 170 that have *lying*. A good number are self-help books, advising people (mostly women) about how to detect truthfulness or lies in their partners.

One has the feeling that the world is filled with land mines and that these books promise to provide a map of them. Many rely on popular versions of work stemming from Ekman's on facial expression. (More on this in the appendix.) There are said to be telltale signs of lying that can be used to diagnose lies of all sorts. Building on Sissela Bok's *Lying* (1979) and on straightforward understanding of what makes something a lie (a contradiction between meaning of words and intent), we can find comprehensive books such as Jeremy Campbell's *The Liar's Tale* (2001) and Evelin Sullivan's *The Concise Book of Lying* (2001).

In addition to the broad writing about truth in philosophy and theology, there are a few gems in linguistics on the subject of "lying." Psychological anthropology also comes into play in helping to see how notions of persons and selves are involved in all human interactions. My major illumination comes from linguistic anthropology, and especially the subfield of pragmatics. You can read more about these theories in the appendix.

Not only do I discuss deception, lying, and truth in China, but I also make explicit comparisons between different cultures' ways of being and valuing truth and deception, including North American ways. It is clear that all anthropologists draw on their own life experiences to point to what they should observe. Many times these baselines are unstated. Psychologically oriented anthropologists know from psychoanalysis that it is essential to examine the observer's background in order to understand the nature of the encounter (see, e.g., Clifford and Marcus 1986; Lutz 1988; Rabinow 1977; Spiro 1996, etc.). So in the interest of disclosure, here is one snapshot of my biography:

My own position is that of a white, middle-class, educated Jewish American female from the Midwest; after having lived in every time zone in the United States I now teach at a midwestern Catholic university. I have been studying China since 1977 and have an undergraduate degree in linguistics and postgraduate degrees (two M.A.s and a Ph.D.) in Chinese literature and in anthropology. I have made four trips to China and one to Taiwan, totaling approximately thirty months residing in Chinese societies. My abilities to read, write, speak, and understand Mandarin are just short of those of a native speaker, though I am more narrow in my experiences than a native speaker would be. I also read classical Chinese. Many of the observations I have made in the course of this investigation are noteworthy because they contradict my expectations—expectations that are often naïve, self-righteous, morally narrow, and so forth.

I will comment in the conclusion about what some of this has meant to me, but here I would like to point out that I also have two children. Many of the values I aim to inculcate as a member of U.S. society have become increasingly difficult for me. This difficulty is another source of information, as

An unchanging identity is ideal. Things have unchanging essences.
Language is part of nature.
Novelty is desirable. Avoid clichés. Be original. Be unique.
Tell the truth.

I propose different guiding principles for China—at least for urban Han China. I will show that maxims for interaction in China include the following:

Consider consequences.
Anticipate others' responses. (theory of mind)
Give and save face.
Consider power and role.
Guard information.
Select script.
Keep track of inside and outside.
Avoid transparency.
Thicken interactions.
Do the right action in context.
Consider bystanders.
Take relationships as primary.
Language is culture, not (only) nature.
Performance counts.
Proclaim loyalty and affiliation.
Trust! And suspect.

It's unlikely that these apply only to China, nor do they apply in all contexts in China. If they apply in Anglo-American contexts it may be with shame rather than pride. In the spirit of broadening our understanding of humankind, I present them here for consideration. I also introduce maxims for Japan and Judaism in the relevant chapters. Each chapter below exemplifies one or several of these maxims and principles.

Explaining Culture

People often want more than description and analysis of apparently odd behavior. They seek explanations of why things are the way they are. Whenever I raise the topic of this book, people will ask me, "Why is it like that?" Then they will think a moment and ask, "Is it that way because of the Cultural Revolution? Because of communism? Because of the Eastern mind?

Because society is so loosely governed now?" Here are some possible types of explanation:

1. China is the way it is because of its cultural essence.
2. China is the way it is because it is/was communist.
3. China is the way it is because it is now modernizing and becoming capitalist.
4. China is the same as everyplace else; it's just human nature.

Each of these is too simple, yet each has countless examples to support it.

I will try to answer the question, "Why is China like that?" by placing it in its historical as well as cross-cultural context. While there are strong continuities with the past, real events in the world have had a substantial effect on the particular personal interactions within Chinese society. Still, human interactions can take only a range of possible forms, and in terms of its views on deception and truth, China may be fruitfully contrasted with a variety of other societies to locate similarities and differences.

Outline of the Book

The remainder of the book takes these issues and examines them first (part II: chapters 2, 3, 4, and 5) from an ethnographic, social, and literary look at the morality of deception and truth in contemporary China. Then, in teasing out continuities and discontinuities in the Chinese record, part III (chapters 6 and 7) traces notions of deception and truth, first in the premodern period, then in the revolutionary period that ended just after the death of Mao in 1976. Part IV (chapters 8 and 9) presents cross-cultural understandings of deception and truth and situates all this within a broader understanding of humankind and language use. The appendix is mostly for my academic colleagues and graduate students, who expect even more explicit theory than I have chosen to include in the main text.

In the end, you will see that there are some peculiarities in Chinese practices, many peculiarities in U.S. practices, and many commonalities across all the cultures mentioned. This should of course be the case. We are all human, which means that we are all involved in the endeavor of surviving individually and collectively with our self-respect and the respect of others. How we use language and silence in negotiating that hard road is the story to be told here.

We start in a hotel in Suzhou, China, in 1982 and end with humanity in general. I'm pleased with that.

Note

1. See Levinson 2001 on ethnographic challenges to Grice's maxims; see also Brown and Levinson 1978; Leech 1983; Wierzbicka 2003.

PART II

CHINA PRESENT

CHAPTER TWO

Tricks and Traps: Deception and Protective Cleverness

The terms truth and falsehood contain so many subtle nuances that, if we invited the sages to debate them, even the learned ones would be unable to explain thoroughly. If there is truth, there must be falsehood; if there is falsehood, there must be truth. If truth increases, falsehood diminishes; if falsehood increases, truth diminishes. And from the beginning of history, in that arena that lies between the poles of true and false, how many games have been run? How many dramas, great and small, have been played out? Play after play, plays within plays, the stage is never silent. To substitute false for true is a source of great pride; to confuse true with false is a talent. But if you were fooled and took false for true, your own poor vision and thinking were to blame. Now don't go getting angry and upset. Weren't there many people who so took false for true that, even on the day they died, they still couldn't recognize the truth? And wasn't the false then true after all? As to the terms true and false, the honest, naïve people looked for the two obvious extremes. The shrewd, clever ones played the middle ground, some making a good living at it.

—Feng Jicai 1994

The Question of Deception

On my first trip to China in 1982 I was "lied to" by the desk clerk at one of the few hotels in Suzhou permitted to accept foreigners. I was a young-looking "foreign expert" (*wai zhuan*) with a little bit of Chinese and a very slight understanding of China. Yet it was not ultimately the words that were the problem.

One cold winter weekend I had taken the train from Nanjing (where I was teaching English to teachers) to the famous tourist city of Suzhou, renowned for its gardens, canals, beautiful women, and gentle dialect. At the hotel counter I set out to book a room. A group of foreign students walked by and said they had just gotten beds in the "dormitory" for ten yuan a night. I went up and said I wanted a bed in the dormitory. "We don't have a dormitory." This had to be a "lie," because one minute earlier the same clerk had assigned the other students to the dormitory.

"Yes there is; they got one."

"Oh, well, there aren't any more beds."

"They said it was empty."

"Well, foreign teachers can't stay in the dormitory."

"Why not? That doesn't make sense." To an American, anyway.

"You wouldn't be comfortable. There is no private bathroom and you have to share the room. . . . You would not be comfortable."

"I would. I'm younger than they are. I would be fine. I don't care about the bathroom. . . ."

Ultimately, it was much more trouble to have me standing there arguing than to risk having me complain about the lack of comfort, so I "won." I slept in a bed for ten yuan a night with other foreigners and walked down the cold hallway to the bathroom.

Many factors are potentially involved in this little anecdote, such as the idea of a role superseding individual identity, which I did not then understand, and the idea of trying to avoid potential unpleasantness in the future by a careful answer in the present.[1] It could be that gaps in our respective language abilities were too troublesome; it could be that there was a quota of permitted guests. It could be that government rules prohibited even revealing the existence of rules. My point is not to blame the clerk, but to observe her behavior. For our purposes, the conclusion to be drawn is that there were many motivations behind this clerk's giving the answer she did, and "telling the truth" was one that was weighed rather lightly relative to other goals.

When I asked people about this incident on subsequent trips, it took quite a bit of explaining just to show why I found the clerk's behavior surprising. None of my Chinese friends found it at all unusual, and they all had similar experiences to recount. A young Chinese woman whom I'll call "Margot" had once helped three American students buy chops (stamps with their Chinese names). Under her breath, the salesperson told Margot she could get a cut on the high price quoted. He assumed Margot was a tour guide, because she was a Chinese woman in the company of Westerners. (They did not buy from this seller.) Another person mentioned that two Chinese women asked if there was a "Western" section of the Cuihu (Green Lake) Hotel in Kunming. They were told no, but in fact there was such a section.

How should such common episodes be understood? Is this just the way people in the 1980s and 1990s dealt with foreigners? Was information so precious that lying was automatic? Some lies for gain—inflating prices—might be easily explained, but lies about simple observable facts? The judgmental American (that I was originally) may seize upon the question of lying (*shuo jiahua*), but this did not strike a chord in my Chinese consultants. What *did* evoke excited conversation was the topic of deception.

Pian, "to cheat, to deceive," is ubiquitous. When asked if people had ever been cheated/swindled/deceived (*Ni you mei you beipian de jingyan?*), people were eager to discuss it, and they offered examples:

Afang, the friend of a friend, both members of the Yi ethnic group, told me of one encounter with a *pianzi*, swindler, in Kunming. A woman approached her, claiming to be a student at a local college, about the same age as Afang. She claimed she'd lost her wallet and needed two Chinese dollars (now worth about a quarter U.S.) to call her teacher in Beijing (more than 3000 km away, by rail), who would come immediately and bring her the money. The stranger promised to pay Afang back if she would only write down her address. Afang noted how preposterous the whole thing was, that one "couldn't call Beijing for two kuai," and a person couldn't come to Kunming from Beijing in one day. She didn't give her the money. Our mutual friend said that she'd had an identical experience. Ridiculous though such cons are, some must succeed.

Afang told another story. On a long bus ride, a young man sat quietly with a can of soda; his friend explained that the fellow was a mute. The young man opened the can and it spilled all over an adjacent passenger's pants. He offered to pay him money for the pants, and an older woman on the bus gave the man 1000 yuan to repay this insult. But it was a setup; ten people were working together in this scam. They all got off immediately, at the very next bus stop. (I take the point to be that others were to follow the young man's example and make payments if they too were responsible for spilling soda on seatmates' clothing. Afang took the point to be so obvious that it required no explanation.)

I have heard many such stories. The targeted dupe is often a country bumpkin; the swindler is often a person with more power—or more desperation. The absurdity of the claims was evident to all and was emphasized by the almost disconnected way the story was recounted. The antidote to attempted swindles is always depicted as cleverness, and the battle is presented as a battle of strategies, not of morality or factuality.

A different but more elaborate struggle to outwit occurred in 1996 in Beijing. I wanted to look around China's premier university, Beijing University (Beida). A Chinese acquaintance I'll call Xiao Ji took me to see the campus in the car she used to carry out the business of her employer, though it was her own private car. At the first entrance we were stopped by a guard.

"Where are you going?"
"I'm taking our foreign guest to look around Beida, because it's very famous."
First strategy: flattery and appeal to national pride.
"Beida is not open for sightseeing. Outside cars can't enter." (*Guard information. Keep track of inside and outside.*)

Flattery failed; rules intervened. Another appeal: to responsibility.

"We're going to see someone."
"Who?"
"I forgot her name."

This being a bald-faced lie, since the answer changed immediately, the guard ordered us to turn around. There was a van behind us, so we could not back up. Could we go forward and turn around? No, no. Xiao Ji brazenly tried to go forward, whereupon another guard from inside the gatehouse came out and began looking sternly at her, holding his hand up and letting her know she couldn't go in. They clearly did not believe that she would merely turn around, since she had just proven herself untrustworthy. But finally it was evident that because of the long line of vehicles close behind us there was no physical possibility of going backwards as they had asked us to do, so they saw they had no choice but to believe her; in the end they let her turn around.

Xiao Ji's status was clearly not great; she was evidently someone hired to do service work, even though she had become wealthy—nouveau riche, by the looks of her permanent wave and fur-edged coat. The gatekeepers had more status because they represented the nation's foremost university. Xiao Ji also appeared flippant, not humble or sincere.

We began to learn what it would take to get me in, and by the final attempt—there were many entrances, each with its own gatekeeper—we had succeeded. A sincere-sounding "We're going to the graduate student building" did the trick. I suspect it was not believed, but it was not so obvious a lie that it required confrontation. Plausibility is one requirement for getting deception across. It may even evoke admiration for its skill. Further, she had learned the proper script for the situation. (*Select script.*)

I felt bad forcing Xiao Ji to lie, but she claimed it did not matter: "If we hadn't deluded him, we wouldn't have been able to go in." (*Bu meng ta, bu neng jinqu*) (*Consider consequences.*) *Meng*, meaning "deceive, delude, pull the wool over someone's eyes," appears light, ethically, as if used with a good-natured shrug.

Xiao Ji had a responsibility to please me, a foreigner. I could have stopped the event—but as an American I probably believed that closed campuses were unnecessary and unfair. I too—unthinkingly at the time—evaluated deception in terms of its consequences. I was relieved that I did not have to utter the untrue words, but I was willing to benefit from Xiao Ji's scheme; indeed we discussed our strategy between the various gates.

This could happen anywhere. Is there anything unique about this story? For me, most striking is that my Chinese friend seemed genuinely nonchalant about her deception and that the guards did not try to dig more deeply into the truth. If Xiao Ji knew how to *seem* truthful, if she was sincere, that indicated enough knowledge for them to permit her entry. (*Performance counts.*)

In striking contrast was an event that occurred in 2002 in the United States. Several colleagues were driving together to a departmental honor society dinner at the end of the year. The parking lot nearest the dining hall was at the campus hotel nearby. The colleague who was driving told the guard, "We're going to the Morris Inn." She turned to us when we got to the parking lot and said, "It's true. We're walking through it, even if it isn't where we're going in the end." And to make us all feel better, we entered the hotel—and then left through the back door. The difference between the two cases is that my colleague felt the need to justify what she felt to be a departure from truth by pointing out that at some literal level it might be partially true. (*Tell the truth.*) It was not a matter of outwitting anyone, but merely of finding some truth to cling to.

Cleverness and Stupidity (Simplicity): *Congming and Laoshi*

Cleverness, being *congming* (pronounced *tsong ming*), permits one to protect oneself from deception or trickery, *pian*, as long as circumstances are not entirely stacked against the target. Cleverness has to do with being able to understand other people's motives and to respond quickly. Often misunderstood by "Westerners" as "intelligence," it has nothing to do with formal education or the kinds of things measured by I.Q. tests, though it may be aided by worldly experience. Cleverness involves cunning, a proper degree of suspicion, and a developed sense of quickness in interaction. It also includes being able to anticipate others' reactions and staying a step ahead of them. This is admired, to some degree. Some people are obviously not *congming*; many deceptions succeed.

Cleverness allows the actor to anticipate the other's response and to act in a way that will bring about the desired consequence. It is the consequences that tend to be evaluated morally, not, in the case of speech, the words in isolation.

Sophisticated urban Han—who are usually regarded as most clever—are said to have an extensive repertoire of roles, scripts, stances, and ways of using language to accomplish aims, whether worthwhile or illegitimate.

Simplicity and honesty—being *laoshi* (*lao* rhymes with English 'how'; *shi* sounds a little like English 'sure')—are hallmarks of most ethnic minorities, according to Han, just as they are of peasants (and, it should be said, children and some foreigners). At least officially this trait is admired. In the 1960s when urban youth were supposed to be educated by peasants rather than by books and teachers, one of the qualities most often mentioned was that peasants were *laoshi*, *pusu*—ingenuous, unassuming, natural.

Urban Han considered *congming* behavior praiseworthy and criticized being *laoshi*; minorities took the reverse view. "Cleverness" resembles to some extent what in ancient Greece was called *metis*, practical cunning, where it often appeared as disguise. *Congming* has some affinity with "street smarts" except that in China the general association is with higher social class, whereas "street smarts" in the West are often the property of people of lower social standing, while the educated are considered "bookworms" who live in "ivory towers."

The frankness and honesty of ethnic minorities leave them vulnerable to the greater manipulations of others. The novel *The Remote Country of Women* illustrates the potential cultural conflict when a Han man falls in love with a Mosuo minority woman. Ultimately the possibility of life together is doomed because of many fundamental differences in viewing the world, including the issue of sincerity. The heroine, Sunamei, had to go to the "outside world, a Han place full of dishonesty and turmoil" (Bai 1994, 347). This is difficult because the Mosuo are so frank and guileless. The book romanticizes the Mosuo (officially classified with the Naxi ethnic group) for their alleged matriarchy and a more "authentic" culture.[2]

Many people make a connection between ethnicity and truthfulness. Recall Ma Qing, the young woman of mixed ethnicity who told me that she contained within her two models of sincerity and found it painful. Han Chinese society, majority society, required mastery of lying, while Hui (Muslim) society admired truthfulness. Minorities in Kunming told me of their own entrapment by Han who were clever; they themselves were incapable of such deviousness. People of several ethnic minorities told me that they themselves were incapable of wily, calculated speech and that unlike the majority ethnic group, the Han, their own ethnic group was known for its frankness. One Yi woman told me that her village has a saying (*shuofa*): "Even the most clever Yi can't compare with the stupidest Han" (*Zui congmingde Yizu bibushang zui bende Hanzu.*) She warmed to the subject: "We Yi are often taken advantage of when we come to the city. At my hometown, no one cheats because it would all be known by everyone." In the capital city of Kunming, she was afraid to go out too much because she feared she would be easily duped.

When I asked a Naxi woman who had been in Kunming for about a year to compare people in Kunming and Lijiang (her hometown, center of Naxi life), she told me, "*Lijiangren bijiao laoshi, bu hui shuohuang; xinzhi koukuai*" (Lijiang people are more honest (*laoshi*), can't tell lies; they are straightforward and plain-spoken [literally, their hearts are direct and mouths quick]). In contrast, Kunming people always say things they don't mean. She gave an example: Her fellow cleaning people may be jealous if she is recognized by the leaders for cleaning especially well, so they may say things that aren't true, or even would go so far as to claim credit for *her* thorough cleaning. I asked if this made her unhappy. No, she said, because she *duideqi tade lian*, she could hold her head up because she has done the right thing. She added that in Naxihua they have a saying: *renbujian, tian jian* (People can't see but heaven can see.) When I asked if this has anything to do with religion, she looked puzzled. I asked if it has to do with *daode*, morality, and she said yes.

A scholar writing about morality among China's southwest minorities claims that *chunpuxing* (honesty, simplicity, unsophistication) of most ethnic minorities should be valued. "They treat others sincerely, honestly and reliably, giving people a sense of security. They do things extremely clearly; one is one, two is two, they come straight and go straight, their moral sentiments are directly expressed externally" (Gao 1990, 229). He claims that in "primitive society" and in the past, such directness characterized all people, but now only minorities truly retain this quality. Words used to describe them are *chengken*, "sincere," and *dushi*, "honest and sincere, solid."[3]

Peasants too were often held up as models of honesty, yet norms regarding *laoshi* are changing even in the countryside. In the 1960s and 1970s, people who were *laoshi* were seen as ideal marriage partners, but by the 1990s they were considered undesirable because they were too easily humiliated outside the village (Yan 2003, 76–80).

> When villagers were confined to their close-knit local community and inter-
> acted only with people in their existing social networks, laoshi meant trust-
> worthy and reliable, qualities that could reduce transaction costs within the
> village society. However, the other merits of laoshi, such as naïveté and hon-
> esty, could be fatal shortcomings outside the local community, especially dur-
> ing the postreform era when villagers had to deal with strangers in the unreg-
> ulated market. In the new circumstances, laoshi invites aggression and
> cheating; a laoshi husband cannot be expected to provide the kind of safety
> and protection that a prospective bride desires. (Yan 2003, 77–78)

By the 1990s anyone who was *laoshi* was an automatic target of potentially
dangerous cheating. It was associated with rural villages; as admiration for ur-
banness, economic success, and prosperity increased, and as urban migration
soared, appreciation for *laoshi* husbands decreased.

In the U.S. we too have mixed views of simplicity and cleverness. Saints,
for instance, are often regarded as protected by God through their own innocence. It is only those with devilish intelligence who can outwit others.
Purity and simplicity are cultivated through asceticism and selflessness. Trust
in God makes it unnecessary for people to be suspicious of others. Even the
notion of seeking too much protection makes it seem as if God's will is not
guiding one, but that one is taking matters too much into one's own hands.
"God will provide" for those with faith. Cleverness is unnecessary. At the
same time we applaud people who are clever and able to succeed. Donald
Trump's *The Apprentice* teaches just the wiles needed to thrive in business.

In urban China there is no virtue attached to being simple, innocent, and
naïve. Still, even the Han have limits to their admiration of cleverness. Another term for cleverness, or slyness like that of a fox, *jiaohua*, is written with
two animal radicals. This term is used of con men and those ultimate immoral people, the Japanese, often with derision and hatred—but sometimes
still with some appreciation of their skill.

It is not only ethnic minorities and peasants that are stereotyped for honesty. Another great divide in China is regional. A survey of regional stereotypes found that people from the northern provinces tended to be considered
honest while those from the southern provinces were considered sly, deceptive, dishonest. These stereotypes have existed for quite some time, perhaps
even millennia (Eberhard 1971 [1965], 305–17).

When I spoke in the United States with an urban, southern, Han intellectual about regional differences, he agreed with this characterization and attempted to illustrate it for me. His example was as follows: If you are served a
bowl of noodles with a big piece of chicken, the expensive part, the northerner will put the chicken below the noodles and the southerner will put the

chicken on top. How, I asked, is this deceptive? (It seemed to me that it was honest, showing what there was.) The southerner, he explained, is trying to show off by promising that it is all chicken, yielding disappointment when the guest finds out that it is mostly noodles, while the northerner is modest and gives a surprise. (Yang Xiaoshan, personal communication, August 31, 2002)[4] I came to see that the key to this interpretation lies in misleading the guest, who will have certain expectations based on what she sees. (*Anticipate others' responses. [theory of mind]*) In the Greek story told by Hesiod, Prometheus similarly tricked his father, Zeus, asking him to select one of two bundles, one with the desirable fat and bones hidden under skin, and the other with bones concealed in fat. Zeus naturally chose the one with fat glistening. As punishment for this deception, Zeus took fire from humans. (Prometheus later stole it and gave it back to them.) The concealment is deceptive.

People from different regions of China are believed to have different degrees of deceptiveness. Kunminger Yan Qimei was adamant that the people most likely to be *pianzi* came from Guangdong province in the south—especially from the countryside, seeking but not finding work, thus in need of help. (She explained it as arising from circumstantial need, not from a character deficit.) A different kind of cleverness, she went on, is that of people from Jiangsu and Zhejiang provinces. They are so clever that they have already thought of new things while people from Yunnan (the province of which Kunming is the capital) are still back on the previous thought!

Cleverness in using language is usually part of the instrumental movement of people in society, but cleverness can also be appreciated for itself. As in other societies, China has stories of tricksters, but they are usually not the weak or oppressed of the society, but rather the powerful—except for some minorities.

Trickery and Ruses: Stories of Cleverness

Chinese stories of rusing, in contrast to stories about Coyote or Br'er Rabbit (Basso 1987; Bright 1993; Lester and Pinkney 1988), do not usually represent the materially oppressed being protected by means of superior cleverness. For example, in collections of con artists and other frauds, the poor are often further humiliated by clever others.

Life in contemporary China is often depicted as filled with traps, scams, cons, misrepresentations, and other forms of danger for the unwary (especially for the greedy and gullible). Clever people (*pianzi*, "cheater(s)" or "swindler(s)" or "deceiver(s)") carefully lay traps and entice dupes to their web; the dupes exercise insufficient caution—or at most predictable caution that is easily anticipated by the schemer—and lose their fortunes. In the 1980s *pianzi* were usually quick to understand where loopholes in the system lay. Popular books such as *Contemporary Swindlers: Uncovering the secrets of all sorts of hoaxes* (Cao and Ma 1988) depict sensational frauds and hoaxes. By the 1990s the *pianzi* had become much more subtle and industrious. *Cautions about the Contemporary Art of Swindling* (Wang Youlin et al. 2000) provides 122 cases culled from recent media accounts, divided into money scams (ninety-eight cases), sex scams (sixteen cases), and government scams (eight cases).

These books, like the newspapers from which many of their cases are drawn, provide sensational accounts of crimes that were discovered and prosecuted. They may almost be regarded as contemporary reality TV (newspaper) versions of *Water Margin* (*Shuihu zhuan*), the Ming novel about bandits, where readers savored the heroes' unbelievable cleverness outside proper social channels. Ultimately in contemporary accounts the criminals are punished. Though the authors always profess their sincere efforts to warn the public about such things, there is no doubt that the public loves such accounts. Here is a fairly typical case from the 1990s:

A Fashionable Young Lady Comes to Collect Taxes; Old Folks Fall for the Ruse

She said she was sent by her superiors to collect the census tax, administration tax, water fees; the old folks turned over the fees according to the rules. But after investigation, the so-called superiors who sent her, and the various taxes and fees, were wholly unreal. She was a con artist.

At about 11 a.m. on June 4, 1999, the Nongqishi 123 group of eleven families were quiet. In each house, there were only the old folks who stayed behind to take care of kids; all the others had gone to the fields to work.

Just then, at the home of retired worker, sixty-plus-year-old He Bingquan, an uninvited guest, a thirty-something young woman wearing the latest fashions, appeared: sunhat, black glasses, a dress, and high heels.

"I have come to do the census, sent by my superiors. I am responsible for the eleven families in this place." After she asked about the situation of He Bingquan's family members, she said, "According to regulations, everybody pays a census tax of ten yuan. Your family has three

---

people, so you must pay thirty yuan." When she was done she made a show of writing down the old man's name and the amount he paid in her "receipt book." When she left, she told the old man, "Grandfather, thank you for your cooperation."

Next she knocked on another family's door. "Grandmother, I heard that some public project workers came to your house. I come from the *tuan* to collect administrative fees. . . ."

Finally, she also went to retired worker He Gongcheng's house. "Grandfather, the leaders of the *li* are busy with work and they can't get away themselves. I am a new secretary-in-training for the *lianli*. The head of the *lian* sent me to collect five months of water fees. . . ." On such a hot day, it wasn't easy to doubt a young woman. He Gongcheng, the old man, believed he was acting "according to regulations" when he turned over twenty-five yuan. After the "formalities" were finished, she quickly left the He household.

Half an hour later, He Gongcheng's son came back from the fields. The old man told his son about paying the water fees. The old man's son felt there was something fishy about it. He immediately got on his motorcycle and looked all around for this secretary-in-training but couldn't find a trace of her anywhere. When he inquired, the *lianli* simply had not sent someone to collect water fees, and the "census tax" and "administrative tax" were simply made up.

So that's how it went. The 220 yuan of the old people from seven households stayed in the ingenious wallet of that modern young lady. The old folks were duped by the woman con artist.

(Selected from *Xinjiang Legal Journal*. Original authors Xu Zhong and He Linxiang)

Comment:
Preventing this kind of con artist is not actually difficult, you just have to ask several question of why? Why did the fee collector suddenly change? Why didn't she come during the standard time to collect the fees? Why were new fees added without their having been previously announced? Maybe this "fee collector" could fabricate these lies, even if it's not easy to believe. Without seeing all manner of receipts clasped in the hands of the stranger and paying the fees according to regulations, if someone had made a phone call to the relevant office then the true face of the con artist would have been exposed.
(Wang Youlin et al. 2000, 90–91; my translation)

The guileless old folks, helpless and trusting while their sons worked, were too simple to question the appearance of a young woman. (There is a certain degree of misogyny implied here, but that's another topic . . .) It is clear that their trust is being criticized; they should have been more suspicious.

Here is another story with even greater consequences:

"Master Teacher" Scams Manager of over 1,000,000

A superstition-fortune-telling teacher and an assistant general manager of a real estate company who spent more than 1,500,000 yuan on "fortune-telling expenses" and "warding-off-calamities expenses" within four years.

In November 1995, So-and-so Wang, an associate general manager of such-and-such, a real estate company in Weihai, Shandong, took a business trip to [the tropical island province] Hainan. Associate General Manager Wang was on the second floor cold drink café in a shopping center in Haikou and rested while drinking his cold drink. He had just taken a seat when three strangers walked in and sat across from him. The eldest of them held a folded fan which had written on it: "On or off the path—has the hero entered or exited? Forecast the cosmos, is it safe or not?"

"Mr. Fortune-teller" spoke first: "I take it you're from the north, sir." Wang nodded. The person across from him continued: "It's difficult to pull off endeavors that are half government and half business; your future has much misfortune and little auspiciousness." As soon as "Mr. Fortune-teller" spoke of Manager Wang being from the north and his position as half government and half business, Wang had some confidence in "Mr. Fortune-teller." For those few days, he had in fact felt that many things had not gone smoothly. He blurted out, "Where does the misfortune come from?" This "Mr. Fortune-teller" called himself "Great Teacher Li." He read Wang's face and read his palm, took out his "eight characters" and counted his "destiny," and finally the conclusion was "much misfortune and little good fortune."

Associate General Manager Wang was fifty-three years old, had traveled widely; this jack-of-all-trades had seen his fair share of life. He naturally didn't believe everything that this "Great Teacher Li" said, yet what "Great Teacher Li" said reminded him of several things, which he felt couldn't be bought for any amount of money. So he handed over 1,000 yuan cash to "Great Teacher Li" and his pals. Li took a ten-yuan bill and folded it into a triangle that he tossed to Wang. He said it would give him luck. Then he took the 990 yuan and walked away.

Two days later, "Great Teacher Li" and the others went to Manager Wang's hotel to help him "make magic." "Great Teacher Li" had spread a sheet of paper on the table, on which was standing a lit cigarette representing incense. They "told Wang's fortune" but no matter how many times they did it, his fate was always "inauspicious." When the incense was finished burning, Li had Wang trace in the ashes on the paper with his hand. As soon as Wang rubbed, the word "unlucky" appeared on the paper. He couldn't stop himself from blanching in fear. Li said to the side, "Mr. Wang, don't worry, an enlightened one is in Hainan right now. I'll ask him to appear, and your misfortune, sir, can certainly be changed." Li recommended two "colleagues" to Wang—"Great Teacher He" and "Great Teacher Liu"—demanded 3,300 yuan from Wang, and left.

Two days later, "Great Teacher Li" brought "Great Teacher Liu" and "Great Teacher He" to Wang's hotel. They brought a tortoise, which they said was expressly to eradicate the misfortune of Associate General Manager Wang. They all filed to the seashore, where "Great Teacher He" removed his shirt and exposed his chest and did exercises for Wang. "Great Teacher Liu" opened up a piece of paper off to the side, stood a cigarette up and lit it, and put the living tortoise out to sea. After a while, the "great teachers" said, "Okay, your misfortune is cast off." Then they had Wang trace in the ash on the paper, but this time the word "lucky" appeared. Wang was very happy and was completely grateful to the "great teachers."

One of the "great teachers" who told Associate General Manager Wang's fortune was Liu Yincai, from Xiantao, Hubei. Liu Yincai had a fellow provincial named Song Aijun who had opened a clothing shop in Haikou. When Liu Yincai walked around Haikou "telling fortunes," he often ended up in Song's shop. Therefore, Song Aijun knew everything about how Liu Yincai and the others "told the fortune" of Manager Wang and asked him for money. He saw that Liu Yincai got money easily from "telling fortunes" so Song sold his dress shop, asked Liu to be his teacher, and went with Liu to dupe people by "telling fortunes."

In December 1995, Song Aijun went to Weihai, Shandong, under Liu Yincai and others' guidance, and secretly learned all about Manager

Wang's situation. Then they found Manager Wang and told him that "misfortune" had come, and that they had burned incense to Buddha and read scriptures for his merit, but this time hadn't been able to transform the disaster, so this time they brought a special "high monk" expressly to eradicate the "misfortune" of Manager Wang. In fact, the "high monk" they brought was Song Aijun.

"High monk" Song Aijun closed his eyes and looked as if he was meditating. After a while he said to Wang, "It is definitely a problem that has arisen with your ancestral graves. To the left of your ancestral graves, sir, is a tree as thick as the mouth of a bowl. This tree is very bad, and you must cut it down. On both sides of the grave perhaps is a ditch, and in front is a shallow stream, which is also bad." Associate General Manager Wang left Weihai City every year to travel ten kilometers to his hometown to clean off his ancestral graves and remember his ancestors, but he had never paid attention to whether there was a tree to the left and a stream in front of the graves. Song Aijun's words silenced him. Liu Yincai and the others added, "Where are your ancestral graves? Go see whether there is in fact a tree, and then you'll know." Manager Wang took the whole group to see his ancestral graves and, lo and behold, the situation was exactly as the "high monk" had said. Wang immediately prostrated himself before Song Aijun in gratitude. That day, they cut down the tree beside the grave and said they would help get a golden Buddha for the Wang household to help the family keep disaster at bay. They guaranteed that from now on Wang would attain all his desires. Wang gave Song Aijun and the others 30,000 yuan and saw them off.

Several days later, Song Aijun and the others indeed brought Associate General Manager Wang's household a statue of Buddha, but the Buddha was clay, not gold. Song and the others said they were going to give Wang a golden Buddha but they had to go to Singapore to have it made and they needed 380,000 yuan in expenses. When they left, the "great teachers" saw that Wang was wearing an enormous gold ring on his finger. They said, "This gold ring is not good, you should only wear it after you inlay it with jade and polish it." So, they took Wang's gold ring to "polish it" and left.

In January 1996, Wang sent seven money orders totaling 293,800 yuan from Weihai to the Sanfu Tanzhen, in Xiantao, Hubei, that the "great teacher" had specified, and Song Aijun would send it to the "great teacher." After this, Song Aijun felt the money orders were inconvenient, so he went to the Agricultural Bank in Xiantao City, was issued a Jinsui card, and had Wang send the money directly to his Jinsui card.

In 1997, Liu Yincai was involved in a case of swindling, and was arrested in Haikou, then sentenced to life imprisonment. After the "master" was arrested, not only did Song Aijun not take this as a warning, his swindling intensified. The Jinsui card that he had previously used had been involved in Liu Yincai's swindling case and had been cut off, so he opened another card. In December 1998, Song Aijun called Wang and said he wanted to build a thirty-nine-meter-tall pagoda for him in Guiyuan Temple in Wuhan, with Wang's name carved on top, and pretended that this matter had been approved by the Master Changming (Flourishing) and reported to the Chinese Buddhist Association, and informed Zhao Buchu. They needed 640,000 yuan from Wang to build the pagoda. In February 1998, they had also asked for 188,000 yuan from Wang to build a pool for releasing live animals (for merit) in the Guiyuan temple.

Aside from these amounts of money, Song Aijun and the others frequently called Wang and asked for money in the guise of building temple gates, polishing, burning incense, etc. Each time Wang gave 20,000 or 30,000 yuan. From late 1995 until February 1999 he had sent money to Song Aijun and the others dozens of times, altogether over 1,500,000 yuan.

In March 1999, Associate General Manager Wang went to Wuhan on business from Weihai. The first matter of business was to go see whether his name was really carved on the pagoda at the Guiyuan Temple. Accompanied by a friend, he arrived at the Guiyuan Temple. He looked everywhere but couldn't see a pagoda. He asked whether they had built a pool for releasing creatures and was told they hadn't. Wang took Song Aijun's business card and asked in the temple whether there was such a person, only to be told there was not. Wang only then realized that the so-called "fortune telling" and "great teachers" were all lies, and that from start to finish it was all one big con.

On March 11, accompanied by a friend, Wang reported the case at the Wuhan Police Station Economic Crime Investigation Bureau.

According to the verifications of the various police inspections, this is an especially large case of fraud. At present, the suspect Song Aijun has been caught, and the details of the case are being investigated.

(Selected from *Law Daily*, original reporter Zhang Yunying)

Comment:

"As soon as 'Mr. Fortune-teller' said that Associate General Manager Wang was from the north, Manager Wang had some confidence in "Mr. Fortune-teller," yet most people can tell quite accurately whether someone is a southerner or a northerner. Associate General Manager Wang was a big fellow from Shandong; for that slick "Mr. Fortune-teller" who watched everyone's every word and expression closely, it was simply too easy a victory. And as for the several things during that time that Manager Wang felt were not going smoothly, "Mr. Fortune-teller" could not "eradicate" them either. Even though Wang had seen something of the world, because he was superstitious he missed the boat and went astray, and was cheated of more than 1,500,000 yuan.

From this we can see that spending money to eradicate misfortune cannot guarantee psychological equilibrium. People who turn their own fate over to others to manage lose themselves, throw out their own independent thoughts and rights to make decisions. If we are incapable, and are bad at managing our own fate, in the end it makes us less balanced. Only people who are not superstitious are clever people who are difficult to swindle and con. (Wang Youlin et al. 2000, 196–99; my translation)

This spectacular case of Wang, a wealthy man being duped of more than 1.5 million yuan (US$181,000) over four years, is explained by the editors as resulting from Wang's superstition. The editors claim that cleverness lies in avoiding superstition. Of course Wang's beliefs in mystical and religious salvation are components, but such an elaborate scam is also made possible by the invocation of information, the carrying out of ritual, and the irrational hopes of a man who encounters difficulty. Many of the other cases in the book involve bogus investments, impersonation of police, and other entirely non-superstitious manipulation of the gullible and greedy. The editors' didactic aim is to show that economic rationality is superior to irrational superstition. Just believe in the new economy, and all will be well.

This case requires the vouching for the "teachers" authenticity by a person who appeared to be a chance acquaintance, with evidence supplied by their apparently knowing facts about Wang that strangers would not know—especially given the assumption that information is usually guarded. (*Guard information.*) The savvy con artists were also adept at giving face to the stranger (*Give and save face.*), something that is not expected and thus might be explained—to a gullible dupe—by their real knowledge. The bystanders' importance is clear throughout, even in the discovery at the monastery and the accusation at the police station. (*Consider bystanders.*)

Whether such cases are accurate portrayals of events, whether they are common or rare, it is clear that people feel themselves quite vulnerable to scams, corruption, falsification, and cheating. In such a context, being *laoshi* would certainly make a person an easy target. One solution is that of Ma Qing's parents: arm their children with the ability to cleverly detect false-hood and to engage in protective falsification themselves.

Chu Chin-ning's popular books on business, *Thick Face Black Heart* (Chu 1992), *The American Art of Thick Face Black Heart* (1993), and *The Asian Mind Game: Unlocking the Hidden Agenda of the Asian Business Culture—A Westerner's Survival Manual* (Chu 1991), show how powerful and determined the successful must be. People must learn the Thirty-Six Strategies, but mostly for defense. "The Chinese maintain that their study of these strategies is not motivated by a desire to deceive others, but rather to recognize and prevent these strategies from being used against *them*" (1991, 44). Thus deceit is rationalized in a modern-day account as defensive.

"To accomplish one's objective, it is sometimes necessary that a falsehood be openly displayed and the truth hidden. An opponent's attention is thereby focused on the false situation, allowing the true objective to be accomplished easily without detection" (Chu 1991, 44).

A story by Wang Shuo, "Wan Zhu" [The Operators] (1993), describes a brilliant "business" established by some hooligans.[5] This business creates a kind of charade whereby they pretend to be whoever is needed for whatever goal: pseudo-business partners, false wives, impostor doctors, and so forth. The story is hysterically funny, a publication forbidden by China's government but widely read nonetheless. Some have told me they think it's funny because it's so easy to fool people. People nowadays are so greedy that they forget to use common sense and common scruples and believe they will really get something for nothing. In the contemporary climate, exploiting this greed is lamentably easy.

Unlike most Han stories mentioned above, where the vulnerable are at the mercy of their superiors' cleverness, the "civilized" minority group, the Naxi, tell stories about the clever Ayidan who outwits his lord, Lord Mu (also Naxi). For example, Ayidan was so poor despite working himself ragged that he could not afford to have his rice pounder repaired. One day, Ayidan rushed in and alerted Lord Mu to an ominous noise that the ruler's sturdy new rice pounder was making. He claimed it made a sound "Mu-clan-de-cline" and was a bad omen ("the decline of the Mu clan"). At first Lord

Mu thought it had to be destroyed, but Ayidan suggested replacing it with his own. Lord Mu was grateful for Ayidan's saving him from a bad fate, and Ayidan was of course pleased with his own ruse (Miller 1994, 214–16).

Ayidan continually bested Lord Mu. Finally Lord Mu issued a challenge: try to make him eat shit within three days. Ayidan vowed to do it in a single day. This is how it happened:

> Early the next day, Lord Mu got up, washed his face, and was about to have breakfast, when Ayidan came running in, panting and shouting, "Fire! Fire! The ancestral temple is on fire. Help!" On hearing the alarm, Lord Mu's family members and servants also joined Ayidan in the shouting and ran outside.
>
> Lord Mu was terror-stricken. When he looked up toward the temple, he saw nothing but columns of thick smoke pouring from its eaves. He treasured the things inside: the shrine engraved with beautiful dragons and phoenixes; the ancestral tablet painted red, with words engraved in gold; the sacrificial utensils on the altar made of gold, silver, jade gems, and precious stones. The thought of all these treasures flashed through his mind and made him run as quickly as he could to the temple.
>
> Just then Ayidan was at the temple struggling hard to unlock the big brass lock. As soon as Lord Mu got there, he pushed Ayidan out of the way to unlock it himself. Strangely enough, the lock seemed to be deliberately mocking Lord Mu. It refused to open. He started to get really worried. By now there was more and more dense smoke, choking people and burning their eyes. It was terrible.
>
> Ayidan promptly made a suggestion. "It won't be hard to open the door if you would just wet the key with a little of your saliva." On hearing this idea, Lord Mu quickly pulled out the key and stuck it in his mouth a few times to get it good and wet. Ayidan burst out laughing. "Forget about the fire! What you ought to be worrying about now is you've just eaten shit!" (Miller 1994, 221)

Clearly, cleverness is valued by people who are the underdog, the oppressed, and desperate. It is not only in contemporary urban China that cleverness is valued, but its value is now seen as especially necessary simply for survival.

Trusting Minorities

Stories from the Jingpo, Hui, Naxi, Nu, and Primi ethnic groups sometimes depict poor clever minority persons outthinking the evil, greedy, cruel majority person. One story, "The Guileless Man and the Trickster," collected from the Primi (a people usually classified as "Yi," on the border between Yunnan and Sichuan; see Harrell 2001), plays with the reversal of the valence between a trickster (*jiaohua ren*) and a guileless man (*benfenren*). The guileless man, on being tricked by the trickster who wants an entire musk deer for himself, lands helpless in a tree outside the cave where they were sleeping. Through luck, he overhears animals telling one another about healing techniques, underground water, and jewels hidden in a tree. He cures the headman's wife, reveals the water source to a village that was completely dry, and finds the jewels.

The trickster wants to have the same luck, so takes the guileless man's place in the cave. He too falls into the tree and overhears the animals, but this time they are angry because someone found out their information. Looking around, they spot the trickster in the tree and eat him in one gulp. The clever trickster is outdone by his greed, in contrast to the moral virtue of the innocent (Miller 1994, 228–31).

Another story from the Yi focuses on honesty. The story is titled "The Magic Shoulder Pole" and tells of a magical bull that can provide enormous benefits, but only to the proper, honest person. An old man watching over a cornfield beats the cattle to get them off the field. Unknown to him, a magical hair is wedged into a crack on his old shoulder pole. When he loads firewood it is as light as if it was empty. A rich man sees the old man carrying an enormous load as if it was nothing and forces the old man to sell him the magical shoulder pole. Since it is cracked and looks imperfect, the rich man has it polished and repaired—which inadvertently makes the magical hair from the bull fall out. Of course, the pole's magic vanishes (Miller 1994, 181–84). Rewards go only to the honest here.

In a Jingpo story, "Mr. Crooked and Mr. Straight," Mr. Straight is an honest and simple man who is outmaneuvered by Mr. Crooked, more clever and wily. Mr. Crooked beats up Mr. Straight and gouges out his eyes. Mr. Straight's sitting crying on a rock attracts the pity of Old Uncle Sun God, who sends a fairy to investigate. Old Uncle himself comes down to earth, restores Mr. Straight's eyes, and instructs him to cook some old rice, put his animals in their pens, and sleep at a neighbor's. In the morning, Mr. Straight finds that his animals have multiplied and the rice has become gold. Mr. Crooked learns about this and asks Mr. Straight how it happened. Mr.

Straight answers honestly. Mr. Crooked gouges out his own eyes and sits crying on the rock.

The fairy comes, and Old Uncle comes down. Mr. Crooked lies and blames Mr. Straight for his misfortune. He is given the same instructions as Mr. Straight, but instead of following them, he uses new rice in order to increase the amount, expands his pens to hold more animals, and sneaks back before morning to peek at his new riches. All he finds is excrement in the pens and the pots (Miller 1994, 205–9). Again, the greedy and wily are punished while the simple and honest are rewarded. The value of being *laoshi* is, as usual, associated with ethnic minorities (and peasants).

Similarly, a story by Tibetan writer Alai (writing in Chinese) (2002), *Red Poppies*, features an "idiot" narrator, the second son of the second wife of the chieftain in decades prior to China's control over Tibet. At the beginning he is fondly dismissed by everyone for his idiocy; everyone is sure that his elder brother will become the chieftain following the father. After an event-filled childhood and early adulthood, in which he builds a grain storeroom while his brother plants opium, it is clear that people harbor increasing doubts about his genuine idiocy. Is it a ruse to make himself appear harmless? If so, it would be extremely clever. Is it inadvertent and genuine? By the end of the book it is clear that he is not really an idiot, but this doubt has been central to his role throughout the rather long novel. Again, though, this is a minority writer using idiocy as a deceptive weapon.

So what are the guiding principles for moral use of language? *Consider consequences. Select script. Anticipate others' responses. Guard information.*

Knowing Truth and Its Others: Theory of Mind

Moral evaluation of deception, rusing, lying, exaggeration, and all their cousins depends on their consequences and contexts. Unlike the first-order approximation in the United States, where such actions are automatically deplored, in the Chinese context we find no automatic criticism of these non-truthful actions. They can perhaps attain a higher good, relying on a higher notion of social truth or justice or welfare.

Complex ruses may be admired for the planning, intelligence, cleverness, and knowledge that is required. Dupes are sympathized with, to some extent, but they are also pitied and criticized for their gullibility, which often stems from greed or desire. If an offer is too good to be true . . . should not a clever person know this much?

Simon Baron-Cohen points out in a fascinating essay on autism (*Mindblindness: An Essay on Autism and Theory of Mind*, 1995) that what most of us do effortlessly—attribute intention and purpose as we observe the actions of others—is impossible for certain individuals who are categorized as having the disorder known as autism, and in particular Asperger syndrome. They can observe someone going into a room and explain it simply as what the person does, perhaps according to a schedule. They have no curiosity about the person's motives or frame of mind. In our society, and according to psychology, medicine, cognitive science, and education, they are not entirely fully functioning human beings. At best, they might be retrained by means of diagrams, behavior modification, role playing, and a host of other interventions to act as if they believed they understood the minds of others.

But however important or unimportant this feature is in general, it varies from society to society. Interestingly, not all societies share the U.S. fascination (indeed mandate) with understanding the minds of others. The Baining of Papua New Guinea actively discourage and condemn people who involve themselves with attempting to guess others' intentions. "Informants do not readily speak or vouchsafe personal opinions about either their own actions or those of others. Evaluations of events do not involve an internal, emotional explanation. The most common response to questions such as 'Why did he do that?' is 'I don't know about him'" (Fajans 1997, 122). The Ilongot of the Philippines are similarly reluctant to venture a guess about what someone else is feeling (Rosaldo 1980).

Even more than in the United States, in urban Han China it is essential to try to predict others' actions. This includes their verbal actions and the consequences that accompany such actions.

If this chapter has focused on deception in China, it is not to say that people in China are always deceptive, nor that they are any more deceptive than people elsewhere. Morality is a central concern in China, just as it is everywhere, but the specific details of what counts as moral behavior differ. The Chinese focus on the effects of language suggests a humanly complex world where it is not adequate simply to blurt out the truth and celebrate one's honesty; rather it is a world where speakers must be guided by others more expert than themselves, to reveal information judiciously, and to trust only when the speaker is verified as trustworthy.

Is China unique? Scarcely. What comes across from the examples given is that Han are especially aware of the many ways language can be used to deceive, to tempt, to protect. Unlike my own odd idiosyncratic ideology of honesty and its rewards, this is a contested area, with urban Han aware of the dangers attendant on speaking. Every time we speak we can reveal secrets or hide them; we can utter soothing words to the dying or we can blurt out the facts. Each person in each circumstance decides—often unconsciously and as the result of training—what to say and what to conceal. In no society could people literally "tell the truth" at all times. How a balance is struck between entirely pragmatic and entirely truthful speech depends on many factors. In the next chapter we will see some of these factors spelled out.

Notes

1. We cannot in this case suspect a desire to earn more money for placing me in more expensive accommodations, for in those days the lack of personal benefit to state-employed clerks, and their attendant lack of interest in selling anything, were legendary. I also misunderstood the notion of rules (the Chinese term is *guiding*), finding that they were best learned by infractions. Another consideration was that the clerk had to honor my elevated status (as a foreign teacher). Even if I didn't know better, my "face" as a foreign teacher had to be preserved, even if it required a "lie" to do so.

2. Written at the peak of the *xungen yishi* (searching for roots) movement in the 1980s, like so many others Bai Hua sought alternatives to China's Han culture in the past or at China's periphery.

3. Even groups such as the Hui, who are often regarded negatively by others, especially by Han, are never accused of being duplicitous. Hui were called violent (e.g., Lipman 1990), unreasonable, separatist, and superstitious, but where ethnic stereotypes were concerned, only the Han were repeatedly mentioned as *congming*.

4. I should note that another Westerner listening to the explanation, an expert on Japanese literature, was as puzzled as I about why the southerner's presentation should be considered deceptive while the northerner's should be considered straightforward. We found them both deceptive.

5. Thanks to Yao Yusheng for this reference.

CHAPTER THREE

For Their Own Good: Benevolent Deception and Flattery

The neurologist warned me not to jump to any premature conclusions, for they still knew very little about the tumor. No prognosis was possible until after an entire battery of tests. I accepted this wait-and-see attitude very easily. It was the only alternative to contemplating the worst-possible-case outcome of the disease. I once asked the neurologist how bad it could get, and, with a pained expression, he answered, "Do you really want to know?" I didn't.

—Robert F. Murphy 1990

Just praise is only a debt, but flattery is a present.

—Samuel Johnson 1969 [1751]

Benevolent Deception

Immediately upon hearing the words *deception and truth*, sociologist Wang Xiao-qing, studying for her Ph.D. in the United States, offered the observation that it is *obligatory* to lie when someone is terminally ill (personal communication, November 11, 2002). The closer people are to dying, the more their loved ones are required to reassure them that they will recover. Everyone must pretend that preparations for a return home have been made. One cannot discuss burial arrangements; to speak of a parent's imminent death is entirely taboo. One can use vague words or speak about someone else's condition, all the while with everyone knowing that the topic is the parent's situation. Xiao-qing was certain that this was the moral position—though her smile and continual explaining showed that she knew it contrasted with American ideals. Her view echoed what I had heard in Kunming from the neighbor of a friend.

A stylish young Han woman in Kunming, whom I'll call Yan Qimei, told the following story to support her view that it is better not to tell people how serious their illnesses are, so as not to increase their burden and to provide peace for their final days. A man was told he had a fatal illness. He went home and put his affairs in order, including writing two letters confessing wrongs to people. The next day the doctor came and said there had been a big mistake, that he was not so sick after all. He was very happy, but then immediately remembered those letters. They had already gone out. A few minutes later, the mail carrier came and brought him the remains of two letters, saying they had been burned and all that remained was the corner with the return address. He was relieved. This was divine proof, for the storyteller, that people should not be told about terminal illnesses.

I had also asked fourteen people to evaluate the following hypothetical scenario: *Feng Zide's grandmother got cancer. The doctor says she won't live much longer. Feng Qide, his parents, and the doctors tell his grandmother she'll soon be well.*

Ten of the fourteen responded that it would be moral, exemplary (*shanliang*), to misrepresent the seriousness of a terminal illness; three of fourteen said it would be okay (*hai keyi*). (One person didn't answer.) No one thought there was anything wrong with it. This contrasts sharply with an American notion of "patients' rights to know." At the least, people would argue about it. (It is easy to forget that in the West such a "right" is recent.) A Chinese doctor argued that it was the family's and the health care practitioner's responsibility to make the patient comfortable and optimistic. What could possibly be gained by saying that she would soon die? What good would come of worrying the ill person? Why not give them peace, if one could? It would be considered a bad act indeed to inflict a burden of anxiety when it was within one's power to avoid it. (*Consider consequences.*)

(Afang, the Yi friend of a friend, said *she* would want to know. We should be careful not to exaggerate the unanimity of opinion on this or any other matter. Just as in the United States, many people have opposing views.[1])

It was obvious that revealing the full truth about serious illness was not merely inconvenient, painful, and undesirable, but that it was immoral, based on the premise that people have an obligation to protect their loved ones. Considerations of the *effects* of the speech control whether it is said. There are other cases where deception may not be obligatory but may still be morally legitimate.

Legitimate Deception

When I asked a group of college graduates in Kunming about occasions when lying or deceiving might be legitimate, such as Kant's example of a murderer asking if one's family members were sleeping inside the house, they were unanimous that there were such occasions. They brought up the film *Schindler's List*, about a man who saves Jews during the Holocaust by elaborate deception, as an example of when lying might be the ideal tool for saving someone from unrighteous others. One young woman, Celeste, brought up an example that had happened that day. Her coworker, Xiao Gao, went to take care of some business. Their boss came back and asked where she was; Celeste responded that she'd gone to get a document or something. It wasn't true, but it didn't hurt anyone to have her say so, and it kept Xiao Gao from getting into trouble. Bosses are often unreasonable and inconsiderate; protecting a coworker from exploitation, she implied, was morally legitimate. Impersonal rules could not command loyalty as much as people with whom one has a relationship. (*Take relationships as primary.*)

As in Gandhi's, Thoreau's, and Martin Luther King's notion that unjust laws should be broken, there is an unspoken sense in China that just reasons can excuse behavior. Most people consider it acceptable to cheat cheaters. I presented the following case:

> A swindler came to sell a very effective medicine in a village. Chen Jun saw through his tricks and said to the swindler, "My father-in-law really needs this medicine. I'll take you to talk to him." The swindler was very happy and was already thinking about how to spend the money he was about to earn. He was thinking about his medicine, and suddenly realized that Chen Jun had taken him to the police station, where he was immediately arrested.

In their evaluations of this case, five people said the behavior was exemplary, seven said it was okay, and two said it was extremely immoral (*feichang bu daode*).

I asked about lying for economic benefit:

> A new rule says that all foreign *tourists* in China must pay four times the rate Chinese pay for train tickets, but foreign *students* in China pay the Chinese price. When John went to buy a ticket, the ticket seller asked for his status in China. He said he was a student. Actually, he was a tourist.

Four said this was okay, seven said it was wrong, and three said it was extremely immoral. This example included a number of issues: the foreign/native distinction, the idea of equality in treatment, economic consequences, and deception. There is no unanimity here, though most regard deception for economic gain as unacceptable.

Polite Sincerity, Flattery, and Face

Asians ("Orientals") are often stereotyped as polite and concerned with "face." As with many stereotypes, there is a kernel of truth to it, but we have to delve more deeply to tease out the actual principles involved. As with the previous chapter, what we will find is a variation in degree between China and other societies, rather than an absolute difference.

A large body of scholarship has emerged around the topic of politeness, taking people's "face wants" as universal and basic. Bluntness contrasts with politeness, showing various forms of sincerity, only some of which involve literally speaking the individual truth.

Face and Flattery

Sometimes politeness seems to produce talk that is, on its surface, untrue, as with flattery and formulaic phrases.

Brown and Levinson describe conflicting desires in human interaction: the desire for involvement and the desire for distance. They term these, respectively, *positive face*—the kinds of pleasure derived from praise, flattery, identification, and so forth—and *negative face*—the desire for what we might call "space" or options, the desire to be unimpeded. In language, we often preserve the desire for distance by use of politeness phenomena. We usually avoid what they term bald on-record directives—unadorned, undeniable commands—such as "Pass the salt," since the only possible responses are compliance or confrontation. Instead, we say "Please pass the salt" or "Could you please pass the salt" or "Would you mind please passing the salt"—adding words, hedges, that all preserve the hearer's options.

Considerations of "face" are ubiquitous in China (as, according to Brown and Levinson, everywhere), and can be seen operating daily. Positive face is often valued more than negative face in China. Its counterpart, positive politeness, or emphasis on producing relationship, prevails in China (*Take relationships as primary.*), and negative politeness, or emphasis on preserving freedom and autonomy, prevails in the United States. (*Be autonomous.*) A simple example can show how.

When a person expects to follow Chinese practices and is given a drink, being presented with choices is interpreted as a marked, unexpected use of language. "Would you like something to drink?" will very likely be answered with "No, thank you, I've just had dinner." (This may or may not be literally true, but it is the expected and proper reply.) A proper host would have presented tea, but the polite guest permits the host to reclaim the proper role by now insisting on giving tea; it is the host's responsibility to make this decision, and by denying desire, the guest will receive tea only at the host's initiative.

I had this experience during my first stay in China, when I was an English teacher in Nanjing in 1982. I invited my students for chats in small groups. About five students arrived and I began to offer them food and drink.

> "Would you like some tea or coffee?"
> "No, thank you, we've just had our dinner."
> I waited, we chatted, and then I tried again.
> "Aren't you thirsty? You rode your bikes here."
> "No thank you, we're fine."
> I let that go, then suddenly was worried.
> "Maybe you don't like tea or coffee . . ."
> This caused consternation. Their proper refusal was making me lose face.
> "No, we like it."
> "Then, why don't you have some?"
> "Maybe later."

Eventually, one person was willing to break the stalemate and the others followed. In time I learned that this is not supposed to be a script of option giving with "true" answers, but of attending to guests' anticipated needs. I now regard it as a triumph if I can get people to accept my hospitality. I have to remind myself, though, to present the tea or coffee without choices.

Yu-hwei Shih explains the principle well:

> When making an invitation, if the guest gives a negative reply, the host is supposed not to take it at face value at the first offer. He should offer again and again, and sometimes impose on the other to take it by various means, such as "Please do come, we will wait for you," "I will ask someone to pick you up," or "If you don't come, there will be no fun for the whole party," and the like. This is a way of showing the host's hospitality and sincerity. Yet the Chinese way of strong imposition often gives Americans a sense that they are "too pushy." (quoted in Wierzbicka 1996, 333)

This emphatic hosting may also appear insincere and the entire exchange dishonest. Giving face here is mandated but it is based on the maxim *Take relationships as primary*; relationships are to be emphasized and furthered. The positive politeness of increasing involvement, rather than American negative politeness of preserving autonomy, requires that hosts and guests follow the script very carefully. Failure to persist means that the host will lose the opportunity to serve in that role.

Wierzbicka elaborates that "it is by disregarding the addressee's expressed wishes, rather than by accepting them at face value, that one establishes the 'sincerity' of one's desire to do something good for the addressee" (1996, 333). Thus the face value of the words is not especially significant.

Positive face is also conferred through "flattery," an idea used often in China: *taohao* (to flatter, to toady), *pai mapi* (to pat the horse's rump, to flatter). Even false praise is understood to have great efficacy though it can be excessive—or at least it seemed so to me in the following event:

At a banquet in Kunming in 1997 my host introduced the participants at the banquet, though I knew most of them already. (As linguistic anthropologists know, language is used to do far more than to convey previously unknown information. Here the introductions permitted status relations to be clearly established.) When my host reached one particular person, he said to me,

"Mr. Wen was your teacher, wasn't he?"

"No," I said, "he taught my students." Everybody roared with laughter. A joke . . . but what was funny? All I did was correct my host's mistake.

"Americans are so *zhi*, so straight, they just say what they mean!"

"What should I have said?"

"You should have said, 'Right, he was my teacher' and then he would have said, 'No, I was never her teacher, *bu gandang*, I can't take credit for this.'"[2]

In a banquet full of such exchanges, we all agreed that I flunked my first culture test of the evening. I would never have been able to bring myself to claim this fellow as my teacher even with a lot of coaching. He simply was not my teacher. That is the pure truth. Saying otherwise would have been like singing hymns of a religion not one's own—and though some people don't mind doing this, it's impossible for others (Keane 1997, 2002). (I also knew some other upsetting things about this teacher; he'd harassed several foreign female students the year before.) Still, I should have attempted—it would have been so easy—to give Mr. Wen face by acknowledging his role as teacher. This sincere role playing would have allowed the script to unfold. Instead, I unknowingly clung to my American notion of expressing my feelings directly, with no consideration of context. (*Tell the truth.*) One aspect of the context is those who are witnesses to it. The goal of performing praise is to cause witnesses to perceive the praised person's merit. (*Consider bystanders.*) It is not sufficient to say what one would have said if alone in a room.

I described this to some young college graduates in Kunming. They laughed and started talking about politeness (*keqihua*) and flattery.

"People all like flattery, especially leaders (*lingdao*)."
"Do they believe it?"
"They do!"
Don't they remember how *they* worked at it?
"Perhaps they forget how easy it is to say things."

In that context one person talked about New Year's visits, when people have to say pleasing (*haotingde hua*) and lucky (*jili hua*) talk: *Ni hen piaoliang* (You're very pretty), *Nide haizi zhangde hen hao* (Your child is really growing), *Ni shenti hen jiankang* (You are very healthy). Under these circumstances, people like to hear the pretty words even though they are all aware that they are required by the occasion. *Keqihua*, politeness, is not believed, yet it is not regarded as lying. (The students were insistent: *keqihua* is not *jiahua*, lying, nor is it *pian ren*, cheating, though it is not exactly a reflection of reality either.) *Keqihua* must *sound* sincere, even while the hearers remain undeceived about the veracity of the utterance.

The dean of a university in Beijing affirmed this: People do say nice things to people to make them feel good. Even though it may not all be entirely true, no one would criticize it since it demonstrates willingness to be kind. This is done mostly with people we don't know well. With family and familiars, he went on, one can be much more frank. I was startled a moment later when he told a foreign teacher that her hat was "very strange." (And it was! It was a kind of aviator's hat with leather flaps that connected beneath her chin—very warm in Beijing's winter.) I was struck by the fact that for Americans this would have been masked by politer comments. Blunt truthfulness can occur in Chinese contexts, of course, when Americans might prefer "white lies," especially about someone's appearance.

Other obligatory offerings can include invitations and refusals of invitations or compliments. As in the United States, an invitation for lunch may be just that or it may be an expression of friendliness (see Chen, Ye, and Zhang 1995, 151–61 on "ritual refusal"). *Youkong lai wanr*, "Come see us when you have a chance," is a common parting invitation. Hearers evaluate speakers' apparent sincerity, and speakers attempt to appear sincere, without deceiving anyone about their purpose. There is a kind of infinite regress as speakers anticipate hearers' reactions to their talk and then anticipate their own reactions to hearers' reactions.[3]

In a similar case—though in Japan, not China—described by Japan-born anthropologist Harumi Befu in his wonderful article "An Ethnography of

Dinner Entertainment in Japan" (1986), he weighs the evidence about an invitation to lunch on a visit to Kyoto. He is not sure if he is really invited, because "Kyoto people are known for extending 'false invitations' more sincerely than other Japanese and are fond of ridiculing others in private for misinterpreting them" (109). In the end he decides to accept the invitation, though he is not sure if it had been genuine. (When he arrived, lunch was indeed prepared.) This case of uncertainty about truth and lying involves two "natives" negotiating the meaning of an exchange; one is never finally sure about what kind of exchange it had been. Politeness in many settings may lead to apparent breaches of literal truthfulness.

Directness is often regarded as undesirable and graceless. At the banquet in Kunming, where all the participants were teachers or bureaucrats, the good-natured and humorous discussion (made more riotous by the toasting with strong liquor) continued, where the topic was Americans' simple-minded direct expression, Thai solicitous politeness, and Chinese indirect politeness.

Teacher Li said, "For Americans what is in their hearts and what comes out of their mouths are *yi*, the same." My host said, "Americans brag and believe everything good about themselves. Chinese people have *didiao* (low tone) in their mouth but *gaodiao* (high tone—pride) in their hearts. They say 'My child is *ben* (stupid)' but they think 'He's great.'"

Teacher Chen said that she spent two years in Thailand, where people are extremely *keqi* and relations are extremely important, but *keqi* is different from that in China. "If a Chinese person uses Chinese politeness and says that their business is so-so, they don't have money, don't have clothes, etc., the next day a Thai person will bring them clothes and money." The politeness of the Chinese did not carry—for Chinese—the sense that the words corresponded to events in the world, but only that the speaker was behaving properly, sincerely, in given circumstances. Thai politeness, according to Teacher Chen, did assume a correspondence between words and worlds. Thai assumed Chinese words did too and acted accordingly.

The ironic and metalinguistic conversation reached its peak when we discussed the polite language used in hosting and guesting behavior. Recall the connection between *keqi* "polite" (literally, "like a guest") and *ke* "guest." Teacher Li said, "You can go to a friend's house and your stomach is growling and they ask if you are hungry and you say 'No, I've just eaten.' So your friend has to say, 'Come eat with us, there's too much food, it's no problem.'" As long as all participants play their parts, everyone knows exactly what to say. (*Select script.*)

My host said, "When Chinese people say *duo chi yidiar* (eat more!) they really mean *shao chi* (eat less!), to the point that they really don't want you to eat anything." "Fine," I said, "if you invite me to your house to eat, I won't eat anything!" Everyone laughed again—not least because of the impossibility of a guest not eating.

Training

While people of lower status in China—minorities, peasants, children—are regarded as honest and blunt, a different view of the value of sincerity and politeness is held by members of the academic elite. In 1991 an American teaching linguistics at Yunnan University (the top university in Yunnan province) agreed to share her students' essays with me. She had asked her students if one could detect a person's level of education through the way she or he speaks. Though we both expected to hear about the use of the standard language (Putonghua) in contrast to local topolects, eight people out of fourteen mentioned politeness, but only three mentioned linguistic variety (and two of these had also mentioned politeness). Here are a few excerpts:

> For example, [to differentiate levels of education] don't use clothes, use speech. When you hear somebody speaking or when you talk with somebody, you can judge his level of education. The persons of lower level of education speak rudely, impolitely, vulgarly. But the persons of high level of education usually speak elegantly, politely, properly.

∞

> A well-educated person learns how to speak, how to talk with other persons, he has good habits. He always listens to the others carefully and never disturbs them. But a poorly educated person is not like that. When he speaks, his hands, arms, even his legs are out of place. He likes to laugh at other persons when they make mistakes. He cannot keep quiet but interrupts and always "corrects" the others while they are speaking.

Here we see that politeness is valued as a property of educated people, which includes "good" (quiet) listening and restraint, even of the body during speech. The most interesting, however, is the following: (The gendered language was in the original; I have corrected minor grammatical infelicities to avoid giving the impression of quaintness.)

> If I have a conversation with a person, I can speak to him, listen to him, and understand what he says. Meanwhile I can watch his manner of talking, the words he uses. Thus I can tell whether he is an educated person or not.

For example: Several days ago, I went shopping. As I went into a small shop, I saw two girls sitting at the counter. One, about sixteen years old, was knitting a sweater; the other, about twenty years old, was reading. They were both in beautiful skirts. I went up to the girl who was making the sweater and said, "Excuse me, can you show me the red plastic washing basin?"

"Don't bother me, don't you see I'm busy?" said the girl.

I got surprised and said, "Are you the shop assistant here?"

"It's none of your business, I'm the boss of the small shop, and I sell everything in it," answered she.

I could hardly restrain my rage. But I calmed myself as if nothing had happened. I thought the girl was little educated. At most, she only finished middle school because she spoke very impolitely. But I really wanted to buy the red basin and I said something with little to do with selling.

"It's very hard for you to do business, you should go to school or go to college at this age." At this time, the other girl who was reading a moment before came up and said gently to me, "Can I help you?" And after saying this she immediately showed me several and let me choose the one I liked best. Then she said again, "The girl is my younger sister. She has run this shop since she finished middle school. I'm in Yunnan Normal University. I'm free today. So I help my sister do business."

After this experiment, I can tell these two girls' level of education according to their different behavior, their vocabulary, words, their attitudes, and the way they speak. The younger girl used impolite words and unfriendly tone. Her manner was rude and she is less educated. The other spoke beautifully, her words were friendly. The way she spoke is superior. She is at a high level of education.

This perhaps idealized example[4] of an interaction and of the speaker's considerations about reception and perception shows how politeness is involved in portraying a selfless—if patronizing—concern with the other's welfare, from a position of superiority (greater age, higher educational level) and of apparently disregarding expression of her own desires (though she tells about them), in this case for the basin. "I really wanted to buy the red basin and I said something with little to do with selling."[5] We could say that she consciously manipulated her hearers' feelings by masking her own feelings and feigning concern, but it is more subtle than that. She was aware of the requirement that people with education act politely and gently; she portrayed her concern as sincerely as possibly, likely meaning what she said even if she also harbored annoyance and dislike. Yet her intention was not especially relevant here. She portrays herself as having acted properly. She was rewarded with both the gentle words of the elder sister and the red basin.

Part of the convention here, invoked consciously, it seems clear, is that superior people are kind, controlled, and other-directed. Another student said the same thing:

> There is a phrase in Kunminghua, "Jian gang." These two words express hard and solid things in Chinese. But the lower-educated people use it with another meaning that will make you feel sick if you know the real meaning of the words. Almost all the people in higher-educated society don't say these two words. . . . On the other hand, talking with higher-educated people, you will feel that they speak gently and politely. They talk with simple and key words. They like talking about your work and study and concern about your life.

Other-regard ("talking about your work . . . study, and . . . life") comes in part through training, which includes the use of euphemism, polite formulae, and indirection (*Language is culture, not (only) nature.*):

> Generally, people with high level of education would use some polite, "big" words, euphemism, whole sentences.

∞

> The educated people use formal, polite words, such as "please," "kindly," but uneducated people rarely use these words. Educated people like to use euphemisms. They never say that a girl is ugly, they only say that the girl is not so pretty, but the uneducated people express themselves very directly.

∞

> First of all we will notice the vocabulary he uses. If he uses vulgar words or popular expressions . . . we can judge that he is not well-educated, probably uneducated. . . . Second, we can learn something about their education from the phrases and idioms people use in their talking. Old, well-educated people often use idioms and old sayings. . . . Sixth, the way he uses his voice also tells a lot. A well-educated person doesn't shout roughly, he speaks in a mild polite way. Seventh, well-educated people use "Chinese Polite Language" more often. For example, they are always saying "Thank you," "I've troubled you a lot," "Be careful on your way home" and so on.

∞

> A well-educated person is always polite and he or she could always use the right words in the right place at the right time. When he or she talks with his

or her friends of the same level of education, he or she would use some jargon and euphemism but when he or she is with workers or farmers, he or she would always get along well with them. He or she would use workers' or farmers' language including some slang. When he or she talks with friends of the same level of education, he or she would say "Wo airen" (my husband) but when he or she speaks to workers and farmers he or she would say "Wo Lao Gou" (also means "my husband" but used only by workers and farmers). If a person could "Do in Rome as the Romans do," he or she has a high level of education.

The assurance of well-educated people that their way is superior comes across clearly, especially in terms of speaking politely and gently, using euphemisms and idioms, and adapting to circumstances. Politeness requires a high degree of training. (*Language is culture, not [only] nature.*) Bursting out simple truth shows lack of training and for urban Han Chinese is not often welcome.

Getting Results

My friend Li Kun brought her nearly pathologically naughty son everywhere. One time he threw heavy bricks at the street, with a gleeful violence. She muttered to him in Kunminghua the Mandarin equivalent of "*Wo da ni*" ('I'll beat you'), which he took as a weak warning. He laughed at it and continued to throw bricks. Andrew Kipnis describes parents saying to children at a clinic "We won't give you a shot" (*Bu dazhen*) (Kipnis 1997, 111). Once the child is calmer, the shot is given. Then the crying child is comforted by "We won't give you any more shots" (*Bu dazhenle*). Kipnis's astonishment may reflect his own American conscious ideal rather than any kind of observation of American practice—but that is the case for a lot of implicit comparisons with a hypothetical "West." When I ate dinner with one family, their daughter wanted to watch TV. While we ate, they kept saying "Don't watch TV, eat." But nobody turned it off. The admonitions served a purpose, but it was not of bringing about action in the world. Rather the purpose was to express their recognition of the ideal. After all, *performance counts*.

Post-Spock American readers may find it appalling that parents would lie so clearly to children, using idle threats or promises. Parenting advice in the United States warns against these tactics. Yet many Chinese parents may sincerely believe they are acting in their children's best interests, especially when the consequences are considered. (*Consider consequences.*) Children are often seen as having no claim to truth on its own merits. We might wish to contrast rights and obligations to truth, sincerity, and authenticity in a variety of domains. (*Do the right action in context.*) Members of a person's own household may expect a certain kind of bluntness in certain domains, such as regarding money, in the presence of dangers, evaluation of conduct, etc.

Members of a shared social circle might expect bluntness with regard to appearance, accomplishment, and so forth. Strangers may have no right to any of these, and in fact in many domains they may have no right to expect anything except the greatest stretching of truth and credulity.

A salesperson might claim that the goods are made of rare metals, made of lead-free paint, and so forth. *Caveat emptor*: every buyer knows that such claims are meant to be insincere. Only the most foolish and foolhardy would stop there and accept the first offered price. But once the exchange has been made, with each side trying to stand her or his ground against the piercing arguments of the other, then one may accept the final, best offer. This is not different from hard bargaining in some markets in the United States where exaggerations are to be expected; Richard Bauman (1996) makes the case that dog sellers in Texas are expected to exaggerate and cannot be faulted for performing according to expectation. At farmers' markets, in contrast, expectations are of honesty and simplicity. Used-car salesmen are the archetype of duplicity. Similarly, in some domains in China people expect more sincere claims, while in others—such as at fruit markets or selling of jewelry on the street, and so forth—the claims may be farfetched and not easily falsifiable.

Within the family, children are often aware of the effects of their actions and words. One very popular eight-year-old girl whom I'll call Tiaotiao, a favorite in her family, was praised because—as her mother said—she really "knows how to say what people like to hear" (*hui shuo bieren zhen xihuan ting de hua*). For instance, she telephones her maternal grandmother and says "*Wo hen chang shijian mei kandao ni, wo hen xiang ni*" ('I haven't seen you for a long time; I really miss you.'). Tiaotiao's mother did not say whether this was genuine or not, only that it was sincere and had a very positive effect.

Ideologies of Politeness and Sincerity

Politeness in the United States is often conceived as "mere" politeness and thus antithetical to real feeling or real meaning. For elites in China, the reverse is the case. Politeness, no matter what the speaker's feelings, is desired and desirable. Failure to be polite is not excused by a surplus of feeling. There is a look of horror that people exchange when children are impolite, even if they are verbally excused for being children. Their parents are certainly faulted for failing to inculcate the proper attitude.

Sincerity is valued, but among educated, urban Han it is a very trained sincerity, a sincerity akin to that of a method actor. As in pre-Qin China, the skillfully trained person comes to act naturally. The more genuine the expressions appear, the more appreciated they are. Authenticity, the spontaneous eruption of feeling into action, is avoided at all cost. Truth alone cannot justify saying something. The result is that to many outside this system, the actions and expressions may appear deceptive. A common response by Americans to Chinese activity is "They are lying!" Yet speakers may be sincere. Still, there are cases in China where deception is lamented for its social costs. The following chapter treats some of these as it discusses corruption, censorship, and media, as they operate in contemporary Chinese society.

Notes

1. There is a lively debate in Western medical ethics about the desirability or need for benevolent deception. Since the 1950s and 1960s when the notion of "patients' rights" arose, along with malpractice suits, in the service of patients' autonomy doctors are charged with being frank about patients' prognoses. At the same time, doctors and nurses *in practice* gauge how to dole out information. A first-level approximation in the United States is that doctors should "tell the truth"—the level of ideology—while a close look reveals greater complexity. In the *Journal of Medical Ethics* a series of articles and opinion pieces in the 1990s discussed the (lack of) justification for lying to patients on general moral grounds (Bakhurst 1992; Hope 1995; Jackson 1991; Ryan, de Moore; and Patfield 1995, Teasdale and Kent 1995), along with a study of Mediterranean (Athens) populations and their attitudes toward medical practitioners' benevolent lying (Dalla-Vorgia et al. 1992). The discussions raised the issues of patients' fragility, doctors' roles in treating the patients' psychological as well as physical health, and whether lying and deception might be differentiated. The interesting question of placebos was raised. Placebos are quite effective for many conditions, but only if presented as genuine with absolute conviction by the medical practitioner. It is clear that in practice, many health care providers struggle with telling the truth, despite a clear ideology that mandates it.

2. One reader found this story hard to believe; I too was amazed by it and wrote down the details as soon as the banquet was over. I am confident of the accuracy of the account.

3. The dyadic model of verbal interaction is misleading in the case of China. Bystanders are often included in any consideration of audience. For anthropological challenges to this simple model of a speaker and a hearer, see Blum 1997; Goffman 1981; Irvine 1996.

4. We do not know, of course, if any of this actually occurred. We are in the realm of language ideology, of reports about language and beliefs about linguistic behavior. Yet the fact that the teller gave *this* report to a question about the level of education and language suggests that she felt it was relevant.

5. She wrote in fairly high-level English. I would like to focus on the *and* linking the two clauses but can't be sure how to treat it. In Chinese there is a conjunction, *er*, that is a combination of *and*, *so*, and *but*. Perhaps she was translating with the closest both phonologically and semantically. I would love to conclude that she meant *so*, but this is not warranted.

CHAPTER FOUR

State Secrets and Fakes:
The True, the Real, the
Transparent, and the Squelched

The structure of social relations in China rests largely on fluid, person-centered social networks, rather than on fixed social institutions.

—Yunxiang Yan 1996

Mundus vult decipi, ergo decipiatur. (The world wants to be fooled, therefore is deceived.)

China has made headlines around the world since the 1990s for its vast increases in gross national product, for its rapidly modernizing cities such as Beijing and Shanghai, for its hosting of the Olympics in 2008. Tourists return from their carefully guided visits with a sense of China's historic scope and of the sweetness of its children. People are amazed at the new wealthy middle and upper classes. Yet alongside these relatively positive aspects is another complex China. China faces a number of significant challenges, including an unemployed migrant population numbering at least 140 million in 2003 by official sources (People's Daily Online 2005a estimates it at twice that), worrisome income disparities of up to tenfold between coastal and inland areas, severe pollution of water and air (among other environmental concerns), repression of religious freedoms (especially Falun Gong and some forms of Catholicism), "trafficking" in women and children, execrable work conditions for millions of workers with no right to protest, and layoffs for millions of urban workers (see Solinger 1999; U.S. Department of State 2002; Weston 2000; Zhang 2001).

Within China, headlines often focus on corruption. Corruption is said to be the primary concern today in Chinese citizens' minds (see Gong 1994, 135) and since 1986 has been considered the most serious social problem (Kwong 1997, 85). It is the cause of many executions and a high percentage of China's legal efforts. The social and economic costs of corruption are in fact staggering. Though impossible to measure with any certainty, corruption was estimated at 1.270 billion yuan (US$154 million) in the last five years, or 17 percent of gross domestic product (Central News Agency 2003). At the National People's Congress meeting in March 2003 it was announced that more than 83,000 officials had been convicted of corruption in the preceding five years (Radio Australia News 2003).

When asked about China's gravest social problems, corruption is almost always mentioned first. Concern about corruption fueled protests in 1979 as well as in 1989. During the demonstrations in Tiananmen Square, Western media portrayed the central concern as that of democracy, while native accounts always mentioned both economic problems (such as inflation and the low stipends given students) and corruption.

Corruption is long-standing; it led to the downfall of the Nationalist Party (Guomindang) and the victory of the Communists in 1949 (Kwong 1997, 79), when "public offices were openly bought and sold, and the going rates were public information. For example, three thousand yuan would buy the office of a district magistrate in Jiangxi for three months between 1930–1933" (79–80).

In a constant rain of cases, newspapers and television are filled with accounts of high officials, whether in government or in private business, guilty of corruption, including, increasingly, tax evasion. In the early 1990s it was often the *gaogan zidi* or *taizi dang*, offspring of high officials, who were implicated. By 2000, it was the officials themselves who were increasingly charged. For example, in 2000, the vice governor of Jiangxi province, Hu Changqing, was executed for corruption (U.S. Department of State 2002, 18). In 2002, Zhu Xiaohua, a bank president and a well-known financial official, a protégé of the (unrelated) premier, Zhu Rongji, was sentenced to fifteen years in prison on charges of bribery (New York Times 2002).

China is not the only nation with a bad case of corruption. In a quick search of the archives of the *South China Morning Post*, there were forty-eight articles on corruption between September 22 and October 18, 2002. (There were eighty-two in a similar search on the *New York Times*, with perhaps about half concerned with cases outside the U.S.; all of the *South China Morning Post*'s cases were Chinese.) In 2006 the U.S. government was distracted in part by the corruption of lobbyist Jack Abramoff. (*Corruption*, like *terrorism* or *evil*, may be so vague as to conceal more than it reveals.)

The International Corruption Perceptions Index, issued annually by Transparency International and Goettingen University, provides a rough cross-cultural measure of corruption, using the idea of "transparency" as its antagonist. The most transparent (least corrupt) country in 2005 was Iceland, at 9.7 of a possible 10, and the least transparent were Bangladesh and Chad, at 1.7. The United States ranked seventeenth of 158 countries, at 7.6, and China ranked seventy-eighth at 3.2. It should be noted that Singapore—an overwhelmingly Chinese society but with a different government and history than the People's Republic—ranked fifth, at 9.4, and Hong Kong ranked fifteenth at 8.3, both above the United States (Transparency International 2005).

Transparency International defines the relevant terms: "Corruption is operationally defined as the misuse of entrusted power for private gain," and transparency is "a principle that allows those affected by administrative decisions, business transactions, or charitable work to know not only the basic facts and figures but also the mechanisms and processes. It is the duty of civil servants, managers, and trustees to act visibly, predictably, and understandably" (Transparency International 2003). This fits with a Euro-American view of ideal social functioning, but it might not be the only way to accomplish such goals. It is possible, for example, to imagine a society in which processes of procurement, distribution, employment, consumption, etc., occur in non-visible and secret ways that are nonetheless according to acceptable principles. Yet the notion that openness and uniformity should guide all societies in every circumstance is applied across all countries—a measure with ramifications for how countries are regarded internationally by powerful institutions such as the World Bank. This notion is that status and role should be irrelevant to access to services and goods, and that information should circulate freely and be unaffected by context. Relationships should be purely affective and have no practical benefit. Transparency means that all transactions should be impersonal, should not rely on connections, gift giving, or reciprocity. There are many reasons that corruption is difficult to eradicate in China. Yet it also serves as a focus for internal and external critics alike.

This chapter looks at corruption, as well as other non-transparent, non-honest forms of activity in contemporary China, including fakes, censorship, and secrecy.

Corruption

Corruption is a violation of trust by those to whom responsibilities and power have been delegated.

—Julia Kwong 1997, 145–46

Corruption (*fubai* or *tanwu*) may be defined as improper use of resources or position for gain. *Fubai* has the implication of something rotten or decayed. (*Fuhua*, also translated "corrupt," carries the implication of a process, with *hua* meaning "having become," so *fuhua* is essentially "corrupted.") *Tanwu* resonates with graft and embezzlement. Together the two words form the phrase *tanwu fubai* or *tanwu fuhua* which are commonly translated as "corruption and degeneration." They connote excessive greed and power.

The particular forms of corruption have varied over the past half-century. In the 1960s, 1970s, and even 1980s, corruption often involved using understood channels—connections, gifts—to assist people's work units in gaining access to otherwise unobtainable resources, such as raw materials. In Gao Xiaosheng's satirical story "Li Shunda Builds a House," we follow a simpleton who attempts to build a house over the course of the 1950s and 1960s. Each time he complies with a political campaign and is on the verge of securing his building materials, the campaign changes. He finally succeeds because he learns to bribe (Gao 1987 [1979]). This story seems quaint today.

Procuring resources has depended on cultivating secret relations with individual officials rather than using impersonal channels (Kwong 1997, 54). Kwong sees bribery as a consequence of state ownership: "In the abstract, state property might be everyone's property, but few felt that way. In dispensing favors for a fee, state officials gave away something that did not belong to them in exchange for something personal and tangible and would belong to them. They would lose only if they were found out, and it was unlikely that their clients would tell" (1997, 63). Since so much of the corruption typically involved private transactions, their secrecy was guaranteed. Kwong claims that had such fabricated reports been done in the West, "the authors would be reprimanded for fabrication and not accused of corruption" (1997, 74).

Not only did the system itself make bribery almost essential, but it discouraged frankness and clarity. The more murky things were, the more possible it was to accomplish aims. There was a tacit agreement that inquiries would not be made. (*Avoid transparency. Thicken interactions. No evidence, no responsibility.*)

Kwong continues to explain the way corruption intersected with power and truthfulness (falsification):

> Ironically, the monopoly of power and its attendant efforts to extract conformity resulted in false reporting and cheating, because the negative consequences of nonconformity were high and the payoffs from meeting expectations were great. Although occasionally there were the humorous surrealistic improvisations for official visits, grass-roots units more often fabricated production statistics and submitted only positive reports to please their superiors. When the perceptive subordinates saw their superiors enthusiastic about new policies, such as the agricultural collectivization of the Great Leap Forward, they were especially willing and eager to comply. (Kwong 1997, 55–56)

In the fascinating memoirs of Yue Daiyun (Yue and Wakeman 1985), the narrator describes, in a completely unself-conscious way, all the gifts she had to provide in her quest to have her children admitted into a university after the university entrance examination system was restored at the end of the Cultural Revolution in 1977. Yue believed that her cause was just and that the children of intellectuals should have a place in the university. (For at least the ten previous years, the primary qualification for admission had been political stance. Intellectuals were at a disadvantage because of their privileged family background.) She was especially concerned about her daughter, who was almost at the upper age limit for university. In a system that depended on such imprecations, she had to do everything she could. Ultimately the office for admissions was moved to a secret location because so many supplicants pleaded on behalf of their children. And, inevitably, someone had connections to someone who worked in the admissions office and tracked it down. Yue never decries the system; she merely complains about how much work it took her to lug all the packages to distant locations on public transportation, all over Beijing. This was simply the way to get things done. It was clear to all that this was the way; interactions had to be somewhat shrouded; the price was known.

Pretense and Reality

The importance of building clientistic relations is apparent in the well-known and well-analyzed play from 1979, "What if I Were Real?" (*Jiaru wo shi zhende*) (See translation by Sha, Li, and Yao 1983 [1979]). A young man claims to be the son of a high-level official. To curry favor with his father and build up credit for their own requests, person after person wines and dines this fellow, who acts as if he is entitled to all this attention. Of course, it turns out that he is nobody. Like a good Shakespearean comedy, the truth is straightened out at the end, and a lesson is learned:

> Zhang Senior: Why did you want to impersonate my son and fool people?
>   Zhang: You can't say I'm the only one fooling people, can you? No. Everyone is in this game. Aren't the people I was fooling all going around fooling others? They not only provided me with situations and opportunities and helped me commit my fraud; some of the people I fooled even *taught* me how to fool others. I don't deny that I've used your identity and your position to get what I wanted for myself. But you can't tell me they haven't also tried to use the identity and position I pretended to have in order to achieve even bigger goals for themselves. (Sha, Li, and Yao 1983 [1979]: 244)

Corruption and deception counter the transparent and the real—in a tragicomedy familiar to all. This play was widely discussed—and banned.[1]

Authenticity and Its Others: Falsification, Piracy, Forgery, Plagiarism, Cheating, and Cons

The baldest form of cheating and deceiving is to falsify either information or goods. Without an effective system of consumer protections, China is filled with easy copying of manufactured items that people buy with relish because of their low cost. One good is substituted for another. Monthly reports (at least) in the South China Morning Post describe fake medicines, fake foods, and other goods that are sold under false pretenses. An article titled "Drinkers of 'domestic' wine being duped" (Jen-Siu 2003) describes the substitution of the very cheapest imported wine from Chile, Argentina, and other countries for wines supposedly of superior vintage.[2] In the 1980s there had been a host of substitutions of inferior goods for superior; "water was added to milk; wool was sprinkled with lead, iron, and glass filings to increase its weight; 0.91 *jin* of vinegar was sold as one *jin*; and part of a measuring rod was cut off to give the customer less cloth" (Kwong 1997, 96). There was little to be done, since there are few quality checks in China. In March 2003, authorities happened upon an ingenious punishment for advertising false goods (medicine, diplomas, identity cards): they developed a computer program that phones the advertised telephone number every twenty seconds, jamming the line until the phone number has to be changed or the advertisers turn themselves in to the Hangzhou Urban Administrative Bureau, which could undo the phoning (Chai 2003).

Every traveler to China glories in the fake Guccis and Rolexes and Mont Blancs, in the two-dollar silk ties and the ten-dollar cashmere scarves readily available in Chinese markets. Successfully buying a host of knockoffs and cheap copies is a badge of honor for students who care more for utility than for the status conferred by the real McCoy. Every market has such items and the trick is not to be cheated too much in the negotiations over price. The initial price is never the final price, and everybody in China is fully aware of this unspoken rule. The usual opening bid is half the asking price, but it could be less. Foreigners usually pay too much, adding to their reputation as easy marks, gullible dupes.

Amusing though such pastimes are, there are many spheres in which fakes and falsifications are dangerous. Fake medicine is often blamed for serious side effects and even death when unknowing and vulnerable shoppers buy them at attractive prices. On occasion poison is present in foods, resulting in expensive illness or death.[3]

In fact, the place [Changsha] has always been awash with inferior and second-rate products. These days people buy imitation wines with counterfeit money and then come to us to complain. It was the same in the Cultural Revolution. Phony revolutionaries were going around denouncing fake reactionaries—and then, after it was all over, they'd appeal to the Central Committee of the Communist Party to be rehabilitated. Things may appear to have changed, but the same old chicanery continues. China is rife with fakes; it's our social pathology, and it's been that way from long before the Cultural Revolution.

Of course, the sheer scale of fraud these days is unprecedented. We make fakes, we sell fakes, we trade in counterfeit currency, and we buy imitation goods. Everyone is a victim, and everyone is cheating everyone else. The whole society is trapped in a vicious cycle. We're all caught up in an endless revolution of revolutions.

There's always a counterfactual reality about anything and everything in China today. *In fact* has become just a catchphrase for the whole society, because, in fact, things are never what they appear to be. When people say what, in fact, is happening, at least you know you might be getting a little closer to the truth. But what I hate most about the use of the expression *in fact* is the tone of voice people use. It's as though they're leaking you privileged information: I'm treating you with particular respect and letting you in on a secret, the truth. But that's not really the case at all, because there's always sure to be much more going on than they'll ever admit to you when they say *in fact*. (Sang 2006, 138–39)

Cheating, Plagiarism, and Authorship

In 2001 and 2002, the *Chronicle of Higher Education* published a series of articles about the increasing awareness of cheating and misrepresentation by Chinese students (students in Hong Kong, Taiwan, and South Korea were also mentioned but with lesser infractions) seeking to attend American universities. Students with perfect scores on the TOEFL (Test of English as a Foreign Language) or on the GRE (Graduate Record Examination) showed up in Cambridge and Berkeley unable to communicate at all. Because of fraudulent transcripts received from some Chinese students, the graduate biomedical and life sciences program at UCLA began to require verification of all transcripts from foreign students (Mangan 2002). The Educational Testing Service is replacing its use of computerized testing (with a rotating question bank) with the earlier form of paper tests because there have been so many allegations of copying tests, memorizing questions, and making tests available to future students. Scores from China were elevated by 100 points (on tests with a range from 200 to 800) because students posted answers to questions on the Web (Wheeler 2002).[4]

The China Educational Service Center, a private company in Beijing that helps students prepare applications for studying abroad, announced its mission as ensuring that talented students secure their rightful places in American graduate schools. A foreign reporter asked one young woman who worked there editing application essays if this would mislead American universities into thinking that the work was the students' own. "'Quite possibly,' she says. 'I hadn't thought about that.' Has it occurred to her that her work might be unethical, maybe just plain wrong? 'Wrong,' she muses. 'I haven't thought about this question'" (Walfish 2001, A52). At the New Oriental School in Beijing, American students are paid substantial amounts to write essays for applicants. On electronic bulletin boards, students solicit "gunners" (*qiangshou*) who can take the GMAT (Graduate Management Admission Test) or TOEFL in the name of an applicant and guarantee a high score. Applications are written in China as a sincere attempt to please and meet the expectations of the receiver.

Clearly, for Americans this represents a crisis. Our entire system of credentials is based on the truthfulness of examinations, transcripts, and other proofs of accomplishment. Robert Hauptman articulates the bedrock belief of American academic practice:

> Academics are committed to the discovery, propagation, and dissemination of truth. They seek it out, confirm it, publish the results of their quest, and teach it to their undergraduate, graduate, and postdoctoral students and protégés.

> Truth may vary depending on perspective, gender, culture, agenda, zeitgeist, and a host of other factors, but the unequivocal goal of the college or university professor is to ascertain the truth and share it with students and peers. (Hauptman 2002, 39)

To be sure, the American educational system has its own difficulty with plagiarism; honesty committees, honor codes, academic integrity, and plagiarism detection are hot news on all campuses. Reports about students' views of cheating suggest that since the 1990s a huge increase in and acceptance of cheating has occurred among students of all ages and levels. My own university has subscribed to an on-line plagiarism-detection service, Turnitin.com, which checks submitted student papers against a huge database of papers, some of which are available (elsewhere) for purchase. At the same time, a university-wide honor code has been bolstered (which stops short of requiring students to turn in other students).

As Ron Scollon demonstrates, we should discuss the issue of plagiarism from the perspective of cultural background (1995, 2001). The American insistence on originality derives from a particular understanding of the source of words, as stemming from an individual's efforts. Those views are not universal, and in China they are quite different. In higher education this is especially evident. In the United States a premium is placed on both tracing ideas and being critical of them, in order to arrive at an independent viewpoint. Chinese students are trained to believe that their words are formed in the context of authority and mutual expectations inherent in a situation. Thus, asking them to produce their own words, in defiance of tradition and authority, is to ask them to negate all they believe is correct.

It is also important to recognize that cheating has been a problem in Chinese examinations for centuries. The civil service examination system, which (in principle) selected bureaucrats on the basis of merit, relied on a three-day test in which people were searched and locked in rooms to ensure that there was no possibility of their cheating. Clearly there was warrant for such extreme measures. The histories are filled with accounts of attempts to cheat and discoveries of people having cheated. Cheating was not acceptable, but it was widespread. Though the matter of cheating is neither new nor uniquely Chinese, it nonetheless is considered a devastating contemporary problem in China.

Communicative Controls: Censorship, Media, and Propaganda

The People's Republic of China, like its early mentor the USSR, has effectively controlled communication from the start, whether blocking messages it considers dangerous or unflattering, or fabricating messages it considers useful. Though most such controls are substantially looser than in previous periods since 1949, there is still a good deal of energy used in either establishing or evading such controls. Kevin Latham, an anthropologist who did extensive fieldwork in Guangzhou and Hong Kong on media, reports that despite significant social change in China, it is still the case that "[a]ll news media in China are considered to be the 'mouthpiece' of the Party" (2000, 637). Amnesty International reports thirty-three cases of people detained or imprisoned for use of the Internet; accusations of publishing "state secrets" could result in the death penalty (Amnesty International 2002).

Censorship is silence that is knowingly non-truthful. It might be considered deceiving through the sin of omission. (News in China certainly does not operate on the principle of "all the news that's fit to print" unless we especially focus on "fit" and the criteria for fitness.) Yet there is no absolute line between ordinary practices that Americans consider appropriate—such as avoiding vivid "swear words" in family television programs or selecting appropriate vocabulary for a given audience—and those considered noteworthy for their censorship.

The outbreak of SARS (severe acute respiratory syndrome) took the world by storm in spring 2003. While the United States was preoccupied with its war on Iraq, the rest of the world struggled with the downside of global interconnection. Dire warnings of disaster in China's economic situation echoed alongside public health appeals for diagnosis, treatment, and prevention.

First detected in November 2002 but believed at first simply to be a strange kind of pneumonia, SARS had claimed scores of lives by March 2003. At that point the Chinese insisted that there were at most a handful of cases in Beijing, with most cases in the southern province of Guangdong, the province that borders Hong Kong. In March 2003 in an article about a mysterious respiratory ailment that seemed to have originated in China, the New York Times cited international health officials who believed that "the government [of China] has not been fully candid." The article explained that "health statistics in China concerning a wide range of diseases are regarded as politically sensitive and so are often misrepresented or never made public. This week the government ordered Chinese journalists not to report on the outbreak of the strange pneumonia" (Rosenthal 2003b, 2003c).

The World Health Organization (WHO) was at first refused entry into China (Altman and Bradsher 2003), but on April 12 it was permitted to investigate (Eckholm 2003b). There was a game of concealment and accusation: In early April a health official declared the illness on the wane (Kahn 2003); the next day retired physician Dr. Jiang Yanyong publicly urged China to reveal "the truth" and not "tell lies" (Rosenthal 2003a); some insiders issued a report on *Time* magazine's website claiming that patients were being concealed in ambulances and hotels to prevent the WHO team from discovering them (*Straits Times* 2003). This game ended on April 20, 2003, with the firing of China's health minister and the mayor of Beijing on grounds that they had covered up the facts. At that point the government vowed to fight SARS and presented as many details as possible to the Chinese public.

But the most interesting aspect of the epidemic is in the charges of "cover-up" and "lying." The English-language Hong Kong newspaper, *South China Morning Post*, featured the headline "Relief and anger after officials finally come clean on real figures" (Jen-Siu 2003). In addition to shock at the huge numbers and concern about travel, many Chinese expressed suspicion about the accuracy of figures. A woman from Beijing is quoted as saying, "This is unbelievable, it's absolutely terrifying. I never believed the official figures released in the past but I'm still totally shocked by this news. I had planned to travel to Hainan for the May Day holiday. I had bought my tickets and everything. Now this has ruined my holiday. I'm so disappointed. I can't understand why we can't have a longer holiday. We need a break."

A recent graduate from prestigious Beijing University said, "I heard some inside stories that 346 cases [of SARS] is still not enough [to be accurate]. I think the real figure in Beijing is about 1,000 judging by what people are telling me. Actually, students always knew the government was not telling the truth and the figure was much higher, but this news is good for the older people. Now everyone is aware of how severe the situation is." In other words, students already know the truth, without being told, but the less savvy older folks are more gullible and stick to the surface report.

A foreigner focused on the truth: "Thank goodness they've finally decided to tell the truth."

The *New York Times* reported on China's admission: "In a rare public admission of failure, if not deception, the Chinese government disclosed today that cases of a dangerous new respiratory disease were many times higher than previously reported, and stripped two top officials of their power" (Eckholm 2003a). Later in the same article it mentioned that the deputy health minister, Gao Qiang, attributed the earlier low figures as "a result primarily of incompetence rather than deceit." Officially, the Chinese refused to acknowledge deliberate deception. Gao's statement is clear: "There is an essential different [sic] between inaccuracy of SARS statistics and intentional cover-up of the situation of the disease" (*People's Daily* 2003b).

One Beijing resident was persuaded by the government: "At least the truth is out now. It's a relief really. I think these figures are accurate."

The bluntest statement, however, came from a question asked by a "foreign journalist" at a press conference in April 2003: "Officials told us at a press conference a fortnight ago that Beijing was safe for the Chinese people as well as for foreigners in China. But the present epidemic situation is becoming more and more serious. Just now you also explained why there were some limitations to the data reported some days ago. What on earth are the problems in Beijing (or in China's health system) that deters you from telling us the truth?" (*People's Daily* 2003a).

Central governmental control of the media and literature has been part of Chinese life since before the founding of the People's Republic in 1949.[5] One could trace it to some of Mao's speeches, such as the Yan'an Forum on Art and Literature in 1942, in which he exhorted revolutionaries to use art and literature for politics, because they were inseparable (McDougall 1980). Thus during the height of the control of expression, there were severe limits placed on what was produced or available. In the realm of dance and opera, there were only eight "model operas" that were performed during the Cultural Revolution. Literature had to be vetted by censorship boards and had to serve the purpose of bolstering morale or lauding heroes.

Newspapers and broadcasts were all centrally coordinated. Broadcasting was ubiquitous; almost every person was at all times in the reach of loudspeakers, which had as their task conveying a constant stream of news and propaganda (*xuanchuan*, also translatable as "promulgating" or making widely known). The English classes I taught in 1982 had nationally coordinated exercise breaks with exhortations from cackling loudspeakers, counting and counting while we did our nationally synchronized exercises on the hard blacktop outside the school. Trains had speakers with constant fuzzy broadcasts, moving from cheerful music to news to urging of political rectitude.

Despite the substantial economic liberalization accompanying China's entry into the World Trade Organization, the government has retained control over all broadcasting media. This is not to say that there are no outlets for independent transmission, but that they always run the risk of being shut down. Publishing in China is lively and an active group of writers attempts innovative and sometimes radical efforts to promote independent views of China, but periodically presses are fined or forced to closed, or particular work is prohibited. In January 2006, the *Bingdian Weekly*, an independent, critical, and influential publication for eleven years, was shut down because of its critical stance about history textbooks' interpretation of the Boxer Rebellion (Wu 2006). (The immediate effect is usually that pirated copies sell wildly in the PRC and that they thrive in Taiwan and Hong Kong!) Many, such as university presses, censor themselves to avoid trouble.

Censorship in the media is usually justified on the basis of its effect on the audience. When a certain effect (optimism, faith in the government) is desired, an appropriate slant is taken in conveying the news. This was especially evident in the Cultural Revolution, when only good news about the successes of the program, or failed attempts to derail it, was permitted. Newspapers are read avidly in China, often displayed in public cases where walkers-by can simply read. Even now, just as in the West, prominence is conveyed through placement and length of articles. But sometimes arguments within writers' circles about the subtle use of particular words revolve not only around how things sound or mean, but around the meaning of their moral valence (Schoenhals 1992).

Despite different notions of the goals of media, most practitioners appeal to a notion of "truth" in their work. Latham distinguishes two types of "truth" on which the media are believed to rely. One is familiar in the West and evident in Hong Kong as presenting all relevant facts. Impartiality is a primary goal. In China, in contrast, evident in Guangzhou, the guiding principle is to "seek truth from facts" in which "truth" includes "the true state of society and the objective world as formulated by Marxism-Leninism-Mao Zedong-Thought" (Latham 2000, 640). This entails the notion that "there is ultimately only one socialist truth which is valid" (641). Beyond that, portraying multiple viewpoints or perspectives was argued by a TV journalist to lead to confusion (*hunluan*) and chaos (*luan*) (649). To prevent this most dreaded of consequences, censorship of news from Hong Kong is supported even by those who themselves seek other media sources.

Debates over censorship, ratings, and access are common in the United States as well as in China. In June 2003 the U.S. Supreme Court approved withholding of federal funds for public libraries that do not filter the Internet (for the purpose of blocking pornography). Some opponents (e.g., Nunberg 2003) argue that, realistically speaking, the software is far too crude to select the proper sites to block. Others argue that the very notion of blocking information is antithetical to the missions of public libraries. Similarly, debates over song lyrics, films, and TV programs point out both disagreement about what is appropriate for children and about how to maintain appropriate standards of decency while retaining freedom for individual choice. During the 2003 Iraq war, American journalists "embedded" in the services were briefed regularly about what they were permitted to broadcast or report. Reports of wounded children, for example, were considered demoralizing and thus were voluntarily concealed. The apparently vivid and real broadcasts were quite deliberately skewed. A nice irony had Chinese media free to present any view of the war they wished, including images such as of wounded Iraqi children that were censored in the United States (Brown 2003).

A furor was sustained for years over the Bush administration's deception of the public in its haste to go to war, having claimed "proof" that there were weapons of mass destruction even though there was ample—if squelched—evidence that the weapons were not to be found.

Unlike the United States, China has never extolled "freedom" or autonomy as primary goals, yet it is clear that conflicting views over access to information of all varieties exist.

Internet censorship is quite tight, though fluctuating, in China. A study found significantly more sites blocked in China than in Saudi Arabia (Zittrain and Edelman 2002). The government appears ambivalent about the economic possibilities of the Internet and the political dangers of the free spread of information. In keeping with the maxim *Guard information*, in this case it is the government controlling which sites are available to viewers with Chinese addresses. The criteria are fluid, as Zittrain and Edelman point out, so that sites blocked at one time may be available at a later time, and vice versa. Political concerns influence which sites are blocked; information about Tibet and Taiwan may be primary targets at one time, while human rights and AIDS may predominate at another time. Since 2005 the crackdown on the Internet has been particularly fierce, culminating in a law (a draft law in place in summer 2006) aimed at restricting news of "sudden events"—protests, diseases, accidents—in any medium, whether print or electronic, domestic or foreign (French 2006a, 2006b; Kahn 2006a, 2006b).

Under authoritarian regimes, people both accept and challenge Internet constraints (Kalathil and Boas 2003). The Internet by itself will not bring freedom to China, nor has the regime chosen to control it absolutely. The authors conclude: "All told, the Internet is likely to contribute to change within China, without precipitating the state's collapse" (2003, 42). The state employs a combination of regulation, policing, threats, and punitive action (27), which in turn lead to self-censorship. Some of the goals of the government include educating and entertaining the populace, conducting business, and making government operations more transparent, but as Kalathil and Boas state bluntly, "Alongside its e-government program, the Chinese government is strengthening its uses of the Internet to distribute propaganda and engage in thought work" (32–33). Government sites are attractive and lively and have carefully selected links.

Journalist Nicholas Kristoff is optimistic about the possibility of the Internet's opening China to the world (2006). Whether that is borne out or not, I think it is clear that the chase between those seeking opportunities to express forbidden viewpoints and those seeking to restrict that expression will occupy a good many people for a good time to come.

Neijing Waisong: Familiars and Outsiders

A well-known and often invoked distinction between *nei* (inside) and *wai* (outside) emphasizes that actions should naturally be different in these two spheres, whether they refer to the family and non-relations, the village and outside, the nation and outside, or some other contrast. In discussing my imminent departure from China, I once mentioned that I wished I could take newspapers with me, but that I knew they were prohibited for export. A bureaucrat laughed and said it would then make it too easy for outsiders to air China's dirty laundry (*jia chou bu wai yang*; don't display the family's ugliness outside) and the government didn't want to facilitate this. (I hid some in my suitcase, nonetheless, and had no trouble with customs.)

Similarly, in discussions of bird flu, officials admitted in 2005 that in order to prevent a panic, they may have toned down reports of the alarm that they actually felt. *Neijing waisong*—worried inside but relaxed outside—is a familiar tactic. Again, consequences are the primary concern. What people say is in the debt of that goal.

The maxim *keep track of inside and outside* functions here to remind social actors in China that certain kinds of activity and expression are appropriate only within intimate circles.

In a society that operates through connections, transparency is unwelcome. When morality is measured by an action's effects, information that would cause undesirable consequences—SARS causing a panic, for instance—is forbidden. When wealth and gain are celebrated, fakes are useful for bringing on prosperity. From these perspectives, some of China's gravest social problems can be understood. Yet within China are many who lament this situation, longing for a more open, more genuine, more transparent homeland.

Notes

1. Not all corruption is regarded negatively. If corruption may be regarded as in part counterhegemonic, then peasant cynicism as expressed in the following slogan may be easily understood: cadres "cheat (deceive) the state and coax the villagers" (*pian shangbian, hong xiabian*) (Yan 1995, 229; actually the terms here translated as "state" and "villagers" are "above" and "below."). And this may not be entirely unwelcome; morality that protects the less powerful may require different rules for different categories of people, as James Scott has argued in *Weapons of the Weak* (1985).

2. Two weeks later, an article in the *New York Times* reported that in the United States several drug companies had been charged with repeatedly airing misleading or deceptive advertising (Pear 2002). My cataloguing of China's misdeeds does not imply that I believe the United States to be free of such tendencies.

3. The widespread availability of rat poison is sometimes offered as an explanation for China's suicide rate. The suicide rate of rural Chinese women is the highest in the world.

4. I am grateful to Irfan Noorudin for these references. Personal communication, Nov. 26, 2002.

5. One could follow Godwin Chu and say that "the concept of using communication for social change is almost as old as Chinese civilization" (1977, 21).

CHAPTER FIVE

Longing for Honesty

The black night has given me black eyes,
Yet I use them to search for light.

—Gu Cheng 1983 [1980]

Lest I leave you with the impression that the current situation with regard to cheating and deception is perfectly acceptable to everyone in China, or that lying is everywhere, in this short chapter I show that some people long for a change in social relations, a change often centered on the topic of honesty and sincerity.

Moral Evaluations

Evaluations of language-related behavior occurred, as do so many things in fieldwork, by chance. On a chilly Christmas Day in 1996 in Kunming, I went with my friend Cui Ji to the Yunnan Minorities Publication Service to meet her old classmate, Rong Ai. It turned out we all had daughters, so after talking business (about minorities) for a while the conversation turned to our children, husbands, and housework. I asked what was the worst imaginable behavior for a child (*zui buhaode xingwei*) and simultaneously they both said "*sahuang*" (lying). I asked what children would lie about and they said it would be about some misbehavior, such as hitting another child. If they admitted their fault (*rencuo*) they would be punished less harshly but would be scolded instead. (Admission of fault permits reconciliation and solution.)

That evening I had dinner with Cui Ji's friend Zheng Lan and Zheng's old friend Chen at a Hui (Muslim) restaurant. I asked what they thought the worst behavior from children would be. Zheng, who is unmarried, said "*meiyou limao*" (being impolite). Chen, who had a four-and-a half-year-old daughter, said it was "*buting fumu de quangao*" (not listening to parents' advice), or at least repeatedly not listening. Cui Ji found this interesting and repeated her answer from earlier in the day. Chen regarded this as overly idealistic and said, "*Sahuang shi haizi dou zuode*" (all children lie). He did not seem to feel it was possible to expect truth telling from little kids.

I continued to ask about this, extending the question to include adults as well. One person said the worst behavior was *canren* (hurting people). A Mencian answer came from Celeste, the young pregnant woman introduced earlier, who said she didn't think children would have bad behavior, and that they learn it from their parents anyway. A teacher who had the extremely naughty eight-year-old son mentioned earlier said that the worst behavior would be *buchengshi*, being insincere. One of the Yi people I asked recited serially that the worst forms of behavior were *tou, qiang, pian, sharen* (stealing, robbing, cheating/deceiving, killing); another person echoed it, saying *yiyang: tou, da, pian ren* (the same: stealing, fighting, cheating/deceiving). Another person said that the worst behavior is *qipian* (deceive, cheat, dupe). Yan Qimei, the stylish young Han woman from Kunming, said that the worst behavior was deceiving someone about their feelings (*qipian rende ganqing*); she gave the example of a man from Guangzhou, the friend of a friend, who was a boss (*laoban*). He said he wanted to "make friends" with her (*jiao pengyou*) because she was so pretty and smart. She asked about his wife. Oh, he said, he would divorce her. The reteller of this story scoffed at how ridiculous this all was; they'd met only that day.

Longing for Sincerity

In 1991, in conjunction with a lesson on paradise in their English-language textbook, my husband asked thirty-seven students to write about the characteristics of paradise.[1] Seven described birds, flowers, flowing streams, sunshine, abundant food; five mentioned having a room or flat of their own; five were adamant about paradise being just a dream; and five said that paradise had to be built with people's own hands in the communist model. A few also wrote about sincerity and honesty:

One person wrote:

My paradise is not immutable happiness and joy forever, sweet love and comfortable life. In my heart, I only wish the earth had less hatred, more fraternal love and kindness, less craftiness, more sincerity, fewer tears and more happiness. I also wish that people who live in the same land would treat each other sincerely instead of each trying to cheat or outwit the other, that making life would become easier, then parents would not work hard for everything, that the man whom I love also would love me deeply, that everything for which I had made an effort could achieve what I wish, etc. . . .

This writer longs for "less craftiness, more sincerity" and wishes that "people who live in the same land would treat each other sincerely instead of each trying to cheat or outwit the other." Aware of the difficulty of consistently attaining such honest treatment, the writer could imagine it only in paradise.

Another student wrote:

There I can show my personality freely, I'll lose no time in deciding what I should speak out and what I shouldn't. There everyone treats the other with honesty and civility. There everyone is equal. No matter whether you come from the lower or higher classes you can obtain an opportunity to compete fairly and beat your rivals.

This writer longs for direct expression ("I'll lose no time in deciding what I should speak out and what I shouldn't"), suggesting that this is not how things are currently done. Direct expression is connected here with general treatment of people in society ("Everyone treats the other with honesty and civility"), even those without relationships.

Clearly these students were quite aware of the need to outwit others and that speakers had to make choices about speaking at all times. Though speakers in all societies make such choices, the fact that these writers were conscious of their choice suggests a particular attitude. The craftiness of Chinese society was deplored, yet acknowledged. The ideology is clearly expressed in the maxims *Consider power and role, Guard information, Keep track of inside and outside*. It is also clear that there is some discrepancy between ideology and practice, as well as potential change in the future.

In 2004 I gave a talk at a university about deception and truth in China. The context was a standing seminar on cognitive science, but in this case the audience was made up almost entirely of Chinese faculty and graduate students who had never before attended the seminar. They were concerned that I would portray China as full of deception, and they were there to contest my story. One person in particular was incensed, and though my ultimate point was that people in all societies lie and deceive, yet all are concerned with truth, he was fixated on my opening stories about China.[2] He found my examples selective and incompletely explained. Why did I not mention, he wanted to know, the people who were willing to sacrifice their lives for truth?

Why did I not speak about parents teaching their children to be honest? Were deceptions not common in all wars, not only in Chinese accounts of wars?

So I feel obliged to include his lament at my account and to show that many people in China do indeed care for and love truth; according to him it is only the government that forces people in contemporary China to lie.

A graduate student at the talk stayed to chat with me later. She commented on a story told during the question-and-answer session. A Chinese student in the United States witnessed someone bumping into a car in a parking lot and leaving a note with his name on it, confessing his misdeed even though there would be no possible way of tracking the miscreant down. The person telling this was astonished and said such an occurrence would never happen in China. The graduate student speaking with me confirmed that there was a difference in likely behavior, but thought it was quite wonderful that Americans would behave in this honest way.

Courage to Tell the Truth

As in every society, no matter what the pressures to present a good face, to think about the consequences, to show loyalty through obedience, China has a variety of heroic individuals who have dared to speak truth to power, to risk life and reputation because they saw things clearly. One such hero is Liu Binyan, who died in December 2005 in reluctant exile from China for his continued stance against Party censorship.

Liu was a Communist Party member and a journalist; he was educated only to ninth grade but was very well self-taught. Because of several published items exposing corruption, he was expelled from the Party in 1956. In the 1970s he was "rehabilitated" and began to publish again, working at China's pre-eminent newspaper, the *People's Daily*. He wrote many explosive pieces of investigative journalism, a genre known as "reportage" (*baogaowenxue*), including the exhilarating piece "People or Monsters?" (1979) that detailed the long-standing corruption of Party officials in Heilongjiang province.

He writes of living among peasants during the 1958–60 Great Leap Forward. Officials told the poor villagers to build a zoo and a fountain. Liu wonders,

> Now, what were peasants who hardly ate meat all year supposed to feed to lions and tigers in a zoo? With no water source—with man and beast still drinking rainwater—how were they to build a fountain? A struggle began to rage

deep inside me: how could two diametrically opposed "truths" coexist in the world? The longings of the peasants were one truth, and the policies of the higher-ups and the propaganda in the newspapers were quite another. Which should I follow? Not until 1960 . . . did I finally get my answer. It was right to uphold the interests and demands of the people. Anything that ran counter to their wishes was ultimately untenable. (Liu 1983 [1979], 3)

This realization catalyzed his work and he became a tireless advocate for the people's interests, even when the cost was extremely high.

"Sound Is Better than Silence" is a remarkable story about a man—a Party member, an avid revolutionary peasant—who pretended to be deaf and dumb to evade the dangers of the Cultural Revolution accusations, being "cured" only in the 1980s after the Gang of Four was tried and the reforms were more firmly in place. Liu concludes: "Old man history tells us that it's better to be a little more noisy. A silent era cannot be a good one" (Liu 1983 [1981], 137).

Liu's fearless exposure of corruption and high-level officials who abused their power made him such a hero that strangers constantly contacted him to tell him their own stories. "Now [the mid 1980s] whenever I set foot in the courtyard of the *People's Daily*, I had to be ready to spend twenty minutes answering greetings from every side. Sometimes people would drop me a piece of inside news. Walking along the streets, either in Beijing or in the provinces, I was often recognized, even if I wore sunglasses" (Liu 1990, 271--72). He was swamped with admirers asking for autographs and photographs, even though his books were banned and his arrival was often unannounced. This shows not only celebrity, I think, but people's thirst for a voice speaking the truth.

Accused of being disloyal to the Party, he later wrote a memoir called *A Higher Kind of Loyalty* in which he celebrated loyal criticism and exposed newspaper censorship (Liu 1990). In the 1980s he came to the United States and was here when the Tiananmen massacre events occurred. He remained here until his death, unable to return home. His book *Tell the World! What Happened in China and Why* (1989) details the events of Tiananmen.

Liu fought censorship, as well as forced praising, considering both of them lying.

In fact, ignoring the truth, inflating achievements, and distorting historical events had been in practice in the media in the early fifties and reached a peak during the Great Leap Forward. The singing of praises for positive achievements and the overlooking of negative aspects prevails to this day. . . . China's papers have never so much as touched on 1 percent of the negative aspects of our society. Isn't that as bad as lying? (Liu 1990, 273–74)

Liu Binyan's writings show a passion for truth that is at odds with what we have discussed until now. What percentage of people in China share Liu's fearlessness and commitment to truth and what percentage share the focus on consequences and pragmatics is impossible to say. The question would be meaningless, even if put to a survey. But as with every society, the tension is important and not obvious.

After Liu's death—not announced in China—a Chinese website devoted to him had a number of poignant recollections. One posting of December 5 titled "Who tells the truth? Mourning Mr. Liu Binyan" extolled Liu's courage at speaking the truth in clear ways that even the writer's laborer parents could grasp. He invited others who speak the truth, other souls who seek truth and righteousness, to join with him and Binyan (Yu 2005).

If you find more similarities than differences with the practices of the United States or other societies, that is fine. My own trajectory was to find differences at first and then similarities. As in all societies, some in China are willing and able to stand up for truth in opposition to conventional thought that urges conformity and timidity. Explaining how this relative proportion came to be requires examination of the role of truth and rectitude in China's past.

Notes

1. The assignment was transmitted through foreign teachers at local universities. For the method and rationale for using essays by students in foreign languages (English), see Blum 2001, 38–39.

2. For a fuller account of this story, see Blum 2005.

PART III

CHINA PAST

CHAPTER SIX

Crooked and Straight: Right Action and Strategy in Premodern China

In China, truth and falsity in the Greek sense have rarely been important considerations in a philosopher's acceptance of a given belief or
proposition; these are Western concerns.

—Donald J. Munro 1969

War is the path of deception.

—Sunzi, The Art of War

Unlike many societies that anthropologists study, China has left a long written record. We do not need to speculate about change and continuity; we
can read the record and really see how contemporary ideas about deception
and truth resemble and differ from earlier ideas. It goes without saying—but
I'll say it anyway—that the record is generally that of literate elites with the
means to secure an education. The nameless, illiterate masses have never
made it directly into history, though we can find traces if we look carefully.
You'll find surprising similarities and instructive differences between China
of the past and China of the present.

The earliest period of China from which we have records is a time of great
violence, suspicion, and fragmentation. If life is not always and everywhere
nasty, brutish, and short, it certainly was this way in Warring States China,
and often in much of premodern China. While stereotypes about Eastern
harmony abound and the trite, fortune-cookie invocation of "Confucius"
shows a peaceful gentleman in a long-sleeved robe, his face inscrutable, the

85

reality is that the invocations of peace were desperate harangues in a world of "sanctioned violence," as Mark Lewis pronounces it. This was an unstable world filled with plotting and fear, a world where alliances were short-lived, and where one's own ancestors and blood kin provided the only certainty.

At the same time—perhaps as a consequence of the uncertainty—there was an efflorescence of philosophical and literary writings that grappled with questions of how to act. Some of the world's greatest philosophical and literary works derive from this period, from the *Analects* of Confucius to the Daoist works, the *Laozi* and the *Zhuangzi*, to the astute writings about politics and governance of the Legalists. Alongside authoritarian and practical treatises ran a thread of paradox, with language not meaning anything discernible and one tradition's right being treated as wrong in another. The crooked becomes straight and the crooked becomes desirable; what is said becomes untruthful and the truth is unsayable. These writings vividly convey the desperate worry of a time when people knew that their questions mattered, and the writings endure, much like the Bible in Europe, as the foundation of all subsequent thought in East Asia.

This chapter introduces some of the earliest coherent writings on deception and integrity, including celebration of cleverness as well as reverence for sincerity.

Truth Versus Right

If some ancient Greeks were preoccupied with Truth, language, categories, and gods, the ancient Chinese preoccupations were entirely different (see Hansen 1992; Keightley 2002; Lloyd and Sivin 2002; Raphals 1992). We might say that they focused not on knowledge of truth but on knowing how to act; they speculated not on speech as emanating from nature but on writing as invented by brilliant culture heroes; they wrote not about categories but about events in the world and what they had to teach about morality; they told stories not of gods and animals but of humans, especially rulers. Like the Greek tradition, the Chinese tradition included strenuous dissent among groups sometimes considered "schools." But also like the Greek tradition, there are some common threads that can be followed for a long time and across many different writers. We might follow the dominant thinkers and differentiate between "orthodox," *zheng* "upright," such as the Ruists (later translated as "Confucians"; see Jensen 1997), and "heterodox," *xie*, which also means "slanted" or "crooked," such as Daoists or Buddhists. Yet the distinction between orthodoxy and heterodoxy is itself suspect; a good bit of Chinese life is compatible with both orthodox and heterodox traditions. Still, there were struggles for dominance; those considered orthodox gained imperial support, tax exemption, and other perquisites.

In contrast to the ancient Greeks' concern with Truth, the ancient Chinese were concerned with what might be phrased as Right or Real. Action rather than thought is often said to dominate the earliest extant Chinese philosophy (pre-Qin [221–208 BCE]) (but see Schwartz 1996 for a critique of this oversimplification). Here we will see the following maxims exemplified:

> *Consider consequences.*
> *Anticipate others' responses. (theory of mind)*
> *Consider power and role.*
> *Select script.*
> *Take relationships as primary.*
> *Language is culture, not (only) nature.*
> *Consider bystanders.*
> *Do the right action in context.*
> *Proclaim loyalty and affiliation.*
> *Trust. And suspect.*

War and Conflict

The 250-year period beginning with the death of the culture hero Kongzi ("Confucius"), allegedly in 479 BCE, and ending with Chinese unification under Qin Shihuang in 221 BCE is known as the Warring States period. A large number of sometimes rival and sometimes allied small kingdoms in the region now called China Proper were unified, conquered, and destroyed, leaving only seven larger "states" (*guo*): Qin, Wei, Zhao, Han, Chu, Yan, and Qi. At the end of this period, Qin swallowed up all the other states and ruled a single territory. Its rule was brief; after only thirteen years Qin was in turn defeated by the Han, which ruled (with a brief interruption) for 400 years. The majority ethnic group in China gets its name from the Han dynasty. Folklore has it that China got its name from the Qin.

Much of the philosophical writing we have from this period was addressed to rulers. Many early thinkers functioned as advisors to rival leaders or offered advice, lamenting that leaders disregarded it. A primary distinction may be made between those who advocated benevolence and those who advocated authoritarianism, and this overlaps with another distinction, between those who saw the ruler's obligation as being straight and direct and those who saw the successful ruler as moving in oblique or crooked ways. In this sense Ruists (Confucians), who often dominated government, may be opposed to strategists, Legalists, and realists (such as those who wrote war manuals, *bingfa* texts), as well as to the Daoists, especially Laozi, who also saw direct rule as both unnatural and unsuccessful. Later the Ruists may also be contrasted with Buddhists, whose views of human life were quite different from the Ruists' convention-worshipping, role-emphasizing precepts.

The traditional philosophies known to Westerners as "Confucianism" and "Legalism" represent tension between benevolence and authoritarianism, a tension still visible in contemporary political approaches. The government that serves as father and mother to the people (*fumuguan*) is not the stern autocrat that kills even its own children in order to retain power. These two views have differing understandings of human nature and of the role of language in interaction, especially with regard to deception. But there are a number of commonalities among even dissenting philosophical approaches.

Training, Not Spontaneity

Almost all schools in ancient China placed a premium on transmission, authority, and training. In contrast to a U.S. premium on naturalness and spontaneity, the aim is for training to be so thorough that it becomes a part of one's nature (Fingarette 1972). This is true for many Asian practices, including archery, calligraphy, and martial arts. Even the Chan (Zen) training in the Gradual School emphasized preparation and study as a way to achieve enlightenment—though the most colorful school (Sudden School), influenced by Daoism, emphasized enlightenment coming without any preparation at all.

For some thinkers, directness (*zhi*) is valued, but it is directness that follows training, practice, and skill. It is not the natural directness of the unsocialized being. Training rather than spontaneity, society rather than nature, were applauded by all who had the benefit of education and literacy in the standard form. (*Language is culture, not [only] nature.*)

Still, there was a middle road to be taken, at least by Ruists, between overpreparation and overritualization on the one hand and natural spontaneity on the other: In the *Lunyu* (*Analects*), Kongzi said, "When natural substance prevails over ornamentation, you get the boorishness of the rustic. When ornamentation prevails over natural substance, you get the pedantry of the scribe. Only when ornament and substance are duly blended do you get the true gentleman" (*Analects* vi, 16; Waley 1938, 119). The "boorishness of the rustic" is the naturalness of peasants, the blunt eruption of feeling. The "pedantry of the scribe" points also to those who have so mastered the rules of politeness that the smooth deceptive mask is all that is seen. Between the two is the Ruist goal—elusive then and still—of speech shaped by truth as well as considerateness and impulse tempered by learning.

Legalists and Rigidity of Authority: Pragmatics, *The Art of War*, and Theory of Mind

Legalism[1] is known for its cruelty but effectiveness (Hansen [1992, 12] calls it "despotic and dirty"; Waley calls its practitioners "realists" [1939, 151]). The first Chinese emperor (Qin Shihuang, 259–210 BCE) had a Legalist advisor, Li Si (c. 280–208 BCE) who, along with the philosopher Han Fei (died 233 BCE), was a student of Xunzi (310–220 BCE?). While Qin Shihuang spent much of his time seeking the pill of immortality, his advisors went even beyond the Legalist teachings in their ruthlessness, from which has derived Qin Shihuang's reputation as a despot. Though the Legalists have been deplored throughout history, some modern political thinkers, including most notably Chairman Mao, invoked this tradition for its autocratic will (in contrast to the more humane Ruist tradition).

Legalists are guided by *fa*, by law and techniques, on the basis of pragmatic principles of power rather than of morality, and have been compared to Machiavelli in their cynical manipulation of people's desires and fears (Bloodworth and Bloodworth 1976).

Many of the Legalists wrote treatises on war (*bingfa*). Sunzi's *The Art of War* (*Sunzi Bingfa*) is the most well-known expression of Legalism and the most obvious proponent of the clever use of people's simplicity to overcome them with superior understanding. The ruler is encouraged to deceive the people in order to increase his or her power over them, justified by the necessity for strength during a time of evident chaos and disintegration. Acknowledging people's weaknesses in order to exploit them, it elevates cleverness to an extremely high virtue.

Sunzi's *The Art of War* has been cited approvingly by millennia of Chinese writers. Like most Chinese books from the pre-Qin period, it probably did not have a single author but was a compilation of sayings that later had an author more or less invented for it. Given the frequency of war and of struggle throughout China's history, warfare should be regarded not as an aberrant condition but as a common one. The realities of feeding an army in enemy territory, of transporting soldiers into frightening situations, of sieges, of identifying the enemies' and allies' chariots are all addressed in some detail in the *bingfa* text. But what is most striking is its grasp of human psychology and of the advantage of outthinking the other.

While Western warfare seems to rely on the brute force of superior arms and the hoped-for grace of a deity on the side of truth (Bowyer 1982), this version of Chinese warfare relies on ruses and wiles, on conserving strength and soldiers. Minford compares it to *taijiquan* (t'ai chi) and other ways Chinese seek "maximum effect through minimum expenditure of energy" (Sunzi 2002, xxvii). Chu Chin-ning (1991) traces a path back from Sunzi, through early twentieth-century author S. W. Lee, to Deng Xiaoping at Tiananmen, advising Western business people about how to understand the "Eastern" way of interacting. She talks about *hou lian, hei xin*, "thick face, black heart," a traditional principle that enjoins people to steel themselves to do the necessary thing no matter what the consequences for their reputation. *Hou-hei xue*, thick-black-ology, is the rigorous study of strategies for success that involve things of which squeamish people are incapable.

A distillation of *The Art of War* and other tactics from Chinese history and literature, known as the *Thirty-Six Strategies* (*Sanshiliu ji*; Verstappen 1999), includes such advice for war—or for negotiations—as appearing weak when one is strong or using the enemies' strength against them. Each strategy is phrased in the form of a *chengyu*, a fixed expression, that is extremely well known and carries with it an entire story. For example, "kill the rooster to frighten the monkey" means that one can use relatively minor means to cause fear in someone more powerful, allowing one to avoid having to threaten the other directly.

Most of the strategies involve clever manipulation of the enemy or of one's own troops, requiring both understanding of how one's actions will be interpreted and anticipation of how that interpretation will be mulled over, so that if the enemy will think that one's actions are intended to mislead, they will decide not to trust at all, leading to suspicion, which one must then alleviate. The theory of mind presupposed here is complex; it fully recognizes that others are as capable of sorting through the obvious as one is oneself. *Consider consequences. Anticipate others' responses.*

The Art of War classifies spies into five categories: *xiang* (local), *nei* (internal), *fan* (double; literally "turning back"), *si* (dead; Ames translates as "expendable"), *sheng* (live; Ames translates as "unexpendable" [Sunzi 1993, 169]). "Expendable spies are our own agents who obtain false information we have deliberately leaked to them, and who then pass it on to the enemy spies" (Sunzi 1993, 170). The ability to use intelligence is considered essential; the best commanders are those who are clever (*qiao*) or wise (*zhi*). There is no excuse for simple-minded trustfulness, especially on the part of leaders. This would only endanger those whose fates are protected by the leaders.

Though there are surely treatises on warfare in Western thought, they do not occupy the central position that the *bingfa* occupy in China. "Everyone" is familiar with the *bingfa* and with the *Thirty-Six Strategies*. They are quoted in everyday life by ordinary people, taking them to be expressions of how the world is. Notwithstanding their discovery in the 1980s by American business, they were not used primarily by merchants or businesspeople—traditionally considered the lowest form of people in the ranks, below farmers—but were part of the repertoire of scholars and officials.

Cunning, Cleverness, Skill, Deception: The Crooked

In confronting a world filled with warfare and struggle, cleverness and strategy are primary tools. *Strategies of the Warring States* (*Zhan'guo Ce*), a compilation of stories about persuasion, artful manipulation, and the battling of wits, demonstrates that strategy is more powerful than strength—especially since one goal is to avoid warfare by convincing adversaries that one's strength is greater than it is (Crump 1964). A premium is placed on this kind of anticipatory or preemptive action.

Persuaders of the time, as exemplified in the fictionalized versions in *Strategies of the Warring States*, merely sought opportunity, not necessarily social order (Crump 1964, 9). We might regard them as mercenary talkers, willing to use guile and deceit for any employer and thus very effective in their confrontations. Here is an example of a clever persuader:

West Zhou Opens the Sluices and Suzi Takes Fees From Both Sides

East Zhou wished to sow its land to rice but West Zhou would not open the river sluices. Zhou of the east was troubled over this but Suzi spoke to its ruler and begged permission to treat with West Zhou for water.

He arrived in Zhou of the west and spoke to its ruler:

"My lord's plans are faulty; by withholding water from East Zhou now he is making her wealthy. Its citizens have all sown to dry grain and no other! If my lord would really do them harm he should open the sluices immediately and injure their seeds. With the sluices opened East Zhou must replant to rice. Then when you deny them the waters they must come to West Zhou as suppliants and receive their orders from your majesty!"

The king agreed and released the waters and Suzi received the gold of both countries. (*Zhan'guo Ce*, Book of Zhou, King Hui, no. 24 (SPTK 2.4b; *Chan-Kuo Ts'e* 1970, 40–41))

"Glib deceivers" were celebrated in texts like *Strategies of the Warring States* and the *bingfa* texts, and reviled by the most orthodox Ruists, who preferred directness and straightforwardness, in contrast to the indirect and even deceitful methods acceptable to most Legalists.

> The importance and permissibility of deceit in *bingfa* texts present a problem that is dealt with in different ways by various philosophers. Essentially two solutions are adopted. One is to relegate the use of deceit to the separate realm of *wu* [the martial]. This is the approach taken by most *bingfa* and to a certain extent by the *Laozi*. In this view, deception in its proper sphere is both necessary and admirable, and the general who uses it is not amoral. This is the view taken explicitly by Militarists and implicitly by Taoists. The other alternative is to condemn deceit outright; this is the solution taken by Confucians [Ruists] both during and after the Warring States period. . . . Mencius and Xunzi advocate the use of *zheng*, straightforwardness, in all circumstances and dismiss the need for use of *qi*, craftiness. (Raphals 1992, 123)

The difference between *zheng* and *qi*, straightforwardness and craftiness, pervades the Warring States. Whether rejecting the crooked or extolling it, it was necessary to engage with it. Almost all rulers seemed to opt for the clever rather than the trusting.

Not all interaction was wily and preemptive. Some states formed alliances. Still, an enormous amount of effort was required to ascertain the trustworthiness of strategic partners; as promises of upholding one's word, both oaths and blood covenants (*meng*) were signed with ritual seriousness, as the graphic form indicates the phonetic component (*meng*, from *ming*) over a ritual vessel.[2] Many episodes in politically oriented works such as the *Zuo Chronicles* (*Zuo Zhuan*) revolve around oaths, verbal and written agreements of loyalty, but these were too easily broken. Lewis writes of the more powerful sealing of a blood covenant during the early years of the Eastern Zhou dynasty, a ritual of fasting, sacrificing an animal, attaching a written textual promise, and drinking the animal's blood. "The blood of the sacrifice marked a supremely solemn and binding agreement, and it was used to forge political ties between men" (1990, 46). The ties had to be continually reaffirmed; promises were frequently broken despite the awe of the blood covenant ceremonies. The *meng* texts were sacred and were accompanied by curses on those who would break them. "A *meng* is an expression of good faith all round, and so it is determined upon in the mind, it is proffered up with gifts of jade and silk, the parties are bound by its terms and by the gods and spirits it is enforced . . . once sworn, it cannot be altered" (*Zuo Zhuan*, Ai xii, 3; in Dobson 1968, 274). Sometimes blood oaths were faked: people buried documents and smeared blood, alleging that there had been a blood oath that was then broken—"framing" the one alleged to have made the promise of loyalty (Dobson 1968, 279–280).

Deception was widespread but not necessarily accepted by all thinkers at the time. Xunzi, for instance (born around 312 BCE), believed that humans are basically evil but that virtue can overcome this. In a dialogue rejecting deceptive methods, he wrote:

> "What is really essential in military undertakings is to be good at winning the support of the people."
>
> "I disagree," said the lord of Lin-wu. "In using arms, one should place the highest value upon advantageous circumstances, and should move by stealth and deception. He who is good at using arms moves suddenly and secretly, and no one knows from whence he comes. Sun Wu and Wu Ch'i employed this method and there was no one in the world who could stand up against them. Why is it necessary to win the support of the people?"
>
> "You do not understand," said Hsün Tzu [Xunzi]. "What I am speaking about are the soldiers of a benevolent man, the intentions of a true king. You speak of the value of plots and advantageous circumstances, of moving by sudden attack and stealth—but these are matters appropriate only to one of the feudal lords. Against the soldiers of a benevolent man, deceptions are of no use; they are effective only against a ruler who is rash and arrogant, whose people are worn out; they are effective only against a state in which the ruler and his subjects, superiors and inferiors, are torn apart and at odds. Therefore a tyrant like Chieh may practice deception upon another Chieh, and, depending upon how cleverly he proceeds, may happily achieve a certain success. But for a Chieh to try to practice deception against a sage like Yao would be like trying to break a rock by throwing eggs at it, or trying to stir boiling water with your bare finger. He will be like a man consumed by fire or drowned in water." (Xunzi 15; Watson 1963, 56–57)

Xunzi thus saw the usefulness of deception by the inferior but advocated against its use by a "true king" or a benevolent man. It is not so much that deception is morally wrong but that it is ineffective in the most important cases to consider.

He continues to dismiss common deceptive practices:

> To attract men to military service and recruit soldiers as [the feudal lords] do, to rely upon force and deception and teach men to covet military achievements and profit—this is the way to deceive the people. But to rely upon ritual principles and moral education—this is the way to unite them. When deception meets deception, the victory may go either way, depending upon the

cleverness of the combatants. But to try to use deception to meet unity is like trying to hack down Mount T'ai with an awl—no one in the world would be stupid enough to attempt it! (Xunzi 15; Watson 1963, 63)

Xunzi's student Han Fei (died 233 BCE), by contrast, the quintessential Legalist, associates wisdom with cunning (in contrast to the *Laozi*, which rejects both). "Han Fei specifically associates wisdom with cunning, in the person of deceptive and treacherous ministers. According to Han Fei, the astute (*zhi*) are not trustworthy, and a ruler may be deceived by the plans (*ji*) of wise (*zhi*) men bent on private gain at public expense. An 'enlightened ruler' (*ming jun*) neither entrusts stupid (*yu*) men with affairs of state nor permits wise (*zhi*) men to practice deceit (*zha*). . . . For Han Fei, 'subtle discernment' consists in carrying out plans before they take shape. Similarly, 'the weak conquer the strong' by the (deceptive) appearance of humility" (Raphals 1992, 83, 84).[3]

The tension between the need and desire for trickiness and the preference for straightforward righteousness is long-standing in Chinese thought. One of the most significant challenges to this straightforwardness comes from the two principal Daoist texts.

Daoist Curves and Circles

Daoism is best known outside China for its two major texts, the *Daode Jing* (also written *Tao-te Ching*), compiled perhaps in the early to middle fourth century BCE but according to tradition written by Laozi (also written Lao-tzu), the Old One, and the *Zhuangzi*, written around 350–300 BCE.[4] The two texts differ in profound ways, but they share the goal of testing received wisdom and convention. *Zhuangzi* is the more radical. Rejecting straightness (*zhi*), it advocates a winding, meandering way of moving (see Blum 1986). Chapter 2 of *Zhuangzi* begins with a comparison between people's speech and the wind, suggesting emptiness and bluster. The image of the universe being composed of the wind making sounds in the hollows of trees and mountains implies that any claims about possessing the definitive truth are bound to be misguided. In fact, speaking is not usually necessary; there is a high value placed on silence and on simply coexisting in a state of harmony. In this tradition, falseness is just as real as claims about truth; lies are no more evil than truth; both are exaggerations of what is possible from humans in their forms. In the *Daode Jing*:

When the government is muddled and confused,
The people are genuine and sincere.
When the government is discriminate and clear,
The state is crafty and cunning.

Sincere words are not showy;
Showy words are not sincere. (Laozi chap. 81; Henricks 1989, 37)

If Daoism provides an indigenous alternative to the other old Chinese traditions, Chan Buddhism (known in the West more commonly from its
Japanese incarnation as Zen) took Daoist elements and fused them with In-
dian Buddhism for an even more radical challenge to notions of truth,
knowledge, and talk. (More common versions of Buddhism in China, usually
called Pure Land and Mahayana, borrow more from Ruist and religious
Daoist traditions of formality and hierarchy.)

Buddhist Distrust of Appearance

Although Buddhism is in many ways incorporated into mainstream Chinese
religious practice, certain aspects of intellectual and institutional Buddhism
are very countercultural. With its basic understanding that the world is full
of illusions, Buddhism reminds people that the hope of saying something true
and real is similarly illusory. Buddhism entered China certainly by 100 CE and
perhaps as early as 100 BCE and was transformed into many varieties of belief
and practice. Chan Buddhism, which arose in China during the sixth and
seventh centuries in part through the indigenization of Buddhism and its
mixing with Daoism, is famous for its mystical and nonsensical sayings
(gong'an in Chinese, kōan in Japanese), such as "What is the sound of one
hand clapping?" The purpose of language is to wake people up, not to utter
definitive truths (though in Buddhist thought there are "Four Noble
Truths"). Gong'an are paradoxical sayings intended to waken the novice from
complacency and to alert him or her to the real nature of reality, ordinarily
hidden beneath appearances (Chang 1969). Questions such as "What is the
nature of a person before he is born?" do not use language as ordinarily conceived. They cannot be analyzed using ordinary notions of truth and falsity;
they suggest that such notions are themselves false.

Legalist, Daoist, and Buddhist challenges to the simple views of reality are
not the only ones found in traditional China. A good deal of literature enjoys and celebrates tricksters and their cleverness.

Tricksters and Cleverness in Fiction and Humor

In the popular novel *Romance of the Three Kingdoms*, attributed to the late Yuan and early Ming (fourteenth century) writer Luo Guanzhong, Zhuge Liang is the most clever of three clever adversaries, the other two being Liu Bei and Cao Cao. Several of his strategies have become legendary and are distilled in the *Thirty-Six Strategies*. The stories of Zhuge Liang were officially considered insufficiently moral, yet they have been extremely popular nonetheless. Zhuge Liang's strength is not physical; it lies in his ability to predict and outthink even the clever ones who anticipate his traps. His theory of mind is quite striking and is explicitly recognized as one of his primary virtues.

A well-known illustration of his cunning is found in the story "Kongming [Zhuge Liang] Borrows Cao Cao's Arrows Through a Ruse" (chapter 46). Zhou Yu wanted to destroy Zhuge Liang, so he challenged him (on his life) to fight Cao Cao. Zhou Yu said he would need a hundred thousand arrows, and that he would have to receive them within ten days. Zhuge Liang said that ten days would be too long; Cao Cao would arrive in just three. He was aided by Lu Su, a man who had also tried to deceive and destroy Zhuge Liang, but because Zhuge Liang had seen through the ruse, Lu Su was now obliged to help him out. In addition to lending him twenty boats, Lu Su put blue cloth screens and bundles of straw on the side of each boat, as Zhuge Liang requested. Zhuge Liang strung the twenty boats loosely together and, on the third day, sailed upriver in a dense fog and beat the drums of war. Cao Cao's men could hear but not see the forces of Zhuge Liang. Assuming that Zhuge Liang's soldiers were preparing an ambush, Cao Cao ordered thousands of archers to shoot at the boats.

Arrow after arrow struck Zhuge Liang's men's boats and stuck in the straw that Zhuge Liang had prepared. Then Zhuge Liang's men easily rode downstream back to their camp. When the fog lifted, Cao Cao's men tried to pursue Zhuge Liang's troops but were too slow. Zhou Yu then had more than a hundred thousand arrows with which to attack Cao Cao. In a single, almost effortless action, Zhuge Liang outwitted three clever people: Zhou Yu (who wanted him dead), Lu Su (who was not really loyal), and Cao Cao (Luo 1991 [fourteenth century], 352–355).

The novel *Outlaws of the Marsh* similarly celebrates cleverness (Shi and Luo 1981 [fourteenth century]). It revolves around 108 heroes (36 major and 72 minor) who form a band of righteous outlaws during the reign of Hui Zong (r. 1101–1125) in the corrupt Northern Song period. Their thieves' honor and cleverness have been well known to Chinese since the book was assembled in the Ming (1368–1644). Beloved for centuries, the book has also been prohibited periodically. Mao Zedong claimed it as his inspiration for the guerrilla warfare of the Yan'an period. The book is filled with apt episodes, but I will summarize one from chapter 61 that reminds me of the Associate Manager Wang who was duped by fake fortune tellers, as recounted in chapter 2. There, I claimed that despite the official position that the cases of cheating should be deplored, in fact readers relished the spectacle of someone getting so obviously taken. This episode, from the fourteenth century, has many common features. (It is a shame to summarize this book, since the unfolding is so pleasurable to read.)

"Wu Yong Cleverly Tricks the Jade Unicorn": Wu Yong boasts that "with the aid of this facile three-inch tongue of mine, I shall go fearlessly to the Northern Capital and persuade Lu Junyi to come to our mountain." Lu Junyi is known as Magnate Lu, a wealthy and strong man also called "Jade Unicorn." Wu Yong takes with him Li Kui—a strong and unrestrained hero from the first chapters of the book whose main problem is his impetuousness. In a humorous flash, he is to masquerade as a mute Daoist acolyte serving Wu Yong. Li Kui has a terrible temper and by the time they enter the Northern Capital he has almost lost his temper twice. Wu Yong gets past the soldiers at the city gate with his false fortune-telling license. He walks up and down the street, followed by laughing children, with his sign advertising fortune telling for an ounce of silver.

The sound disturbs Lu Junyi, whose assistant is sent to ask Wu Yong to tell his fortune, on the assumption that someone asking such a high fee must be truly scholarly. Wu Yong naturally foresees a dreadful fate for Lu Junyi—unless Lu leaves his home and journeys a thousand *li* to the southeast. Wu Yong creates a rhyme that predicts the eventual auspicious ending, providing Lu follows Wu Yong's advice.

Lu Junyi summons his household and informs them that he is indeed leaving for several months. His steward, adopted son, and wife all implore him to disregard what they believe must be a fake fortune. Listeners and readers must enjoy the complexity of their plea: They speak what is actually the truth but it appears from Lu's perspective to be quite mistaken. The steward says, "Everybody knows fortune tellers are slick talkers. You shouldn't listen to that fellow's claptrap." His adopted son says: "Don't believe that fortune teller's wild story. He's probably a plant from Mount Liangshan, sent to stir you up so that they can trick you into joining them. It's too bad I wasn't home last night. With two or three phrases I could have exposed the fellow and made him a laughing stock." (Shi and Luo 1981 [fourteenth century], 985–986)

"You're both talking rot. Who would dare to deceive me!" Lu Junyi insists on going. The entourage of ten carts and forty or fifty animals, plus staff, head southeast. At an inn, they are told of the bandit stronghold in Liangshan and warned to avoid it. Lu Junyi relishes the opportunity to engage with a worthy enemy, and he prepares to fight the bandits. When he enters the wood, he and his men are surrounded by four or five hundred bandits. Li Kui introduces himself as the mute acolyte and laughs: "Magnate, you've fallen for a clever ruse by our Military Advisor. Come and take your place in a chieftain's chair" (990). In succession, several of the fiercest bandit heroes come and challenge Lu Junyi, who enjoys the engagement until he sees that all his carts have been stolen. He fights and nearly escapes into the marsh but is "rescued" by another hero and surrounded by bandits who all wish to have him join them. The entire episode reads as yet another case of the clever and ultimately righteous bandits recruiting more capable people to their side. Much of the delight in reading this novel—and others—derives from the play with reality and fantasy, truth and deception, and good and evil.

Beloved writer Pu Songling (1640–1715), whose collections of odd and fantastic stories have long been treasured, writes in the story "Fraud (Number Three)" of a man who cheats through a most clever and patient combination of verbal lying and misleading actions. A Daoist named Cheng buys a post—this was acceptable in those days—in a certain district in order to forge an apparent friendship with a man named Li who possesses an ancient and magical lute.

For at least a year Cheng never mentions the lute; then he leaves one lying around, causing Li to admit that he too is a connoisseur of the lute. After more time passes, they play for one another. One day, Cheng laments that he does not have a better lute to play with. Li finally takes out his magical lute. Cheng says his wife can play even more skillfully than he can, so he passes the lute behind a screen. Li, who had been drinking much wine, is urged to return the following day to retrieve his lute, and to hear Cheng's wife play masterfully. When Li returns, the entire compound is deserted, and his lute gone with Cheng and his wife.

Pu concludes with the moral: "There are many angles from which to practice deception in this world. In the Taoist's case, there was a certain refinement in his trickery" (Pu 1989, 291).

In cases of trickery, if people are harmed it is lamented, and yet in other cases there is a certain admiration for cleverness, patience, perseverance. To set up a person for a robbery over a period of several years demonstrates much cleverness. (It too reminds me of poor Manager Wang in chapter 2, cheated for four years by people pretending to have religious powers.) Cheng was masterful in his anticipation of Li's reactions, playing Li like a lute and getting him to do just what he wanted. The ruse here involved setting the stage with a lute, protestations about Cheng's inferior lute, lute playing, a screen, claims about a wife, all with perfect anticipation of Li's response. (*Anticipate others' responses. (theory of mind)*)

Collections of humor also include examples of cleverness, sometimes sought by the duped themselves.

"A Trick," from *Elegant Banter,* a Ming collection by Fubai-zhai Zhuren [Master of the corrupt studio]

Zhu Gumin was learned but fond of joking. One day when he paid a call on Scholar Tang at his studio, the latter said: "You are known to be full of tricks. If I were sitting in a given room, could you induce me to go outdoors?" Zhu replied: "It is presently quite cold outside, so I am certain you would be unwilling to step out of doors, but if you were to stand outside this room it would be much easier for me to induce you inside; you would veritably be forced to comply with my will."

Believing him, Scholar Tang went out of the house and said to Zhu: "Alright, how can you induce me back inside?"

Clapping his hands, Zhu replied: "But haven't I already induced you out?" (Kowallis 1984, 64–65)

"Telling a Lie," from the *Xue Tao History of Humor,* Ming compilation by Jiang Yingke

A young cad from Wuling was good at telling a convincing lie. On the street one day he met an old man who said: "People say you lie all the time; well, just try one on me, you young whippersnapper!" The youth replied: "There's no time to talk now. I've just heard they are draining the water from the East Lake and everybody there is busy picking up free fish from off the ground, so I'm hurrying over there to get me one, too!"

Believing his words, the old man dashed to the East Lake but found it still full on his arrival. Only then did he realize that the youth had been lying to him. (Kowallis 1984, 79)

Both of these humorous stories show that even when inviting someone to cheat them, most people are such simpletons that they believe the untruths. But the appeal of the stories comes from the general knowledge that language is always potentially deceptive and yet is often regarded with credulity. The tightrope that must be walked between suspicion and trust is always in people's awareness. (*Trust. And suspect.*)

Some ruses are judged for their justice or cruelty, while others are merely regarded as elegant. In the story by Pu Songling about the lute theft, we find admiration for the cleverness of the duper and disdain for the guilelessness of the duped. A higher truth, though not a profound one, might be seen to emerge from this episode, with greed and love of music and propriety overcoming the more common sense of caution. It is important to note, however, that the harm done to the duped is not mortal in this case. His blinding love of his lute made the loss of it almost just. It is often the case in China that the innocent and trusting are easily manipulated and deceived by the cleverness of superiors.

Forgery and Authenticity

A final aspect of deception in premodern China to be considered here involves art and forgery. Art historian Wen Fong pointed out in his article "The Problem of Forgeries in Chinese Painting" that there was a great tradition of copying in China, to the point that some people were specialists in copying and copies were often cherished along with original works (1962). Even beyond that, there have been many benefits to Chinese copying of art; among these benefits is that prior to photography many famous paintings are known to us only through later copies. Sometimes the later copies are taken as original, and disputes arise when a dealer attempts to pass off a copy as an original and issues of authentication are brought to bear on it. Lists of criteria for authenticity circulated, but these were known as much to the forgers as to the connoisseurs, and the forgers were often able to meet the criteria deliberately. According to Wen, however, the issue was not a moral one.

> It should be noted that art forgery in China has never carried such dark connotations as it does in the West. Since the aim of studying art has always been either aesthetic cultivation or pure enjoyment, rather than scientific knowledge, the acquisition of a genuine masterpiece—and by the same token, the ability to create a perfect forgery—was a matter of virtuosity and pride. The legal or ethical problems of an "honest business transaction" never entered into the picture. As a matter of fact, it was precisely for very good reasons of ethics

and even better ones of tact, that the owner of a forgery was usually protected, as far as possible, from knowing the truth. Scientific truth certainly had no immediate bearing on art appreciation. If someone is gullible enough to buy as well as derive pleasure from forgeries, why spoil the poor man's illusions? (Wen 1962, 99)

In fact, even those who attempted to ascertain the authentic versions sometimes appreciated the cleverness of the deception. Yet the matter of an original, truthful identity was generally not considered relevant in assessing art.

In his seminal study of forgery, Anthony Grafton (1990) writes of more than two thousand years of forgery in the Western literary tradition, in which the cleverness of forgers went in step with the cleverness of authenticators. Forgers had to convey a text that was originally created at some historical distance from the forger and then to convey an artifact that was at some historical distance from its creation. At the same time, the forger had to appear genuine in the discovery of the document. Some tactics employed by forgers include use of deliberately archaic language, darkening of parchment (often using tea) to give the impression of age, and use of quotations from contemporaries of the alleged author.

One very clever forger, medieval Dominican friar Giovanni Nanni, used quotations from Greek texts to denounce lying and forgery, "giv[ing] Nanni's texts an air of moral as well as factual superiority" (61). Reception is the easy part; quoting J. B. Mencke, Grafton suggests that "the world wants to be fooled" (*muntus fuld tezibi* or *mundus vult decipi*) (55–56 and 131 n.36).

A long, complex study of the forgery of documents at the central Asian site of Dunhuang on the ancient Silk Road shows how Grafton's general study of Western forgery might apply in China. The Dunhuang caves in Gansu province, northwest China, were repositories of Buddhist scriptures and other documents written in Chinese, Tibetan, Uighur, and other languages. It is likely that the documents were sealed into the cave by approximately the year 1000 CE (see Demiéville 1970; Whitfield and Wood 1996). The cave with the largest number of documents, Cave 17, was discovered in 1900 and the documents were taken to be the oldest forms of several classic works. Immediately it was discovered that a number of documents sold as Dunhuang manuscripts were forgeries. (There are many fascinating aspects of the case, including the paradoxically dual nature of the documents as objects and as texts.)

Monique Cohen defines a fake as "a deliberate desire on the part of its maker to mislead or to present a work as something other than what it is" (2002, 22). She claims that there were more fakes and copies made in China than anywhere else because of the values placed both on collecting and on the past (23). John Fields and Kenneth Seddon define forgery as "a false document, painting, or object, created with the deliberate intention to deceive or defraud" (2002, 34). They then claim that scientific analysis cannot detect forgeries since the crux of the matter lies in the producer's intention. Certainly this is always true for any assessment of truth and deception; the producers' intention is beyond the reach of others to ascertain definitively. And in some cases in China it is not especially crucial.

Between Truth and Lies

China's most pointed social critic prior to the revolution, Lu Xun, criticized people's tendency to change according to circumstances and to tailor their answers to please. This 1925 satire of the Chinese propensity to lie suggests a yearning for honesty:

On Expression and Opinion[5]

I dreamed I was in the classroom of a primary school preparing to write an essay, and asked the teacher how to express an opinion.

"That's hard!" Glancing sideways at me over his glasses he said: "Let me tell you a story—

"When a son is born to a family, the whole household is delighted. When he is one month old they carry him out to display him to the guests—usually expecting some compliments, of course.

"One says: 'This child will be rich.' He is heartily thanked.

"One says: 'This child will be an official.' Some compliments are paid him in return.

"One says: 'This child will die.' He is thoroughly beaten by the whole family.

"That the child will die is inevitable, while to say that he will be rich or a high official may be a lie. Yet the lie is rewarded, whereas the statement of the inevitable gains a beating. You . . ."

"I don't want to tell lies, sir, neither do I want to be beaten. So what should I say?"

"In that case, say: 'Aha! Just look at this child! My word. . . . Did you ever! Oho! Hehe! He,

hehehehe!'" (Lu 1973 [1925], 126)

Clearly truth would be punished, as would lies—leaving the only solution to say nothing that could possibly be pinned down. Lu Xun's criticism of China's weakness is exemplified by this oily dream-teacher.

❧

The possibility that one is being duped seems long-standing, as does the notion that people should form alliances and trust their partners. *Trust. And suspect* is a maxim that would seem both ubiquitous and paradoxical. Still, paradox and skepticism are also long-standing elements in China's cultural collection. Pure consistency is seen as neither necessary nor possible.

Many of the maxims that apply to premodern China, including *Do the right action in context, Take relationships as primary, Select script, Consider power and role, Consider bystanders, Language is culture, not (only) nature,* and *Performance counts* are also relevant in the present. Yet there are differences as well. In contemporary China, the notion of rectitude has come to be seen as feudal or old-fashioned. The goal of advising leaders has essentially been pre-empted by the Party, which seeks no counsel. If we seek the roots of contemporary practice, we cannot find a seamless line back to China's beginnings, but we can recognize commonalities, in Nietzsche's genealogical sense.

But the present is not a mere step from the past. There was a huge chasm between them, the upheavals of the twentieth century leaving gaps and piles of rubble. What happened as a result of that continuing revolution is the subject of the next chapter.

Notes

1. I share Chad Hansen's rejection of "school analysis" as a way of grasping the history of Chinese thought (1992, 11–14), just as I reject it as adequate or even accurate for a history of anthropological thought. The tendency is to put others in a school and reject the labels others invent for oneself. It is convenient, of course, to simplify a strain of thought into a one-word descriptor: "legalist" or "structuralist." Alternative ordering traces texts, ideas, or people.

2. The original meaning of *truth* was related to *troth*, faithfulness pledged in a promise or covenant, very similar to *meng* (Oxford English Dictionary 1989).

3. In analysis of what she calls "metic intelligence," cleverness, Raphals (1992) examines the enormous vocabulary related to the notions of cleverness and deception in traditional works of Chinese literary and philosophical writing. An extensive and subtle vocabulary distinguishes between "crafty and roundabout" (*qi zheng*) and "versatile craftiness" (*bian qiao*), with a range of "deceit" (*wei*) and "schemes and deceit" (*zha mou*) and more. She translates a large number of terms as "deception": *zuo*

wei (126), *zha* (83, 110, 113, 126), *gui* (112), and *yin* (11). Related terms include: "deception and dissimulation" —*wei zha* (113), *gui zuo* (113); "deceit"—*wei* (120); "perverse"—*guai* (100); "stealth and deception"—*bian zha* (46). Similarly, quite a number are translated as related to cunning: "cunning"—*jue* (126); "cleverness," skill, trick—*qiao* (17, 33, 38, 46, 61, 62, 67, 105); "artfulness"—*qiao* (46, 76); "crafty language, artful words"—*qiao yan* (11, 15, 32); "crafty and roundabout" vs. "straight-forward"—*qi zheng* (110, 111, 124); "crafty, cunning"—*jue* (33, 100, 113); "versatile craftiness"—*bian qiao* (39); "treachery"—*jian* (11, 78); "wiliness"—*qi* (113). Another set of related terms involves strategy and plans; the core key term is *mou*, translated as "strategy, plans, counsel, cunning, crafty counsel" (11, 17). Other related terms are "schemes and deceit"—*zha mou* (124); "scheming and plotting, wily plots"—*quan mou* (24, 45); "uncanny plans"—*qi ce* (125); "plans"—*ji* (13, 14, 15, 17, 67, 83), *ce* (121), *mou* (62, 67, 127); "plans and schemes"—*mou lu* (55); "strategies" (*mou*, 106, *ce*, 127); "skill"—*quan* (121); "advisors"—*mou* (121); "calculations"—*ji*, (107); "devices"—*ji* (39).

4. The nature of these two texts has been the subject of much scholarly inquiry. The *Daode Jing* has been found in Mawangdui fragments from before 168 BCE but in a different order (*De-Dao Jing*) (see Henricks 1989) and was assembled no earlier than the Warring States period (403–222 BCE) despite the traditional view that it was written by a man called Laozi around 500 BCE. See Lau 1963 and Henricks 2000. *Zhuangzi* has been persuasively analyzed as consisting of three types of texts: original (inner), later (outer), and mixed. The earliest chapters are probably from about 250 BCE. See Graham 1981.

5. Thanks to Sylvia Li-chün Lin for pointing out this story to me.

CHAPTER SEVEN

A Social Theory of Truth: Language in Revolutionary China

All humanity will consist of unselfish, intelligent, highly cultured and skilled communist workers; mutual assistance and affection will prevail among men and there will be no such irrationalities as mutual suspicion and deception, mutual injury, mutual slaughter and war. It will of course be the best, the most beautiful and the most advanced society in human history.

—Liu Shaoqi 1964 [1939]

Truth is a thing of this world: it is produced only by virtue of multiple forms of constraint. And it induces regular effects of power. Each society has its régime of truth, its "general politics" of truth: that is, the types of discourse which it accepts and makes function to distinguish true and false statements, the means by which each is sanctioned; the techniques and procedures accorded value in the acquisition of truth; the status of those who are charged with saying what counts as true . . .

—Michel Foucault 1980

When we lie, we're not doing so with malicious intent. It's certainly not like in capitalist countries where people wallow in lies and hypocrisy. . . . In those societies people wear masks all the time. These few little tera-diddles of ours, on the other hand, are simply a way of getting by. . . . The world we live in, with all its speeches, all its meetings, is a blend of truth and falsehood. . . . Since ancient times Chinese have been caught

between lies and the truth. Why do I have to take it all so seriously?
When you can, tell the truth, when you can't, lie—what's wrong with
that?

—Shen Rong 1983, 214, 217–18

In both China and the United States, when I talk about the theme of deception and truth, some people attribute a prevalence of deception to something in China's unchanging character, and others blame it on the excesses
of China's Cultural Revolution or its Communist experience. The previous
chapter introduced ideas about truth and deception in China's more distant
past. Continuities and differences were evident, permitting assessment of the
first explanation. This chapter focuses on the revolutionary period in order
to evaluate the second. You will see here some of the ways the simultaneous
explicit extolling of "truth" was contradicted by actual encouragement of falsification, leading to an ever-changing sense of the true throughout the second half of the twentieth century. Effects of this disturbing period linger in
the present.

It may be a slight exaggeration to argue that the Communist revolution
centered on language and truth—but only slight. This period of bloody and
violent transformation of the world's most populous country has been explained in countless ways, from military to biographical, but I will follow the
thread of truth telling as a guide through the labyrinth of detail. The extreme actions of the period of high revolution, culminating in the conflicts
and agonies of the Great Leap Forward (1958–61) and the Cultural Revolution (1966–76), can be understood as a struggle between factions to command the truth and to have it uttered and enacted. Understanding and uttering the single permitted powerful truth—a view of history and of
humanity's roles in social change—was the goal of education, politics, and
social suasion. Power is thus connected to the holder of the truth. Power
equals command over truth.

Truth occupies a central position in every society, with claimants to truth
having more or less persuasiveness because of their social position. Truth may
be claimed by the powerful, such as government leaders or the wealthy, or by
the subordinate, who have innocence on their side. This chapter examines
truth claims and their relationship to power, looking at revolutionary moments in China's history involving the Communist dominance of the twentieth century and in particular at Cultural Revolution manipulations of
truth. While there were many moments of breathtaking sincerity during the
first years of Communist China and even during the Cultural Revolution, it
is clear that many people played fast and loose with the truth, at the same

time that explicit admonitions to be truthful—learning from the simple peasants—abounded and that the Party claimed explicitly to have the truth. The communicative patterns and structures invented during the high revolutionary period were central to the transformative endeavors of the revolution. Many of them revolve around issues of confession, sincerity, suffering, and accusations, all controlled by the Party.

The maxims that are especially relevant for this chapter are:

Consider consequences.
Guard information.
Thicken interaction.
Performance counts.

While there is continuity between the past and present in the above maxims, there was conscious opposition during the most revolutionary years to *Give and save face*. Though in fact face had to be considered in some cases, it had to be provided under the guise of revolutionary candor and spontaneity. There were also some explicit maxims that operated solely during revolutionary times:

Disregard face.
Be frank.
Everyone is equal.

These had to be asserted and performed regularly, as they involved the ideological yearnings of the revolution, but alongside them were the longstanding maxims. A general precept, *Survive*, operated as well. Not everyone was able or willing to follow this. The deaths and demoralizations of the revolutionary period are a reminder of the power of ideas in human life.

In order to weigh claims about the Communist responsibility for contemporary practices, you must first be introduced to the events themselves. Rooms full of books have been written about that history, and many are still to be written. Nonetheless, a general overview can suffice to introduce the sweep of the past and situate the more specific claims that will follow.

The Chinese Revolution

In the previous chapter you were introduced to Warring States China, with its bloody wars and desperate pacts, its Ruist appeals to people's better natures, and its Daoist and Buddhist acceptance of paradox and flux. Throughout

China's long history one can observe striking contrasts between the gruesome material suffering of many of what would later be termed its "masses" and the opulence of its ruling elite. (This disparity has returned with striking speed in the early twenty-first century. See, e.g., Beijing Review 2006; Conover 2006; Kahn 2006c; Rahman Khan and Riskin 2005.) The end of imperial China was marked by the famous dual (and rhyming, in Mandarin) tragedies of internal chaos and external trouble (*neiluan waihuan*), with the court and society filled with corruption and greed, and China being assailed from outside by foreign powers determined to gain from China's huge market.

By the late nineteenth century the Qing dynasty—Manchu rulers of China—was so weakened and despised that alternatives were clearly needed. Students and activists studied other nations' political systems and organized into groups devoted to overturning the imperial system and replacing it with a different system, in part motivated by nationalist sentiments.

The entire twentieth century of China was spent in search of a system for administering and organizing the huge and unruly mass of Chinese people as it became ordered into a modern nation-state. What form that state would take has been much disputed; how the cultural order of China would reflect or shape the state, and how society would function, have all been at the forefront of lively and often violent and bitter disputes. Some of the choices have endured; others have been fleeting.

By 1937 the two major political groups, the Nationalists (KMT or GMD) and the Communists (CCP), were fighting a three-way war with each other and also with the Japanese, who had invaded China. After 1945 the struggle was between just the two parties. The CCP was victorious in 1949, and on October 1 Mao Zedong declared the foundation of the People's Republic of China.

This period of revolution has been explained and evaluated in countless ways. It has been regarded as an era of mass psychosis as well as a time of sincere utopian experimentation. It is clear that both elements indeed existed. Among the Communists' genuine positive accomplishments upon gaining power was that the Party had won grudging support from peasants and intellectuals for its integrity and principle in fighting and then in ruling. While the Nationalist army, for instance, was always considered a scourge, demanding food and raping women, the Communists were famous for paying for food from peasants and being upright and courteous. The Communists went out of their way to exemplify helpful selflessness. This was novel in China's history, and some people responded to it enthusiastically, from peasants to intellectuals, during the 1940s and up through the middle 1950s.

The example which the Communists set in their everyday lives was as decisive as the words which they spoke or the plans which they suggested. In the last analysis, it was the superior moral character exhibited by the revolutionaries, their integrity, their dedication, their willingness to suffer, their honesty in facing mistakes, their acceptance of criticism, and their capacity for self-criticism that moved the peasants. It was because the Communists set public interests ahead of private interests, long-range interests ahead of short-range interests, and the general good ahead of any partial good, and did so in their own personal lives, that the peasants were willing to follow them. (Hinton 1966, 607)

Peasants supported the Communists because of their integrity, and the Communists set about to undertake "socialist reconstruction," which included transformation of the entire structure of the country. Although intellectuals were regarded with suspicion, many were genuinely drawn to the revolutionary cause. But even they often suffered from the revolution's caprices. There were genuine attempts to eradicate special privilege but also—as you will see later in this chapter—violent and cynical attempts to destroy people who dared defy the leaders' claims about commanding a new reality.

People frequently differentiated "old China," with its particularistic connections and status, from "new China," with a focus on fairness. In some cases bribery and *guanxi* (connections) were no longer effective. Two American graduate students trying to get permission to return to the United States recall in their memoir:

Harriet [Mills] attempted through a girl friend, who had connections with people in the Peking Public Security Bureau, to find out why the permits had not been issued, and when this attempt failed she and Rick [Allyn Rickett] began visiting all the influential Chinese they knew to solicit help in the matter. Such methods might have worked in the old China where it was always just a question of knowing the "right people," but in the new China we ran into a blank wall. (Rickett and Rickett 1973, 23)

During the 1950s the Communists created a system that overturned centuries of privilege on the basis of birth or wealth; those whose privileges were removed found the new system unfair. *Everyone is equal* expresses the profound anti-privilege stance of the regime. (But, in Orwell's apt words, some were more equal than others.)

There were excesses, and these are legendary. But for the first decade, there were also welcome successes. William Hinton's *Fanshen* (1966) describes the processes of sorting through people's class standing and allocating basic resources to everybody. Honesty and sincerity—or at least the appearance of honesty and sincerity—lay at the core of this endeavor.

The myth making that was central to the revolution emphasized the uprightness of the People's Liberation Army soldiers, the trust of people whose lost goods were returned to them, and other examples of genuinely selfless actions on behalf of the social good. The exemplar of the revolution—upright, beloved, selfless, and a teacher of new methods and ideas to improve the peasants' lot—is seen in the main character in the film *Yellow Earth* (Chen 1984), a People's Liberation Army soldier whose job is to go to remote areas of northern China to collect folk songs to write new, revolutionary words to them. Expecting the worst, the local people are surprised to find that he is a wonderful, helpful person who pays his desperately poor hosts for their hospitality.

Communicative Rituals and Structures: Small Groups

One of the first and most enduring approaches to the principal goal of transforming the hearts, minds, and bodies of China's masses was the use of persuasion. Patiently making the case for its radical transformation, the Party brilliantly employed a variety of tactics, all unified under the rubric of *xuanchuan*, usually translated "propaganda." *Xuanchuan* implies spreading, sharing, overwhelming, propelling information and ideas. People were persuaded by slogans written and oral, by stories, by lectures, by meetings, by social pressure. Accounts of the 1950s and early 1960s give the impression of earnest, endless talking, so that the enlightened ones who possessed the truth could persuade those who had not yet encountered it. During the first years of "new China," communication was at the heart of political transformation; people were obliged to interact virtually day and night. (*Thicken interaction.*)

Even before the Communist victory, people had meetings to classify people, meetings to distribute basic necessities, meetings to organize a local Peasants' Association, meetings to "settle accounts," meetings to struggle against landlords through "speaking bitterness." Initially a group of people who had never assembled at all, the villagers that William Hinton came to know assembled frequently: "The classification . . . laid the basis for economic and social action that affected every family and every individual in the most fundamental way. . . . Because this was so the peasants took an extraordinary interest in the classification meetings and gathered without complaint, day after day, to listen, report, discuss, and judge" (Hinton 1966, 276–77).

Beginning in 1949 but peaking during the 1960s, most people in urban China were assigned to small study groups of eight to fifteen people, in which new directives were discussed and affirmed. Consensus was obligatory. Innocuous- and simple-sounding, small groups (*xiaozu*) were carefully constructed and nurtured as a way to ensure that the revolutionary message was promulgated throughout the entire populace. Every individual was required to participate. Communication went both vertically, in both directions (messages down from the leaders and up to them) and horizontally as members analyzed one another. Unlike ordinary, natural "primary groups" in traditional China, these were made up of people with no other necessary connection to one another (Whyte 1974, 22). These groups existed for study, *xuexi* (again, an ordinary term that picked up specialized meaning during the revolutionary period), for carrying out various campaigns of surveillance and indoctrination, and for criticism and self-criticism in the service of transformation of attitude and behavior (see also Liang and Shapiro 1983, 40–41). People had to be taught to overcome their aversion to speaking publicly, and especially to face the likelihood of losing face among a group that had no especial loyalty. (*Disregard face.*)

Criticism and Self-criticism

Small groups were used to disseminate policies and to collect "grassroots" viewpoints, but one of their most creative and memorable functions was to provide a framework for criticism (evaluation) of others (*piping* and *pipan*) and self-criticism (*zi-wo piping*), one of the cornerstones of ideological transformation. Criticism involved scrutinizing a person for political or personal shortcomings, and self-criticism involved examining one's conscience to recognize one's faulty thinking and making a public or written report about one's findings. This method had been developed by the Communists even before they came to power in 1949 to win the support of China's largely uninvolved peasants. It was used with varying amounts of zeal through the 1950s and into the 1960s, culminating in the Cultural Revolution. At that time group study and self-criticism became one of the people's primary daily activities. People often merely went through the motions. Nien Cheng describes a study group in 1973:

> Hardly anybody was listening. Many women had brought their knitting and mending, while the men were either smoking in a relaxed posture or dozing. The study group was a mere formality. People came to it because they had been told to by officials they could not disobey. It was not a serious effort to indoctrinate the people, and the result was nil. Nobody became more pro-Communist or anti-Communist as a result of attending study group meetings. (Cheng 1986, 401)

Despite the hypocrisy created by enforcing attendance at study groups, they endured even into the 1980s and 1990s though with increasingly transparent nonchalance and irrelevance. By the 1980s and 1990s people were openly contemptuous of *zhengzhi xuexi*, political study. In Kunming's Friday afternoon meetings, people told me, many took advantage of the time to knit or nap. Still, they attended.

But at its peak it was a fearsome tool of Party propaganda. Self-criticism (like in Alcoholics Anonymous) was done in ritual settings and on demand. Some became so adept at performing convincing, moving self-criticisms that they were essentially on call at all times to get things going. Chu cites an account written by An Ziwen (An Tze-wen) about various rectification campaigns:

> When a campaign comes, there are people who would prepare themselves in every conceivable way. They pretend to be progressive and sincere, as if they were really engaged in a relentless struggle against all wrongdoings. At a mass meeting for self-criticism, they would cry, moan, and confess all their mistakes. After the campaign is over, when the "storm has calmed down" they go back to their old selves. Their self-criticisms are tossed aside, and they do whatever they want to do. (Chu 1977, 77–78)

As an appendix to his book about "brainwashing," psychiatrist Robert Jay Lifton includes the autobiography of a philosophy professor who had spent many years in the United States (1989, 473–84).[1] People with connections or experience abroad—only the wealthiest and the elite—were frequent targets of political pressure as supporters of imperialism. Titled "Criticizing my Idealistic Bourgeois Pedagogical Ideology," the article begins with his description of "My Crust of Selfishness" and ends with "My Determination": "He who loves New China well must know that in New China the people are on their feet and have come into their own. . . . From now on . . . I shall strive to become a new man and a teacher of the people in substance as well as in name." Puyi, the last emperor of China, wrote such a confession as well. (He was persecuted throughout the 1950s and 1960, and eventually committed suicide.)

Liang Heng recalls what he saw in a temple gateway:

> The people were criticizing an old monk, and I was very curious because I had never seen a monk before. He had a little wrinkled face and his head was shaved bald. His clothes were faded black, with little black slippers of a style I didn't recognize. He was kneeling and beating a gong before a broken stone tablet on which I guessed was inscribed the history of the temple or some Bud-

dhist scripture—I couldn't read it as the words were all in the old-style script. As he beat the gong, he chanted, "I have tricked the people, I should be punished," and "Buddhism is a lie, only Marxism-Leninism-Chairman Mao Thought is the truth." I thought he looked old and tired, especially in contrast with the excited young people shouting at him, and I wondered what he would do now that his temple was a forbidden place. (Liang and Shapiro 1983, 91)

Intellectuals, religious figures, artists and writers, the wealthy, and many other classes of people were required to repudiate their earlier lives and to do so as publicly as possible. As Jonathan Spence points out, though, "It is impossible to tell if such confessions were sincere or not. The party rejected confessions it regarded as insincere or self-censored, but the use of irony was always hard to catch" (1990, 565). The performance was necessary, and paramount. (*Performance counts.*) Whether the confessions were genuine or fake, they were required.

Speak Bitterness

Another performative genre of the People's Republic was that of speaking bitterness, *suku*. The common phrase, *chiku*, to withstand adversity, is a great virtue in China. *Suku*, by contrast, involved publicly recalling past trauma, usually mistreatment at the hands of elites or suffering because of past conditions, in order to make the point that the present was much better. People who were especially adept at the retelling of the terrible pre-Liberation experiences were often brought out to get things going. Some could always be counted on to produce tears in their listeners, much as politicians in the contemporary United States love to bring individuals on stage who have been helped in some way by the politician, evoking sentimental tears.[2] The occasions on which *suku* occurred were predictable and the effect known in advance. (It was intended to bolster people's resolve against the injustices of the regime.) A premium was placed on sincerity, as evidenced by tears and shouting, but such performances could be repeated exactly and still be judged sincere.

This sincerity was a performance of physical expression of suffering, but it was not entirely new in revolutionary China. Anagnost connects the Cultural Revolution *suku* performances to May Fourth (1919) literary activity:

The spontaneous cry of the body became a privileged signifier of the "real" for May Fourth intellectuals, providing them with the means by which the "wheels of history" could be actively grasped through literary practice. But this literary appropriation of the body was only the first of a series in which the body and its pain are made to speak a kind of truth. In revolutionary practice, a poetics of the body and its insults moved from literary representation to the spoken words of uneducated peasants. (1997, 18–19)

Peasants' performances required bodily evidence (tears, frowns, sweating) of the genuineness and thus the truth of the message being proclaimed, or in Anagnost's terms, "the spontaneous truth of the body in its pain, speaking a 'language' of blood and tears" (23). As people recounted the evil of the past, the truth and sincerity of their statement was made concrete in their physical and verbal performance before an audience whose presence justified the retelling. *Suku* was not spontaneous but was mandated by certain situations.

The centrality of linguistic performance to the revolutionary project should be evident by now, but there is yet another verbal dimension of the revolution to be considered: storytelling in the service of "higher truths."

Mao's Revolution as Storytelling

More important even than Mao's extraordinary prowess as a military and political strategist was his mastery of revolutionary storytelling. The stories were orchestrated to yield the theoretical and political conclusions that Mao had in mind before anyone spoke, but the process of creating the stories itself helped create loyalty to the outcome. And the conclusion was considered an ultimate truth that required revolution.

> Like virtually all great political ideologists, Mao Zedong was a great storyteller, especially during his Yan'an days. There he and his associates combined storytelling and truth telling. They drew from individuals the materials out of which they formed a collective mythology. In turn, this mythology was made to yield higher truths. (Apter and Saich 1994, 71)

History was told as a story of struggle and victory. Even before they heard the words, listeners assented to the inevitable truths about the need for control, about Mao's leadership, about China's recovery from the insults and dissolution of the early part of the century. Once the story of the past was established, the path forward was also clear. Mao's leadership and revolution were seen as inevitable, a foregone conclusion.

Exemplary Model Behavior: Honesty and Candor

Transformation was the dominant goal of China's revolution: transformation of social structure, of production, of value, of psychology, of family, of education—virtually every aspect of both collective and individual life. Party members were to serve as models (the "vanguard") for everybody else. One of the targets of psychological and social transformation was the traditional focus on face-saving and politeness, to be replaced by sincerity, honesty, frankness, candor, and truth. Some of the persuading was accomplished by explicit exhortation, some by selection of models for emulation.

Liu Shaoqi exhorted Communists to be sincere. Liu was chairman of the People's Republic during the Great Leap Forward and widely regarded as Mao's right-hand man until he was engineered as a traitor during the Cultural Revolution and died in prison in 1969 (because Mao saw him as a threat to his own predominance). His book *How to be a Good Communist* [*Lun gongchandangyuan de xiuyang*: Self-cultivation of a communist] was published in 1951 in the Communist publication *Hongqi* (Red flag), based on lectures he had given in the revolutionary base in Yan'an in 1939. It was cited and studied for its insistence on the class nature of morality and on the gradual, unrelenting self-cultivation of all who would be Communists. (It was criticized vehemently during the Cultural Revolution as "revisionist" and "bourgeois" [Spence 1990, 613].) In a list of five characteristics of a Party member, the fourth revolves around matters of truth and sincerity:

> [H]e [*sic*] is the most sincere, most candid and happiest of men. Because he has no private axe to grind, nothing to conceal from the Party and nothing he cannot tell others, he has no problems of personal gain or loss and no personal anxieties other than for the interests of the Party and the revolution. Even when he is working on his own without supervision and is therefore in a position to do something bad, he is just as "watchful over himself when he is alone" and does not do anything harmful. His work bears examination and he is not afraid of having it checked. He does not fear criticism and at the same time he is able to criticize others with courage and sincerity. (Liu 1964 [1939], 49–50)

Criticizing others was not done easily and frankly but more often was done behind their backs. Later in the book Liu elaborates: "They cherish their own comrades and brothers, whose weaknesses and mistakes they criticize frankly and sincerely (and this shows genuine affection)" (67). The maxim *Be frank* is one that had to be justified within a tradition that valued relationships over abstract truth. Criticism and frankness may be said to stem from affection. The attack on *Give and save face* is supported with claims that frankness is a sign of affection. *Be frank* is a maxim that applied only in revolutionary times, not before or since, and even then it applied more in exhortation than in practice.

Liu also attacked Ah Q-ism, the chameleon-like tendency to please others by transforming unctuously according to their interlocutor, from Lu Xun's story "The Biography of Ah Q" (Lu 1960 [1921]). "There are people . . . who shift and hedge. . . . [They] are always opportunistic in their personal behaviour, curry favor with all sides and try to please everybody. They tailor their words to the person and the circumstances, tack with the wind and show no principle whatsoever. . . . They have the traits of the old-fashioned merchants" (Liu 1964 [1939], 69). Merchants were, of course, the most despised element of the old society because of their wily, clever use of others and their movement around all segments of society. And merchants, Liu claims, "tailor their words to the person and the circumstances." The revolutionary fervor for transformation indicates awareness and resolute rejection of this tendency.

The Party urged ordinary people to learn from the peasants and emulate their simplicity and honesty. *Laoshi*, the term discussed in chapter 2, involves being straightforward and simple. Blurting out the truth—especially when it corresponded to the truths the Party urged—was seen, suddenly, as desirable. The heroes set up for emulation were all presented as guileless, almost robots programmed to perform moral acts with no concern for self-protection or even anyone's face ("cogs in the machinery of socialism"). All the ordinary concerns about social grace, about politeness, about status and roles, about positions, about reputation—all this was to be overturned by the heroic acts of honesty and bluntness.

Three Hard Years

Some of China's early "reconstruction" in the 1950s was quite successful; people were largely fed and clothed, and the worst poverty was alleviated. The Three Hard Years (1958–61), the so-called Great Leap Forward (Dayuejin), interrupted this positive development, with perhaps thirty million people dying of starvation and disease because of policy errors compounded by drought and other natural disasters (Becker 1996). This information has never been made public; Jasper Becker describes it as "Mao's Secret Famine" in his book on the topic. The cover-up is a perfect example of the maxim *Guard information.* (See also Mueggler 2001 on the lasting effects of the Great Leap Forward.)

The greatest calamity of this period was that people who told the truth about bleak and disastrous conditions were punished, those who upheld the rosy, false claims about excellent progress were rewarded, and millions of people were sacrificed to Mao's theoretical principles.

Nearly everyone in the country—fisher folk, orchard keepers, pastoralists—was ordered to grow grain. Peasants' intimate knowledge of agricultural conditions was ignored. All products were taken by the state for redistribution by the newly organized communes. The unprecedented catastrophic results—famine in every region of China—could not even be mentioned.

One particularly zealous first secretary of Xinyang prefecture in Henan, the first commune in China, Lu Xianwen, oversaw a brutal, murderous war against peasants who dared say they had nothing to eat. Tens of thousands of people were tortured and murdered; a hundred thousand in the area died of starvation—yet the granaries were filled with enough grain to feed everyone. The leaders refused offers of help from the province, claiming they had a bumper harvest. "In the atmosphere of terror, no cadre at any level dared admit the truth: Liang Dezhen, the first secretary of Huang Chuan county, turned back relief grain because he suspected that it was a ruse to trap him into making a political mistake" (Becker 1996, 120).

When Mao toured the province, local officials dug up all the grain they could find to replant in the single, apparently successful field that Mao saw. Everything he saw was staged, and no one dared reveal true figures; exaggerations up to three and ten times the actual harvest were common (Becker 1996, 123).

Only Peng Dehuai dared tell the truth. Peng, the celebrated hero of the revolution and the Korean War, challenged Mao's authority at the Lushan Plenum in July 1959 when he contested the apparent successes of the Great Leap Forward (Lieberthal 1993). This was the fact, based in reality, which is what Mao had urged people to face—but for his truthfulness Peng was immediately sent down to "study" and kept under house arrest for sixteen years. As Red Guards tortured him, he is reported to have shouted "I fear nothing" (People's Daily Online 2005b). He was rehabilitated posthumously in 1978.

Hu Yaobang, later party secretary and party chairman, was sent to Hunan to observe conditions. "On the eve of his audience [with Mao], he paced up and down smoking, unable to sleep. Should he tell Mao the truth? Hu's courage failed him. As he later explained, 'I did not dare tell the Chairman the truth. If I had done so this would have spelt the end of me. I would have ended up like Peng Dehuai'" (Becker 1996, 237). Hu was forced to resign in 1987. His death in 1989 was the catalyst for student demonstrations, which began as mourning rituals in Tiananmen Square.

Eventually enough reports came back that Liu Shaoqi and others restored policies that restored a modicum of prosperity, a prosperity and calm that lasted a scant five years. The successes of the revolution were quickly followed by internal dissension and abuse of power. In part to address these internal problems—but giving rise to an unimagined new set of disastrous problems—the Cultural Revolution was launched.

The Cultural Revolution

Since 1949, when the People's Republic was established, and indeed even earlier, the Communists grappled with ways to be both more effective and more persuasive, often vacillating between persuasion and force.

One campaign led to another. The 1951 Three-Anti Campaign (*san-fan*) targeted three types of misconduct: corruption, waste, and obstructionist bureaucracy. As with so much of the political activity in contemporary China, a good part of the impetus was internal. In this case, the particular target of the campaign was Party members, other bureaucrats, and managers (Spence 1990, 536). This campaign later merged with the concurrent Five-Anti Campaign (*wu-fan*) (1952), which in turn grew into the Socialist Education Campaign (1963) and then the Four Cleanups (*Si Qing*) (1963–64). But the most often recalled campaign was the Cultural Revolution.

The Great Proletarian Cultural Revolution (*wuchan jieji wenhua da ge-ming*) was initiated by Mao Zedong in August 1966 with his cry to *zaofan youyi* (It is right to rebel), to "bombard the Party headquarters" and to create "uninterrupted revolution" (*buduande geming*).

The Cultural Revolution (1966–76) was presented as an opportunity for society to be turned upside down. It would be a thorough reorganization of the entire society through a focus on "culture"—meaning (as anthropologists do) every aspect of life. The Party would oversee these transformations through constant and intimate scrutiny of people's lives, especially in major cities. (The countryside was largely spared its major effects.) What had been on top (such as intellectuals and elders) would now be on the bottom; what had been good (such as education and tradition) would now be bad. People's Communes would take care of everybody; official entities would control all the arts and all entertainment in the service of revolution. The radical and speedy implementation of all these changes occurred with the help of mobilized young people known as "Red Guards." They were allowed to travel without payment on trains throughout the country, and they were drawn to Tiananmen Square, where they might glimpse a deified Mao in million-people rallies and "exchange experience" (*chuanlian*). Families were forced to "draw a line" between revolutionary and reactionary members. Children were urged to denounce their parents. The climactic moments were almost impossible to believe. As Liang Heng, then a child, puts it, when he saw his own father denounced on a poster, "I would never believe the ground was steady again" (Liang and Shapiro 1983, 53). Humiliation and fear were the primary effects of the struggles. Lies, hypocrisy, madness, suicide, and paranoia were everywhere.

Justified as an attempt to avoid calcification of position and rebureaucratization, the Cultural Revolution had multiple causes, effects, and side effects, including Mao's fear of loss of power (Leys 1977 [1974]) or retribution for people who disagreed with him about the Great Leap Forward (Becker 1996), which are difficult to sort out.[3] This period is now usually referred to as the "ten years of madness," *shi nian luan.*

Frankness and Cunning

During the Cultural Revolution, the most avid revolutionaries rejected the traditional notions of valuing cleverness (*jing*) and scorning foolishness (*sha*). Sharp-eyed historian Michael Schoenhals found a pamphlet, clearly written during the Cultural Revolution, at a shop in China in 1981, where it was about to be used to wrap candy. The author, Lü Yulan, was a member of the Central Committee of the Chinese Communist Party, and the title of the brochure was "Why Do Some People Call Me 'Foolish,' and How to Regard 'Clever' and 'Foolish.'" "Foolish" here, *sha*, contrasts with *jing*, "clever, sharp, skilled." It deliberately values a kind of stupidity that is naïve and far from self-serving—upside-down from ordinary values. "I don't know how to enrich myself at public expense, I don't know how to take advantage of a situation to benefit myself, and I'm not good at scheming or calculating. So, if that's what you call being stupid, well, then, I am indeed stupid" (in Schoenhals 1996, 192). "It's only when you're unselfish that you will be fair and truthful" (193). The entire piece is a diatribe against the personal in favor of serving the public, and focuses on cleverness and truthfulness.

Urban youth sent to rural areas under the "up to the mountains and down to the countryside" (*shang shan xia xiang*) policy were distrusted as deceptive: "[P]easants and village cadres have expressed apprehension at the prospect of 'sly' or 'cunning' city slickers in their midst" (Bernstein 1977, 133). Yet sometimes positive views could be formed. A "rightist" dispatched to the countryside found to her delight that some rural residents were frank, as when an older man, with his wife, took Yue Daiyun in as a daughter and spoke very openly with her. Among other things, he admitted that he married late because as a young man he had been not only poor but afraid of women. "I admired his honesty and directness" (Yue and Wakeman 1985, 72). She knew that city dwellers would never have been quite as frank.[4]

Efficacy

Like advertising in the West, Chinese experts in *xuanchuan* debated the effects of words on their hearers (Stranahan 1999). Focusing on the charge of words and on the kinds of statements that would mobilize peasants and others, many hours were spent discussing the ways to persuade.[5] Many Western analyses of lying excuse it in the case of war but deplore it in the case of mere profit as in advertising. It is tempting for Westerners to criticize propaganda in China for its Orwellian doublespeak but to overlook it closer to home. The U.S. propaganda surrounding such undemocratic actions as the Patriot Act or the Blue Skies initiative (permitting air pollution) and Healthy Forests Initiative (permitting logging) were equally cynical manipulations of language.

In any case, during this period in China language was explicitly regarded as efficacious (*Consider consequences.*) even though it was supposed to be spontaneous. This contradiction gave rise to one of the most striking aspects of language and indeed life during the Cultural Revolution: falseness and performance. Tracing truth and truth telling here become more difficult. Most observers conclude that "truth" was invoked falsely and that the impossibility of establishing real truth, in contrast to manufactured, ersatz truth, made so many people despair.

Falseness and Performance: *Biaoxian*

A key concern that emerges from recollections of the Cultural Revolution is of how false (*jia*) so much of public life had become. (Only in the most intimate settings, impossible for outsiders to observe directly, would honesty prevail.) False accusations of counterrevolutionary attitudes, circulated by whispers or in secret meetings, were sufficient to sentence someone. A scholar of Chinese literature, Yue Daiyun, recounts in her memoir *To the Storm* her accusation and inevitable conviction of being a "rightist," an enemy of the people, based on her earlier suggestions about starting a literary magazine. The event itself was not fabricated, but the conclusions drawn from the evidence and the facts were not inevitable. The Party said that top universities like Beijing University "should uncover even more rightists than the 5 percent expected of other work units" (Yue and Wakeman 1985, 32). Thus zealous rightists must be found; Yue's conviction was needed. Her story begins with her utter faith in the Party and ends with her 1979 "rehabilitation"—restoration of her rights and reputation—more than twenty years following her fall (in 1958).

Sent to the countryside for reform as a rightist, Yue Daiyun was advised to compromise by an old friend, also sent down as a rightist. He counseled her "to be careful, to adapt quickly to the new circumstances, and above all not to offend anyone" (62–63). She resisted his advice:

"Now we are enemies of the Party," he counseled me, "even though for years we have devoted ourselves to the revolution. At present we must admit we are guilty and acknowledge that we really are criminals, for only in this way can we resume our normal lives and at the same time help the Party by confirming the correctness of its policy. You must acknowledge that you have done something to oppose the Party and concede your guilt."

"But," I protested, astonished, "that would be a denial of the truth."

"There can be no absolute standard for truth and falsehood," he replied firmly, "for what is true depends always on necessity and circumstance. If you can prove you have a deep consciousness of your mistake, you can return to the side of the people, and that is what matters most. Above all, you must never offend the sent-down cadres, for they control your destiny. Even if they do something you know is wrong, you must pretend not to notice it."

Such an expedient, dishonest approach to life was totally repugnant to me, but I could see how this philosophy had served Lao Wei well. . . . Having learned how to function as a rightist, he sincerely wanted to help me adjust. (Yue and Wakeman 1985, 62–63)

Yue Daiyun rejects her friend's advice to *Consider consequences, Consider context, Performance counts*, clinging to her own notion of *Tell the truth*. Ultimately she was vindicated but in the medium-long term (twenty years) she suffered enormously for maintaining what she saw as absolute truth.

False and secret accusations were a common part of Cultural Revolution life, with dossiers that followed people from institution to institution yet were never visible to their subjects. In betrayals of intimates, people were never quite sure of others' relations, forcing them to build social relations on a foundation of quicksand. Parents could not trust their children's loyalty; even spouses turned one another in for counterrevolutionary activity. Accusing others helped exonerate the accuser (Yue and Wakeman 1985, 32).

Falseness existed not only in interpersonal relations but also in public activities. Statistics have been notoriously unreliable in China (and are far less exact than most people believe, in any case; see *How to Lie with Statistics* [Huff 1954] and Best 2001). This may be explained in part by the knowledge that statistics reported are all consequential. (*Consider consequences.*) In his evaluation of false reports, the ever-insightful Mao reveals his awareness of the pragmatics of reporting. In his first, oral announcement of the Great Leap Forward, Mao said the following (amidst a huge number of details and grand pronouncements), at the Zhengzhou conference, November 9, 1958. Note how sensible he sounds:

[We should] encourage seeking truth from facts: [people] should not give false reports, shouldn't give out someone else's report on pig [raising] as their own;

. . . and 300 catties of wheat should not be reported as 400. This year's [re-ported] 900 billion catties of grain are at most 740 billion catties; that should be taken as the [real] figure. It would be more appropriate to consider the re-maining 160 billion catties as being falsely reported. . . . The main emphasis has to be on solving problems of work style, [that is] party leadership, the mass line, seeking truth from facts. (MacFarquhar et al., 1989, 460–61)

In this passage Mao seems to be cautioning against taking reports at face value and deploring the tendency to falsify reports—mostly because they don't succeed in fooling the enemy. Yet Mao acknowledges that there are both bad and good kinds of falsification: The bad kinds include claiming that certain accomplishments have been made when they have not been; good kinds include hiding output so it can be retained (MacFarquhar et al. 1989, 507–10). During the Great Leap Forward, overreporting led to overly opti-mistic plans about using harvests and dropping subsidies.

As to the question of falsification. . . . There is a people's commune which it-self had only a hundred pigs. To cope with a visit [by leaders inspecting their productivity], they borrowed another two hundred fat pigs, and returned them after the inspection was over. If you have a hundred, you have a hundred; you don't have what you don't have—what is the purpose of making it up? . . . I think there still is some falsification around. There are some people in this world who are not all that honest. . . . There is nothing in the world without a bit of falsification; where there are true things, there will by necessity be fakes. Without having fakes for comparison, where would there be truth? This is just human nature. The serious question at present is not only that the lower levels fabricate, but that we believe them. . . . The masses, in fact, do achieve successes. Why write off the successes of the masses? But by trusting fabrica-tions, one will also commit mistakes. . . . [R]eported successes should be dis-counted, split 30/70—can three out of ten be taken as fake, and the seven as true? (MacFarquhar et al., 1989, 507–8, 509)

Human nature, for the realistic Mao, necessarily includes falseness, but offi-cials need to know just how much there is. Like most urban Chinese, Mao has a formula that strikes him as plausible: in every report, take three out of ten as fake. He seems to appreciate a certain amount of this game.

Then there is a kind of fabrication that also has its benefits. . . . Zhongnanhai has a cadre who went down to the countryside; he wrote a letter back saying that a [commune] had determined to pull up three hundred *mou* of maize and plant sweet potatoes; on each *mou* 1.5 million clusters of sweet potatoes would be planted. But the maize had already grown above a man's head, and the masses felt this was deplorable, and thus the maize was not pulled out. They pulled it out on only 30 *mou*, but reported 300 *mou*. This kind of fake reporting is good. . . . At present there is an atmosphere in which there is only talk about successes and not about shortcomings; when there are shortcomings, there is loss of face; and when you speak the truth, no one listens. If you say that a cow's tail grows on its rump, no one listens; if you say it grows on its head, that's news. Fabrications, much talk, that's glory. Education is needed. Speaking clearly and being honest and truthful—if we achieve this within a few years, it would be good. (MacFarquhar 1989, 510)

Mao clearly grasped the need for protection from unreasonable policies as well as the tendency to portray overly optimistic successes. His policies, however, encouraged just the intensification of falsification that he simultaneously deplored.

It is now well documented that the leaders' lives were the reverse image of the lives of ordinary people (Li 1994; Witke 1977). As Mao and his wife Jiang Qing watched foreign films, ate banquets, and generally lived as they pleased, the ordinary folk watched the same six ballets, ate coarse grains, and were constrained in every deed. That this was standard for emperors was beside the point; the Communist Party was supposed to be a party for the people. Mao's personal physician Li Zhisui depicts the utter decadence of Mao's life with horror and fascination, portraying himself as guileless and honest and thus shocked by breaches of integrity.

Li had worked as a physician in Australia but returned to China in 1949. Seeking a job, he was advised to use bribery:

The friend with whom we were staying in Hong Kong introduced us to a man named Yan, reputed to be a high-ranking member of the Communist party and charged with recruiting intellectuals to return. Our friend encouraged us to give Yan a gift to pave our smooth return. "With Yan's help, you might land a good-paying job in a medical college in Beijing. Maybe you could give him a Rolex watch. He pays the seafare for the people he sends to Beijing, so you would still save some money."

I doubted that Yan was paying the fares out of his own pocket and detested the bribery that had plagued Chinese officialdom for so many thousands of years. I believed that the Communist party was aloof from the corruption that had turned so many millions of people against the Guomindang. I refused to give Yan a gift. "The Communist party is honest," I told my friend. "I can depend on my own abilities to earn my living."

In 1956, when I told Mao the story of my friend's encouragement to offer Yan a bribe, Mao laughed uproariously. "You bookworm," he chided me. "Why are you so stingy? You don't understand human relations. Pure water can't support fish. What's so strange about giving someone a present?" (Li 1994, 41)

Mao spoke about honesty, urged everyone to rely on truth, yet was fully aware of his own clever manipulation of human relations.

In revolutionary China a notion of performance, *biaoxian*, became a key term in the revolutionary description of action. *Biaoxian* has to do with making visible, displaying, revealing, acting, as opposed to invisible thought and feeling. People with strong commitments are expected to reveal them in their acts. Thus acts can be taken as indices of revolutionary zeal. Party membership and promotions were made in part because of people's attitudes as active advocates of revolution. *Biaoxian* figured into regular assessments of merit. "Usually the raise was based on a mix of four standards: work and skill level, years of experience, relations with others, and the impression of each individual in the eyes of the leadership. This includes political *biaoxian*, which at the time [the early 1960s] meant not telling the truth about the Great Leap Forward, saying it was a success" (Walder 1986, 137). People were quite conscious of the possibility of manipulating *biaoxian* to make a favorable impression.

It is easy to advocate truth. The question is, what is considered true, and what is done with alternatives to truth? Who is in a position to determine what is true? During the entire period of revolutionary China, truth and its criteria have been explicitly and publicly debated. Acknowledging that those who are permitted to claim knowledge of truth are in command, in power, China's leaders have declared themselves the irrefutable holders of singular truth. Who could argue against truth? Against facts? Against reality?

From the 1930s to the 1950s Mao claimed that one must "seek truth from practice" and that "Genuine knowledge comes from practice" (*shijian chu zhen zhi*). In 1978, following Mao's death in 1976, an alternative view, "seeking truth from facts" (*shishi qiu shi*) was proposed. At stake was command of the account of reality and acknowledgment of the pragmatic consequences of the debate. The future of China's economic and political policies was being determined, and much of it revolved around the debate over "truth criteria."

Truth Criteria Debates

Mao's original formulation in 1937, spelled out in the polished version of his famous essay "On Practice," firmly attacks idealist conceptions of reality in favor of materialist conceptions:

> Marxists hold that man's [sic] social practice alone is the criterion of the truth of his knowledge of the external world. What actually happens is that man's knowledge is verified only when he achieves the anticipated results in the process of social practice (material production, class struggle or scientific experiment). . . . The truth of any knowledge or theory is determined not by subjective feelings, but by objective results in social practice. Only social practice can be the criterion of truth . . . social practice alone can give rise to human knowledge and it alone can start man on the acquisition of perceptual experience from the objective world. . . . The history of human knowledge tells us that the truth of many theories is incomplete and that this incompleteness is remedied through the test of practice. Many theories are erroneous and it is through the test of practice that their errors are connected. That is why practice is the criterion of truth. . . . Discover the truth through practice, and again through practice verify and develop the truth. (Mao 1967a [1937], 55, 56, 60, 63–64, 67)

This anti-theoretical view of truth permits consideration of actual societal norms and leaves open the possibility that truth is what society says it is. His anti-intellectual standpoint is also evident in the next passage.

> To take such an attitude is to seek truth from facts. "Facts" are all the things that exist objectively, "truth" means their internal relations, that is, the laws governing them, and "to seek" means to study. We should proceed from the actual conditions inside and outside the country, the province, county or district, and derive from them, as our guide to action, laws which are inherent in them and not imaginary, that is, we should find the internal relations of the events occurring around us. And in order to do that we must rely not on subjective imagination, not on momentary enthusiasm, not on lifeless books, but on facts that exist objectively; we must appropriate the material in detail and, guided by the general principles of Marxism-Leninism, draw correct conclusions from it. (Mao 1967b [1941], 167–68)

> Knowledge is a matter of science, and no dishonesty or conceit whatsoever is permissible. What is required is definitely the reverse—honesty and modesty. (Mao 1967a [1937], 59)

While in his early speeches Mao appeared to have believed in a universal, objective truth that could be known independent of the knower, over time, he moved away from this notion. In terms strikingly similar to other social truth theorists including Foucault, Harraway, and others, by the late 1950s and 1960s Mao began to speak of "class truth," knowable only by those with proper class positions (i.e., the proletariat). What this "truth" referred to was not always clear; it was not scientific knowledge but rather grasp of revolutionary consciousness.

> The Maoist insistence in the late fifties and sixties that truth can emerge only through struggle, and the tendency to define the proletariat increasingly in political terms lead me to argue that Mao's use of terms such as class knowledge or class truth was misleading. During this time his concern was not with truth or falsehood in the ordinary sense, i.e., as errors of cognition, but rather, true or false consciousness, where the latter confirms the state of human servitude to impersonal objective-historical processes and the former leads to an awareness of the possibility of emancipation, de-alienation, recovery of species essence, and so forth. (Misra 1998, 33)

Here *truth* has several meanings, only some of which correspond to the simple one of matching conditions in the world. As presented, a hearer of Mao's claim could only assent. How could anyone argue against the notion of class? Of truth? Of the centrality of class struggle? In Mao's China, no one could. *Truth* is an epithet hurled against enemies.

Zhou Enlai upheld this view in a letter he wrote in 1966 about this topic, "Mao Zedong Thought is the Sole Criterion of Truth." The guiding principle is that of "'adhering to the truth while rectifying one's mistakes.' In the course of this Great Proletarian Cultural Revolution of ours there can be only one criterion of truth, and that is to measure everything against Mao Zedong Thought" (quoted in Schoenhals 1996, 27). Clearly Mao Zedong Thought exploded at the center of inquiry and eradicated all other possible versions of truth. Thus "truth" came from power.

Yet in another account of the Cultural Revolution, an intellectual reports that when he was sent to the countryside for re-education, he was discouraged from reading Mao's essay "On Practice." He became involved in an argument about the difference between absolute and relative truth, as a way of applying the formula "one divides into two" to Mao Zedong Thought. Zhao Yiming asserted that this difference was discussed in Mao's essay itself. He earned quite a bit of trouble for this insistent reading and failed to join the Party because of the incident, but in the end he was vindicated and participated in the 1978 conference about truth criteria (Schoenhals 1996, 333–36).

Two positions emerged after Mao's death in 1976: that of "radicals" who maintained the centrality of class struggle and ideology and that of "pragmatists" who sought more technological and economic solutions to China's problems. Ultimately, since the late 1970s the pragmatists have largely prevailed.

At stake was the guidance of the country itself. Was it to be shepherded into the future by Maoism, on the grounds that Mao's brand of Marxism-Leninism had been proven? Subtle epistemological arguments about the nature of verification and theory building filled newspapers and technical political and philosophical journals. Policies about economic directions, population control, and so forth were evaluated according to their truth value.

On May 11, 1978, in *Guangming Ribao*, an official newspaper of the Party, an editorial appeared claiming to elaborate on the statements issued by Mao in the 1950s about "seeking truth from practice"; not only that, but people should "seek truth from facts." That is to say, it was not adequate to follow established practice or habit; just because people said things were to be a certain way did not mean that they really were this way. Thus an attack on the status quo was in the making; mass psychology or socialist ideology was no longer sufficient to make claims for how things worked. Now, a more "objective" criterion was to be introduced.

Akin to the old discrepancy between "red" (ideologically ardent) and "expert" (technologically or practically efficient) approaches to practices in the world, this new pragmatic approach made "reality" the primary criterion of assessing value. Though the editorial was written by Party theorists (Sun Changjiang and Hu Fuming), there was great consternation after it was published, but this was settled in a matter of a month following Deng Xiaoping's championing of the position.

Deng Xiaoping's claim that "I don't care whether the cat is black or white, as long as it catches mice" was considered counterrevolutionary during the height of the Cultural Revolution, when the only basis for acceptable behavior was ideological, and Deng suffered greatly as a rightist. This debate over truth inaugurated the economic reforms that currently lead (if in a desultory fashion) the country as it has opened the gates for its protectionless, Wild West capitalist experiments.

As rhetoric, even more than as argument, the position was unassailable. During the Maoist period, the guiding principle was "Genuine knowledge comes from practice" (*Shijian chu zhenzhi. Shijian*, "practice," gives rise to *zhenzhi*, "genuine knowledge.") In contrast, in 1978 the principle was "Practice is the sole criterion for testing truth." (*Shijian shi jianyan zhenli de weiyi biaozhun.*) The change was from the dominance of theory (*lilun*) over expertise to focus on practice (*shijian*). Though truth, *zhenli*, contrasts in the United States with falseness and deception, in China the contrast called up here is with irreality, impracticality. Who would defend lack of actual knowledge in favor of abstract theory? In fact, in the editorial where the question was first raised (*Guangming Ribao* 1978), the contrast translated as "error" or "falseness" was between the terms *zhenli* (truth) and *miuwu*, translated as "error" or "falseness." *Miuwu* could easily be involuntary or inadvertent, as in a mistake, so that the pair is more like the right answer and the wrong answer. Truth in these contexts is a quite different kettle of fish from the one that involves sincere confession or accurate knowledge of the world.

And Now for Something Completely Different?

Since the Cultural Revolution was finally laid to rest and the Gang of Four convicted in 1980 of all its excesses and crimes, China has been on a path of great transformation once more. The memories of the revolutionary period are both painful and inspiring; people invoke them in some contexts while criticizing them in others. Just after the trial, novelist Shen Rong wrote a short story called *Zhenzhen Jiajia* (True or false; it is translated into English as "Snakes and Ladders"). It follows a group of intellectuals for three days while they prepare for and hold a "meeting" to discuss an article criticizing the literary analysis of one of their colleagues. Xu had written in complimentary terms about literary modernism and was criticized for "groveling at the feet of the Western bourgeoisie." The entire office was required to contribute to the discussion.

Everyone is conscious that it is no longer "that time," the Cultural Revolution. People no longer have to spend hours preparing for meetings (essentially, scripting each person's contributions); they can allow some spontaneous talk. Yet they are reluctant to leave things to chance:

> "Carrying out ideological work is a painstaking and meticulous job," Ji Zikuan chimed as he pulled up a wooden chair. "You may have told them about tomorrow's session all right, but you've failed to tell them what we're expecting of them. Nor have you got any of them to prepare speeches and statements relating to the discussion. Frankly, I don't see how it can be a success."
>
> "This is the way things are done nowadays. No one lines up prearranged speeches anymore. . . . This way no one feels under pressure and people end up saying what they really think. It makes for a far more lively and natural atmosphere. Of course, on the debit side people sometimes go off on a tangent and the main issues may be forgotten."

"My point exactly. What you end up with is an informal get-together at which people gab away heedless of the topic in question. How can such waffle produce concrete results? . . . A meeting requires adequate preparation. As Chairman Mao said, don't hold a meeting unless you're fully prepared. How can you organize this meeting without arranging a few speeches; you need a few catalysts to get things moving." (Shen 1983, 129–30)

Everyone struggles to decide what to say at the three days of meetings. False criticism is taken as praise; irrelevant self-denunciation satisfies the political supervisor, because it fills time. At the climax of the story, a man named Wu, a former "rightist" who had been "rehabilitated" after the condemnation of the Gang of Four, decides that despite all the suffering he and his family had endured, he nonetheless had to tell the truth.

Everyone had suffered enough from lies. Fabricated reports, insincerely motivated political activism, fake exposes, false denunciations and untrue confessions . . . how many people had fallen into such traps? How many homes had been wrecked? Even now, when the Party strongly advocated the telling of the truth and opposed falsification and hypocrisy, it was still so terribly difficult to tell the truth! They continued to live in a thicket of lies. (221)

Wu spoke honestly about the pain of the meeting, the insincerity of the confessions and criticism, and the need to speak frankly.

The writer whose work lay at the center of the criticism session was upset at Wu's honesty: "There's a time and a place for the truth," Xu said. "Whether that is in front of so many people in a meeting, or after the meeting in one-on-one sessions, now or later—all this must be decided on the basis of possible consequences" (231). The Party office representative ended the meeting, praising the various participants and relieved that the session could be ended.

A Social Theory of Truth

Communicative practices in revolutionary China involved a good deal of social pressure to say certain things in certain ways and to speak often, especially about one's revolutionary fervor and optimism regarding production. The very structures of communication both reflected and created desired changes in consciousness as China embarked on its ambitious program to transform its people virtually overnight.

It is tempting to conclude that all manipulations of truth in revolutionary China were cynical, from advocating the honesty of peasants while practicing deception, to claiming that truth is relative to class standing. At the least it was performative, bringing about desirable results. Ultimately the ground for truth was fought over whether truth depended on one's social position, whether truth was knowable, how one could know, and how education (whether ordinary or political) about truth was to occur.[6] "Truth" served not only as the center of epistemological debate, however, but also as a rhetorical emblem—everyone would be in favor of something called "truth"—with disagreement over the nature of theory and experience. All along, everyone understood exactly what the political consequences would be all around, whichever way the debates were decided. "Theory" meant orthodox Maoism and Party leadership. "Experience" or "practice" meant relaxation of the Party's grip on defining reality.

A social theory of truth (Shapin 1994) consciously manipulates the outcome in favor of a particular result. Yet a consciously social theory acknowledges the power of words in addition to the power of knowledge, and is less committed to a wishful model of disembodied and neutral, objective, and floating theory of truth. Still, it conflicts sharply with more ordinary notions of truth.

Revolutionary views of language in China have some continuity with earlier Chinese views, yet certain aspects of language were strikingly novel. Though language was viewed as having pragmatic consequences in the past, during revolutionary China and especially during the Cultural Revolution the social effects of language were consciously emphasized, as an entire propaganda department took over the government. All words and communication were politically charged, and people had to become completely conscious of the effects of their utterances, knowing they would be scrutinized. At the same time, a premium was placed on the spontaneous eruption of profound feelings of revolutionary ardor. This forced many people to pursue a path of performance, of masking feelings they could scarcely acknowledge to themselves.

A society that already had social expectations, roles, face, and other aspects of social life as part and parcel of all communicative norms simply went as far as it could pursuing the logic of that view: individual feeling was not only submerged but eradicated, replaced by proper sentiment. Like industrialized society in which marketing shapes people's very notions of what tastes and smells good, what is desirable in a mate, how to shape their bodies, China was profoundly successful for a short time in its persuasive efforts. There was contradiction, however, in the demands placed on individuals for spontaneity as well as for following the script. Such schizophrenogenic conditions, to use Gregory Bateson's formulation, or a double bind, ultimately destroyed some people, while forcing others into ever greater distrust of society and of others' words.

Since the end of the Cultural Revolution, however, and as China's intense efforts to mold people's consciousness have tapered off, one might ask how much the effects of those efforts have remained? How much residual masking, replacing, performing have endured?

Clearly the Cultural Revolution anti-tradition maxims—*Be frank. Disregard face. Everyone is equal.*—have been discarded. The societal scrutiny of people's every action is long past (see, e.g., Lynch 1999). While appeal is still made in the name of socialism and the CCP (Kluver 1996), it is not necessary for praise to be literally true. Kluver writes of the importance of the audience in Chinese politics: "Chinese Communist leaders do believe that language changes social conditions, and if saying something achieves an impact, then it is correct" (Kluver 1996, 131). According to Alan Liu, "The underlying assumption of the Communist Party is that the social effect of news or information is much more important than the truthfulness" (quoted in Kluver 1996, 131). These approaches have been part of Chinese practice for millennia, and still are, but the stranglehold of the Party and the asphyxiating sense of hypocrisy in every direction have gradually died away. But, as we saw in part II, honesty is still not seen as the inevitable best policy. The thicket of truth and deception endures without a clear map.

Notes

1. The confession had been published in the propaganda newspaper *Guangming Ribao* [April 17, 1952]; cited in Lifton 1989, 473–84.

2. The Latin American genre known as *testimonio* is similar but seems to be less administered and more spontaneous.

3. One of the most thorough examinations of the Cultural Revolution is Roderick MacFarquhar's three-volume *The Origins of the Cultural Revolution* (1974, 1983, 1997). Countless accounts were written, most in the 1980s, showing the horrors of the Cultural Revolution on the lives of intellectuals, the people most vulnerable to attack in the new order. A large number of them have been translated into or even written in English. Notable examples of this "scar literature" (*shanghen wenxue*) in English include *Son of the Revolution* (Liang and Shapiro 1983), *To the Storm* (Yue and Wakeman 1985), *Life and Death in Shanghai* (Cheng 1986), *Born Red* (Gao 1987), and *Wild Swans* (Chang 1991). These memoirs are largely unsympathetic to the aims of the Cultural Revolution. Feng Jicai's *Ten Years of Madness* (1996) is quite illuminating, as well.

4. In order to eradicate the "three great differences" (*san da chabie*)—between manual and mental laborers, between the city and the country, and between workers

and peasants—an extremely unpopular policy of sending urban youth to "learn from peasants" began in earnest in 1968 (Bernstein 1977, 2). (It also addressed the shortage of urban jobs and to a much lesser extent provided labor and education for rural development.) They went "up to the mountains and down to the countryside" (*shang shan xia xiang*)—both undesirable places. The city youth were generally useless to peasants; weak and ignorant of agriculture, they were a burden to the farmers who nonetheless had to feed them. (They were subsidized by the central government, and paid a salary.)

Given CCP control over residence, issued in the form of *hukou*, household registration, city youth either had to remain in the countryside and hope to be permitted to return soon, or to sneak back illegally to the cities and subsist on shared rations with family members who did have a right to urban residence. Control over population movement was possible because social benefits depended on registration. All commodities and resources were redistributed by the state, which took it upon itself to know what people needed. Few items were exchanged solely on the basis of money; usually both permission (in the form of ration coupons) and money were required. Rationing as the primary form of redistribution was discontinued only in 1984–85. In 1982 I needed such coupons to buy cotton cloth or to eat in a restaurant. In 1991 they were still used to buy staples, such as oil or noodles, at state-run stores.

All told, perhaps 10 percent of China's urban population—about 125 million people—participated in this transfer at some point (Bernstein 1977, 2). Cadres (officials) and others were also sent to the countryside as punishment, sometimes instructed to be "retrained" by peasants. Some of this was effective; some intellectuals gained appreciation for peasants, though others merely had their stereotypes reinforced.

5. It is legitimate to wonder how different this is from recent U.S. names for war—Operation Enduring Freedom; Homeland Security, both from 2001, Operation Desert Storm of 1991, Shock and Awe of 2003, Operation Iraqi Freedom—or the misnaming of sizes of drinks at Starbucks, where medium is called "grande" and small is called "tall" (see, e.g., Lutz 1989 on doublespeak).

6. Such debates should be familiar to anyone who follows philosophy of science or postmodernism, where exactly the same questions of interest and disinterest are raised. Nothing of this level of intellectual sophistication ever reaches the mainstream American media, to be sure. (Imagine a headline in *USA Today*: "Postmodern Epistemology Challenged by Theological Pragmatists.")

PART IV

HUMANITY AND LANGUAGE

CHAPTER EIGHT

Truth and Deception across Time and Space

A culture's assumptions about how language works are likely to reflect local folk theories of human agency and personhood.

—John W. Du Bois 1992

In part III I assessed two potential ways of explaining a prevalence of deception in China, both historical. One explanation is that such practices are enduring aspects of Chinese culture. The second is that such practices arose with communism and peaked with the Cultural Revolution. Both these explanations have some merit but are not entirely adequate. This chapter considers a third possible explanation: that they are universal practices, and that deception is scarcely unique to China. This is, of course, a statement I wholeheartedly agree with. Yet I believe there are also facets that are specific to China. Some of what is unique are (1) the domains in which deception is practiced and (2) the ways specific instances of deception are regarded in the context of other behavior.

A number of studies of lying have been published in the past two decades. Most pick and choose among examples from as many places as possible, usually their own society, sometimes dipping into examples from elsewhere and from earlier times. Some of these fine studies, such as Evelin Sullivan's *The Concise Book of Lying* (2001), Philip Kerr's *The Penguin Book of Lies* (1990), Jeremy Campbell's *The Liar's Tale* (2001), Michael Farquhar's *A Treasury of Deception* (2005), and J. A. Barnes's *A Pack of Lies* (1994), have been inspiring and helpful compilations. These context-free compilations aim to synthesize their findings into a single theory. However, it is the contention of this book that attitudes toward deception and truth are not everywhere and always identical, and that they may be understood best by looking at other aspects of the culture within which they are found, including aspects of language and selfhood, to see if there are consistent principles. (I believe there are, though they are not so simple that we could create a mathematical formula.)

This chapter examines some of the ways truth and deception are regarded in white middle-class Anglo-American society, with a few cross-cultural mentions. I then summarize some of the ideas about truth and deception in two other societies, Japan and Judaism. Specialists will perhaps find my summaries unsatisfying. I include them to provide a sense of the range of human thought on similar topics. They also provide illuminating contrasts with Chinese practices and beliefs. Readers can no doubt supply their own knowledge of a variety of other cultural practices.

Despite all the theological and philosophical injunctions against lying (e.g., Bok 1979), lying is widespread in all societies and at all times (Bailey 1991; Barnes 1994; Bowyer 1982; Nyberg 1994; Sacks 1975). Morality is always associated with these issues—but morality is contradictory and incomplete. The human struggle for a reasonable accommodation to the needs and demands of self and society leads to tensions and inconsistencies, yet is definitive of our being as both individual and social. As individuals we attempt to get our own way; as social beings we wish to be trusted and admired. Selfish individuals might deceive frequently, but they would be scorned and snubbed—ultimately making it impossible to fulfill their social desires. So we walk a fine line between doing everything we can, including lying, to get our own way, and being honest because in the long run it is most effective. Most social systems weigh in heavily on the side of morality and honesty, but all have to consider a place for breaches as well.

White Middle-class Anglo-American Society

It is difficult and dangerous to generalize about any society, and it is easy to attack general accounts. Here I offer one version of the ideologies of deception and truth. Actual behavior often contradicts the explicit precepts. This slippage between overt extolling of truthfulness and actual, frequent lying leads me to charge Americans with self-deception.

Truth-telling: *Honesty is the best policy.*
Folktales are filled with stories of truthfulness rewarded. For example, "The Fisherman and the Golden Hatchet" illustrates this value. A fisherman loses

his hatchet; a fish brings him a series of increasingly valuable hatchets from the riverbed, urging the fisherman to take them. The fisherman—poor and honest—refuses them all because they are not his. In the end, he is richly rewarded for his honesty when the enchanted fish gives him a golden hatchet to sell for a large sum of money.

One of the most clichéd American stories is that of George Washington and the cherry tree. Revisionist historians might query the veracity of the story—invented by Parson (Mason Locke) Weems (1918 [1800], 1814 [1806])—but anthropologically speaking what matters is its use by people in society. This story is told—often to children—to convey the importance of telling the truth, the consequences involved in covering up truth, and the rewards for telling the truth.

Similarly, in U.S. law (and in Chinese law, for that matter), confession is rewarded by leniency or bargaining for a lighter sentence. Perjury (lying under oath) is considered the ultimate danger to law, since it calls into question the entire edifice of our truth-based and trust-based system. Swearing on the Bible invokes the power of an all-knowing authority to assess the veracity being sworn to. In cases where fear of such power is suspected of being inadequate, external judgments such as lie detectors may be brought in.

In socializing children in the United States, the bromide "Honesty is the best policy" is often used. Children are incapable of lying effectively before the age of approximately five, but after that there are many occasions on which a good lie will get them out of trouble. In order to reward them for resisting this temptation, many middle-class white American parents refrain from punishing children who admit their own misdeeds. Young children are often amusingly transparent in their lies.

At the same time, children are admonished: "If you can't say anything nice, don't say anything at all." Clearly telling the whole truth is recognized as quite dangerous and often undesirable.

Many scruples are associated with telling lies. People who nevertheless wish to permit an untruth to stand will go to great lengths to avoid uttering a bald-faced lie. A colleague of mine posed the question: "What do you do when someone asks you 'How do you like my new haircut?'" If you don't like it, and the asker is not a most intimate person (such as a family member) to whom truth is owed, you might just say, "Oh, it's *interesting* . . ." Your feelings are conveyed, you have followed the expectation that you will not unnecessarily insult someone else, yet your words are literally true.

There are of course a number of segments in American society (as in any society) and I have generalized here only about white middle-class America. In working-class and many non-white communities, norms of truth telling are quite different. Some forms of verbal play appear to stretch or disregard truth. Folklorists have termed one common verbal practice "ritual insults"— carried out especially among young African American males (see Abrahams 1983 on both African Americans and the West Indies, and Heath 1983, 174–84, where it is called *talking junk*). Fanciful and wildly exaggerated insults, often rhyming and always rhythmic, are hurled at the target, who is thereby tested to see how quickly and cleverly he can return an insult. Dueling, playing the dozens, is an especially long-lived verbal form of escalating insults ("slander" of female relatives, especially mothers) that have nothing to do with expressing information about reality. In fact, Smitherman points out that " [a] fundamental rule is that the 'slander' must not be literally true because truth takes the group out of the realm of play into reality" (1994, 99–100). Winners are often social winners too (Smitherman 1977). Yet even in the African American community there are differences with regard to language. Anne Bower (1998) shows that among elderly poor women, sincerity is greatly valued, in sharp contrast to the unanchored play of young men.

Information: *Free circulation of information is desirable.*

White middle-class Americans almost always state, upon first reflection, that the purpose of language is to communicate information. I begin every course I teach about language with an open-ended inquiry about what language is, and every semester students offer some variation on the following: "Language is a tool for communication of information and emotion." It seems to be a generally unremarkable good to offer and receive information of all kinds. Whether it is about the time or directions or where we found our blue jeans, Americans are happy to answer questions and to ask people for bits of information about the world. We meet strangers on planes and tell them our life story. People clamor to be on talk shows and reveal a version of their past experiences to total strangers and to the unseen viewers. In interviews and on surveys people are generally eager to give their views about any number of things or to give information about their past activities. We usually assume that these are to some extent truthful and are offended when they are found to be embellished or distorted.

White Lies; "Sugar": *Some people—other people—use language for purely social, but deceptive, purposes.*

Almost everybody will permit themselves to utter an occasional white lie, such as telling a touchy child that her clothes look good or praising food that is less than delicious. A regional stereotype in the United States has it that southerners are skillful at manipulating language in order to flatter and praise and generally smooth social interactions, and that northerners (or eastern-ers) are blunt and honest, and hence show disregard for others' feelings. White lies are often seen as lying in the realm of social graces and sometimes as an aspect of politeness.

I met a friend's parents for the first time. Her mother looked my children in the eye and asked questions about their day, their schools, activities, food preferences, and so forth. When I mentioned her mother's ease with children the next day to my friend, she said, "She was lying! She puts on a good show. She's not really interested in kids at all. But this is the southern way; it was designed for southern men, but it works for everybody. She takes her con-versational partner as the center of the universe and directs all her attention at them, asking questions and drawing them out on their interests. She didn't mean any of it!"

A film called *American Tongues* shows the diversity in American spoken language, with a special focus on southern language and stereotypes about speech (Kolker and Alvarez 1986). One scene presents some older southern "ladies" sitting around talking about the difference between northerners and southerners. They say that northerners cut off their speech, saying things like "Yes" with falling intonation, abruptly, while southerners add some softness, so that they produce things like "How are you, darlin'?" and "That would be fine, sugar" with rising intonation, indicating incompletion and invitation. While not directly deceptive, these social niceties can be regarded as fake or false by those who are not part of the system. According to the American language ideology that holds language to be designed for efficiency, extrane-ous words there simply for politeness are a kind of mask.

Lies That Serve a Higher Purpose: *Avoid lying at any cost.*
The kinds of lies that Augustine and Thomas Aquinas worried most about are the ones that lead to the slippery slope that will invite speakers to play dangerously with niceties of truth telling. Examples include flattery, evasion of responsibility when no possibility of being found out exists, telling a lie to unjust authorities (justice being viewed as "higher" than truth), and protect-ing the powerless. Sometimes included here are instances where a person knowing the truth will suffer needlessly (as in covering up prognoses in in-stances of terminal illness); "What good would it serve to tell her?"

Assurances to the dying that everything will be fine were quite common in the United States until the last several decades. Medicine now institu-tionalizes "patients' rights to know" that includes all aspects of their condi-tion. In practice, doctors and nurses often confer with the patients' families to modify what information is told the patient. Since medical research has begun to show the positive effects of "hope," it is clear that simply blurting out all the facts, including prognosis, may have deleterious effects in some cases. In chapter 3, we saw some of what my consultants in China had to say about cases such as this.

Lies that have benevolent intentions are called *officious* lies by Augustine and are included in the category of *paternalistic lies* by Bok. Whether these are permitted or not depends on which is more important, truth or kindness. Which can be more easily sacrificed, truth or justice? Which matters more in healing, truth or peace of mind?

Elevation of truth above all other goods is a hallmark of Judeo-Christian morality, and most particularly of the puritanical Christian morality that dominates in the United States. In arguing that all virtues are secondary to that of truth, Aquinas concludes that "every lie is a mortal sin." He cites as evidence the Ten Commandments, which include "Thou shalt not bear false witness." Sissela Bok argues that even if good were to come from such lies, a society must be based on trust. "Trust and integrity are precious resources, easily squandered, hard to regain. They can thrive only on a foundation of respect for veracity" (1979, 249). This is a practical justification for a deeply held moral belief.

War, Sport, and Strategy: *Deception is acceptable in war and play.*
It is well known that clever use of strategic deception is expected and indeed desired in war. The Trojan Horse that permitted the Greeks to enter Troy without a battle is a classic example. Contemporary governments, like those of the past, have large bureaus devoted to "intelligence" and "counterintelligence"; anticipating deception and misinformation, each tries to outthink (outfox) the other. During a war, the place of deceptive strategies is elevated. Bowyer (1982) discusses at great length some of the deceptions carried out by the United States during World War II; the military has published numerous examinations of these past strategies in the hopes of perfecting them. George W. Bush's government has paid Iraqi (and U.S.) journalists to deliver positive news about the Iraq war.

Yet for hundreds of years, throughout the medieval period in England and Germany, only blunt, brute strength was considered fair and useful. (This is Bowyer's account; it may be overly simplistic.) Warriors sat on their increasingly heavy armored horses and pointed their implements at one another in a "gentlemanly" contest of force and stamina. Any strategy was seen as cheating and unsportsmanlike.

> One universal [of the otherwise disparate Holy Roman Empire] was a disdain for the practice of guile in combat. . . . The etiquette of chivalry did not allow

for cheating on the field of combat, on the field of honor. There is scant evidence of deception for eight hundred years. The European strove for victory by hard fighting. . . . The joust for pleasure was simply war written small—two ponderously armored knights thundering toward each other. No maneuvering, no deception, no retreat—they simply ride into each other. (Bowyer 1982, 27)

Bowyer shows how peculiar this attitude is in the context of warfare worldwide. Naturally, the simple-minded Europeans were defeated by the clever Muslims in the Middle East and by the devious Mongols from Central Asia, under the direction of Genghis Khan. Sounding exactly like Sunzi in China, Ibn Khaldūn extolled the virtues of deception in war: "Trickery is one of the most useful things employed in warfare. It is the thing most likely to bring victory" (Ibn Khaldūn 1976 [1377], 253). Machiavelli, Sunzi, and Laozi all suggested the superior value of cleverness. Why risk the lives of good soldiers if one could save them by a clever ruse?

Sports and physical play also employ deception (Mawby and Mitchell 1986). Even the play of humans and dogs involves setting up expectations and then violating them (Mitchell and Thompson 1986a). The message that a particular act is playful was a puzzle to Gregory Bateson: How can dogs and other animals know to sink their teeth only superficially rather than going all out? How can athletes use their opponents' expectations to compel them to act in a disadvantageous way, knowing that the opponent knows that the other will try to seek every advantage? Convincing, sincere movements in a particular direction might be sufficiently misleading. Using theory of mind in social interaction is often seen as too suspicious in a general American ideology of action, but in these domains it is welcome.

Lies That Fool No One: *We know advertising is one big scam.*
In the United States, consumers are understood intellectually by some to have an adversarial relationship with advertisers, as journalists have with politicians, though the public largely responds as predicted to advertising, journalism, and politicians. (This is one ideal; journalists who take political press releases too loosely are criticized—or at least were criticized in past decades.)

In January 2003, a judge dismissed a lawsuit directed against McDonald's that claimed the plaintiffs had become obese because of McDonald's advertising. He gave advice for how to proceed: if McDonald's had used deceptive practices and claimed that Chicken McNuggets (he called it a "McFrankenstein" creation) were pure rather than a creation of chemistry, then there was possible cause to hold them responsible (Cohen 2003; Wald 2003a, 2003b;

Weiser 2003). Even though everyone knows McDonald's food is unhealthy, there would be a window for complaint only if it was revealed that its advertising deliberately misled about what it was selling.

Examples could be multiplied endlessly, but it is important simply to recall the point that advertising is known to be suspect yet succeeds brilliantly in persuading Americans to act in certain ways, buy certain things, and even alter their own bodies to conform with images portrayed in advertising. Humans can simultaneously suspect and believe.

Tricksters; Tricks, Deceit, and Lies that Protect the Powerless: *Tricksters, properly, protect the powerless.*

Almost every society has myths, stories, and legends about how dominated people employ language with great cleverness in order to overcome those who would like to prey on them. Often conflated as "tricksters," they are usually marginal figures, crippled or poor or young, with the capability of transformation. Br'er Rabbit, Coyote, Hansel and Gretel, and many other figures in fairy tales use clever deception for self-preservation. Youngest children, innocents who unknowingly make bargains with evil ones (Rapunzel's father), learn to deceive though disguise or guile, exploiting the greed and smugness of the ones who put them into that position (Rumpelstilskin). Anansi, the African trickster, is both good and clever, and he is always worth a laugh. In Africa, stories of animal tricksters represent a combination of cleverness and being the underdog (Roberts 1989, 22–23). Coyote and other tricksters of Native American folklore often show the humorousness of using clever deceit in order to evade danger (Basso 1987; Bright 1993).

Lewis Hyde's *Trickster Makes this World* (1998) concludes that artists and other creative individuals often have much of the trickster in them. Many tricksters are also punsters. They are so clever that they manipulate language without lying. Zhuge Liang, the central hero in the novel *Water Margin*, is one of China's beloved trickster figures. Zhuangzi in China could almost be considered a trickster in this sense. China's Monkey from the Ming novel *Journey to the West* (*Xi you ji*) is well known as a trickster figure. Maxine Hong Kingston's surreal and postmodern novel *Tripmaster Monkey* revels in Monkey's playfulness (1989).

Like ethnic minority stories in China, Br'er Rabbit stories from the slave South in the United States show the vulnerable rabbit holding his own in a universe of much more powerful beings, outwitting them through his cleverness. As Julius Lester points out in his appreciative introduction to a collection of Br'er Rabbit (Uncle Remus) stories, "'shameless untruthfulness is a property of the world' (Kerényi); and therefore, a property belonging to each of us because we are human. To be moral about it does not always tell us how to live with it. Through the tales we live with, laugh with, and love, something of ourselves which is beyond our power to redeem" (Lester and Pinkney 1988, xii). He further says that "Trickster's function is to keep Order from taking itself too seriously" (xiii). In a manner reminiscent of Bakhtin's discussion of the carnivalesque, Lester says, "Through [Br'er Rabbit] we experience 'what is not permitted,' and thereby we are made whole. Not perfect, but whole. The ideal of human perfection is one of the most dangerous of human delusions. To be human is to be whole. To be human is to love our irredeemable imperfections with the same passion as our virtues" (xiii). If we can laugh at the misfortunes of the wicked and powerful, so much the better.

Silence; Lies of Omission: *If you can't say something nice, don't say anything at all.*

When asked a question that requires an unpleasing answer ("How does this outfit look on me?") many Americans prefer to evade the question, nevertheless conveying their views. "Well . . ." This connects to the cliché "If you can't say something nice, don't say anything at all." Many people hesitate to answer untruthfully, even if there would be no cost.

Michael Agar describes his own discovery of this problem through fieldwork in Mexico. When a goal of social interaction is to "have a pleasant moment" and certain facts could challenge that pleasantness, the facts are disregarded. Nothing is said, even if in the American context it would mean that businesses are not told the truth (1994, 156–60).

Tact and Greetings: *Everyone has to lie when greeted.*

In his usual patient fashion, Harvey Sacks demonstrated the complexity of a greeting such as "How are you?" in his article "Everyone has to Lie" (1975).[1] When people ask this question, they expect to hear "Fine" and not a lengthy, accurate, truthful account of the status of their health or well-being. Quoting Emily Post and Amy Vanderbilt, he shows that "tact" is expected, and it would be quite rude to interrupt the flow of conventional exchanges by giving more information than is warranted by the recipient or the setting. This, then, requires a lie on the many occasions when a person is not feeling fine. In other societies, greetings may take other forms: In China, one of the most common greetings is to ask "Where are you going?" (*Ni shang nar qu?*) and another is "Have you eaten yet?" (*Ni chi fan le ma?*) Both are to be answered similarly tactfully: "To town" and "Yes" are the unmarked replies. In India, the similar greeting is asked as "Are you going to the *ūr?*" to confirm what the speaker expects. On occasion, such as when foreign anthropologists are going to unusual places, elaboration of the answer provokes tense conversation (Daniel 1984, 63–67).[2]

Flattery: *Beware of flattery; it's dangerous because people are gullible.*

In some contexts, flattery is not expected to be entirely genuine, though if it is too obviously exaggerated, it can serve as either irony or an insult. Comments on appearance, clothing, and general delight in seeing someone are to be uttered in the United States while attempting to appear sincere. Some people are known to be "flatterers" in the sense of exaggerating or extending their compliments to more people than might deserve them. In some regions, such as the U.S. South, flattery is a much-practiced skill—or at least this is the stereotype. Responses to and proffering of compliments is a complex subject (Holmes 1998). Accepting them may be construed as assenting to their truthfulness; rejecting them may question the complimenter's judgment.

Domains of Frankness: *Avoid the topics of politics, money, weight, and age in polite conversation.*

In some settings and among some relationships, some topics are candidates for frank discussion; when they are not, they are considered blunt.[3] Such domains differ from setting to setting. In China, for instance, the most shocking topics (according to American sensibility) that are freely discussed are money ("How much money do you make?" "How much did that briefcase cost?"), weight ("You've gained weight."), and age ("How old are you?"). Middle-class Americans are much more likely to discuss clothing, jobs, and feelings. In France, notably, political disagreements are freely aired.

Humor: *We laugh at the misfortune of the evil ones.*

Many forms of humor revolve around playing with truth and falsity. Those who can mislead while never lying are especially noteworthy; those who deceive for the greater good or to protect the powerless are also applauded. The American film *The Sting* (Hill 1973) depicts a series of cons played elaborately by a society of grifters that runs parallel to respectable society during the Depression. Though everybody portrayed is engaged in various illegal schemes, some do so honorably and others with selfish and violent disregard for others. The climax of the film shows a Chicago mobster who had ordered the murder of a beloved older grifter being conned into losing everything in a fixed gambling scheme. The fascination for the audience is the elaborate care that is taken to produce a very "real" setting to convince a suspicious, dishonorable boss to trust that he had found an authentic opportunity to outwit the horse-racing establishment. The honorable, smaller-time con artists, guided by the brilliant Henry Gondorff, very much engage in fourth-level deception (see appendix); they are quite aware of the active nature of their victim's mind and attempt (successfully) to anticipate his doubts in order to provide a settling of his suspicions that appears natural and enduring.

Magic: *Suspend disbelief! You'll like it!*

Magic (in the sense of entertainment, not the anthropological sense of religion, sorcery, etc.) involves a willing suspension of belief in the truth of what you observe, knowing that you are being deceived by the skill of the manipulating deceiver. Bowyer's theory of cheating points out that the manipulation involved in magic is pleasurable to and desired by those who are deceived (1982). The setting creates the expectation about magic. The pleasure lies in the skill with which perceptions and expectations are manipulated, and the skill in turn depends on extremely acute understandings of ordinary people's assumptions. When the eye moves to watch something, it will not detect the other slight movements that move the object to another side or will not know that it is a mirror that is showing the back of a box rather than the box itself. Still, the sigh of relief when the scantily clad beautiful woman emerges unharmed from the saws or arrows is real; all who enjoy the trick also share a sense of its risk.

The Rhetorical Power of "Truth" and "Lie": *Liar, liar, pants on fire!*

Proclamations of "truth" declare the speaker bold, honest, deserving of an audience, daring to speak the truth no matter what the consequences. "Speak truth to power"; "truth and reconciliation"; "truth and justice"; "He is the truth"; "learn the truth about Bill Clinton (or Julia Roberts or Walter Cronkite)." A newspaper in Indiana proclaims itself the *Elkhart Truth*. "Truth" sells newspapers and products; it prefaces confessions; it promises to open up reality, as if there is a simple key to knowing the universe.

Just as "truth" cannot ever be repudiated, accusations of "lie" are shed only with difficulty. If headlines shout "Senator X lies on the stand," Senator X better find a job heading her brother-in-law's lawn service company. "Why people lie": the very sound appears profound. "You're lying!" children shout at one another. Even worse than just lying is to be a liar. "Liar!" In the very youngest children this indicates only a sense that something untrue—even mistaken, sometimes just undesirable—has been said, but they know how their adults bristle at the very word (just as they know the power of swearing, even if they have no idea what the words mean semantically; pragmatically the effect is crystal clear), so it seems a powerful epithet. In studies of verbal play among children, the expression "Liar, liar, pants on fire" has great geographic

and historic sweep, with variations on the phrase that follows; one twentieth-century version is "Nose as long as a telephone wire."[4] (See the remarkable study of children's taunts and rhymes in Opie 1960.) A liar is indelibly
cast as doomed to lie; all utterances are suspect. Political humor books by Al
Franken, *Lies and the Lying Liars who Tell Them* (2003) and *The Truth (with
Jokes)* (2005) exploit this easy and vital slur.

Truth as Morality and Psychology: *Be (true to) yourself.*
One version of the person in the United States includes the injunction to remain identical in all contexts. As one student said, "I am the same all the
time except in front of teachers and priests," suggesting that it would be a
false representation if he altered according to circumstances. In this view, integrity requires identity and lack of consideration of consequences.

All these examples, which could be increased endlessly, show that there is
power simply in invoking the words *truth* and *lie*. The power is both philosophical and metaphysical, indicating a particular relationship to reality, and
pragmatic and social, indicating a particular social effect based on strategic
use of the words. Like a sleight of hand or a well-crafted advertising campaign, claims of one's own truth telling or others' lies must be made judiciously. They can't occur every day or they would be considered empty. One
must save them for the right moment.

Japan: Inside and Outside

> [The] association of the kokoro (or inner self) with truthfulness gives rise
> to the paradoxical notion that the 'real' truth is inexpressible. Thus
> words and speech as means of expression are often regarded as poten-
> tially deceptive and false, and silence as indicative of the true kokoro
>
> —Takie Sugiyama Lebra 1992

When I told my colleague Satsuki Kawano that I wanted to touch on Japanese notions of politeness in my book on deception, her immediate response
was "Yes, to Americans, this seems like lying." The implication is that to
Japanese it is not; politeness is only deceptive to someone who expects some
kind of pure unadorned information from language. Only with a shared expectation of bald frankness would utterances intended to produce positive
feeling be considered deceptive. Yet a person who feels that much Japanese
communication is deceptive is herself by origin Japanese:

Kyoko Mori spent the first twenty years of her life in Japan and the second twenty in the United States. In her memoir tellingly titled *Polite Lies*

(1997), she describes her discomfort upon returning home to Japan from the United States at the many lies she is forced to use.[5] Politeness is required: "The Japanese announcement welcoming us to the flight reminds me of the polite language I was taught as a child: always speak as though everything in the world were your fault. . . . [The] politeness is a steel net hauling us into the country where nothing means what it says . . . where I can never say what I feel or ask what I want to know" (1997, 5). Mori writes about how painful it is to be forced to say things that are in opposition to what she believes and feels; she is frustrated at all times by the indirect way people make requests: they provide a hint at the reason for the action being requested but never make the connection for the listener. They rely upon the listener's sensitivity and judge the listener according to how well she or he took up the hints.

As in the Midwest of the United States where Mori currently lives, in Japan people use what she calls "the code of Never Say No and Always Use a Disclaimer" (8) but more deceptively. In the Midwest, to indicate good will, people utter vague, timeless invitations ("We should get together sometime"), but in Japan people give their insincere invitations a great deal of detail and precision. "In Japan, there are no clear-cut signs to tell me which invitations are real and which are not. People can give all kinds of details and still not expect me to show up at their door or call them from the train station. I cannot tell when I am about to make a fool of myself or hurt someone's feelings by taking them at their word or by failing to do so" (10).

Mori associates politeness with lying. Though it is usually used for benevolent purposes like saving someone's face or making people feel good, it can be used for ill effect as well. Late in the book Mori recounts the discovery that when she was a teenager her (evil) stepmother, Michiko, had been concocting an elaborate series of lies about her. Michiko told Mori's father and others in the family that Mori had sent many love letters to a boy she met through a family friend. In fact Mori had met the boy only once. The family friend was told a different but equally effective lie and Mori did not see her again for decades.

> Ironically, during this time when I worshipped the truth, I was being fed some big lies by my stepmother. I believed all Michiko's lies because she was such an unpleasant person. To me, liars were people who pretended to be nice, whose sweet words and malicious actions didn't match. Michiko never tried to be nice to me, spare my feelings, or save my face, so I assumed that she was being truthful to me. I even thought that blunt honesty was one of her few good qualities. I couldn't have been more wrong. The whole time we lived together, she was actually trying to isolate me from anyone who could have made me feel loved or valued, and her strategy almost always involved lies. (Mori 1997, 213)

As in any society, only sociopaths in Japan use lies to create an extensive, sustained pattern of wounding another. What is more common, yet for Mori just as difficult, is the politeness encoded into language. Different verb forms and nouns are used for people of higher and lower status. Politeness requires knowing people's status, categorizing them accurately so that the proper linguistic forms can be used; strangers cause a problem since their status is not usually known precisely. The solution is to avoid interaction with strangers.

At the same time, while detailed and precise talk is obligatory, much is unsaid and unsayable. Mori feels oppressed by the silences that make public information clear and uniform but keep private information a secret, even from those affected. Subway information, for instance, is completely accurate, helpful, and available. But in private matters, information is carefully doled out or entirely suppressed. Her father and her aunt were never informed about the cancers that killed them.

> In Japan, doctors usually inform the immediate family of terminally ill patients and ask them to keep quiet. The patients, the doctors advise, may lose heart and die in a few weeks if they find out the truth. "Don't discourage them and shorten their lives," the doctors warn. "Besides, they should be happy and content in the short time they have left, not worried and afraid." Most families agree. They tell the truth to relatives, old friends, and a few business associates, but always with a warning: "Of course, he/she doesn't know, so don't let on." (Mori 1997, 39)

Yet people must know, sometimes, given signs such as being sent home from the hospital after serious surgery without mention of further treatment. Still, even when they perhaps subconsciously know, they are complicit in their own ignorance. Mori suspects this was true of her father, Hiroshi. "Hiroshi must have realized the seriousness of his illness, but he never asked his doctors or his family to tell him more. Perhaps he was afraid. Or else he did not want to put [second wife] Michiko, [son] Jumpei, or [sister] Akiko in the awkward position of having to lie to him. My father was not a fearful or polite person by nature. For him to keep up his end of the mutual secrecy and pretense pact, the taboo against demanding the truth must have been potent" (42).

Social pressure against inquiring about serious illness has many dimensions, like all powerful taboos. Relationships are reinforced through appearance of trust, exercised and performed frequently. (*Perform trust frequently.*) Trust in one's relatives, like trust in doctors, leads them to have no need for knowledge. "The less they know, the more they rely on trust. The more they trust someone, the less they need to know" (55).

Politeness, lies, face, trust, the distinctions between private and public—all these are a source of strong feeling and even conflict for Mori, who feels herself both uniquely herself and a product of the two cultures in which she has made her life. She longs for truth and expression of reality, but she also wishes it to be mitigated by circumstances, so that people's feelings are sometimes taken into account.

Mori is horrified by blunt, pain-inducing statements, especially in the face of sorrow, when "I would rather hear a cliché or a platitude that may be a polite lie. When we say that someone 'had a good life and didn't suffer much' or 'had no regrets,' it may or may not be true. But I prefer these polite lies to harsh truths—that someone's father must have died of sorrow or that someone's mother suffered terribly in the last two months of her illness" (79). Considering further, she moves her analysis up a level: "Maybe it isn't even a matter of truth versus lies. The platitudes and polite lies we say are not true in the sense of accurate, factual statements, but they make an appeal to a larger truth—the truth of our good will" (79). Despite her deploring of polite lies, as a first approximation, she ends up with a much more nuanced view of the power of language to create relationships and to have effects in the world. Apparent lies may actually contain deeper truths.

Similarly, in their book *The Art of Lying*, psychiatrist Sakai and writer Ide discuss the many paradoxical benefits of lying, along with an appreciation of truth telling. They acknowledge many fascinating things, such as that Americans are especially prone to value truthfulness, and that despite exhortations to be truthful in Japan, everyone knows to produce lies on some occasions. "People who are 'sincere' or 'hardworking' are sometimes the most unaccommodating and stubborn people around! . . . A lie can be a remedy for life. In addition, when one goes beyond a lie and the common truth to 'true wisdom,' the real truth becomes clear" (Sakai and Ide 1998, 218). Here too Sakai and Ide question a notion of truth as blunt expression of reality in favor of "real truth" which involves wisdom and considerateness.

Another psychiatrist, Takeo Doi, discusses apparent surface and reality, expression and thoughts, face and heart.

As face may reveal, mask, distort, or conceal inner intention, so does all speech move between silence and expression. In selecting what is to be expressed, words reveal only partially what lies beneath them.

> Words both express and conceal the mind, and so does the face, but these two acts of expression/concealment are not always concurrent. . . . Words conceal the mind even as they express it, but this act of concealment is by no means limited to deliberate concealment. Every time we say something, we also conceal,

in the instant we put it into words, everything outside it, by choosing not to put it into words. This is an extremely selective act. There are also times when we find ourselves trying to say something that is difficult to express in words. Japanese have an expression for the feeling that arises in this situation: "Somehow, when I try to put it into words, it sounds like a lie." (Doi 1985, 31)

Thus words are always a difficult tool in the human realm of attempting to convey one's inner thoughts (*ura*) through public expression (*omote*)—the only means. (*Words express and conceal the mind.*) *Ura* is fundamentally unknowable but is always sought nonetheless.

The key point here is that inside and outside (*uchi* and *soto*) must be properly ordered.[6] Human beings' most important characteristic, *kokoro* (heart, mind, soul, intention), is never visible, but is known only through actions that are public. And this makes deception and hypocrisy possible:

The existence of hypocrisy and deception, in which words and actions seem to express *kokoro* but in fact misrepresent it, is possible because this is true [that *kokoro* itself always is hidden]. Of course, if the person who is the object of hypocrisy or deception is astute enough, he or she may see through the pretense. Thus, the fact that *kokoro* is hidden is not what makes hypocrisy and deception evil. Rather, it is the fact that the person has pretended that there is something in his or her *kokoro* that is not there. (Doi 1985, 107)

Kokoro is by nature private and inner; its unknowability makes possible the notion of secrecy, which is always a danger as well as an opportunity for society as a whole. Yet Doi ultimately rejects the simple-minded equation of public as good and private as bad, surface as bad and interior as good. He views mutual dependence, in context, as the prerequisite for love and independence. Secrets form the basis of love and charm, and words live in the greater realm of silence. He explicitly contrasts Japanese acceptance of apparent contradiction with Western insistence on choosing one of a pair of opposites. Westerners deplore contradiction and believe only one of two opposites can be true at any moment. "The urge to eliminate ambivalence for a higher integrity is generally weak among the Japanese" (152–53).

Japanese sometimes have feelings of superiority toward Westerners, who in their eyes cannot easily become one with nature. The Japanese never experience the splitting of the body and the soul that occurs in the consciousness of Western people. And they are not afflicted by the Christian conflict between spirit and flesh, nor burdened by the severe dichotomy of subject and object that is inherent in the Western philosophical tradition. This may be true. But the Japanese are afflicted, nevertheless, with the splitting of the consciousness into *omote* and *ura*, and we must not forget the fact that we seek to become one with nature precisely because of this affliction. (Doi 1985, 155–56)

Like many other societies, but notably unlike the United States, Japan may be characterized as emphasizing "interdependent" or "social" selves, in which relationships define interactions, rather than encouraging independent unique individuals. What becomes clear from a reading of the material on Japan is that every act, whether spoken or other, is consciously shaped by its multiple contexts. A singular identity with a singular message and a singular truth is entirely alien to this system and violates all its precepts. Hence the explicit understanding presented in *The Art of Lying* is only partially facetious. It also stems from ideas held dear about the value of shifting and shaping one's actions. Bluntness is undesirable; the forms of indirection in Japanese are multiple and complex.

Maxims that stem from some of the material presented here include:

Inside and outside are complementary.
Audience is critical in evaluating actions.
Perform trust frequently.
Face expresses and distorts intention; words express and conceal the mind.
Kokoro is unknowable.
Silence must be interpreted.
Keep track of inside and outside.

Some Japanese views of language should seem familiar from the Chinese world in which consequences and contexts are primary. Both traditions emphasize the importance of context, of face, of relatedness, of differentiating inside and outside, of audience and performance. Both have a notion of sincerity that includes zeal for the expected behavior; both have subtle views of truthfulness.

Next we will encounter a tradition that is quite clearly different in its explicit valuation of truth and its perhaps hair-splitting rationalization for exceptions to truth telling: Judaism.

Judaism: Truth and Its Permitted Exceptions

Death and life are in the power of the tongue; and they that indulge it shall eat the fruit thereof.

—Proverbs 18:21

Oh God, guard my tongue from evil and my lips from speaking falsehood.

—Siddur (Jewish prayer book), Amidah

The Jewish tradition, like the Chinese, traces many of its practices back
thousands of years. At the same time, there is a modern variant that exists
both in Israel and elsewhere, sometimes distinctly unlike the past. Discussions of truthfulness in the Torah (the Five Books of the Hebrew Bible) often point out the duplicity of the patriarchs and matriarchs, either condon-
ing them because they are living out their fated lives or condemning them
for their imperfections.

One of the best-known stories promoting truthfulness is that of Jonah and
the whale (Lev. 18). God told Jonah to "proclaim against" the wicked people of Nineveh. To avoid this charge Jonah ran away on a ship, but God created a terrible storm that was correctly interpreted by the sailors as indicating that someone on board was responsible. They cast lots to determine who
this person was and identified Jonah. Admitting that the tempest was the result of his actions, he told them that if they wanted the storm to cease they
would have to throw him overboard. They did, reluctantly, and the sea
calmed. Jonah was swallowed by a "large fish" that God sent to rescue him.
Jonah was grateful, became submissive, and was released. He warned the people of Nineveh of God's impending punishment, whereupon they promptly
repented and were forgiven. There are several lessons to be learned here, but
one common lesson is that there is no escaping the truth, because God
knows/sees everything. (God knows the truth.) Attempts at flight—and covering up of the truth—are doomed, ultimately, to failure.

Biblical morality is scarcely simple; there are many accounts in the Bible
of attempts to deceive and conceal and lie. Some say that even God uses this
tactic on occasion, as in the sacrifice of Isaac, usually treated as a test of
Abraham's faith (Gen. 22). God tells Abraham to take Isaac to Mt. Moriah
to sacrifice him; Abraham conceals this purpose when he tells Isaac to go
with him. At the last minute, an angel tells Abraham not to sacrifice Isaac;
a ram appears instead. Was it in fact God's intention to deceive and test
Abraham? The lesson—vague, sketchy—is troubling.

God also manipulates appearances to reveal a greater truth, as when
God's angels make Isaac's face like that of Abraham to quiet doubts about
his paternity.

The patriarchs and matriarchs also deceive quite often. Rebekkah, wife of
Isaac, encouraged her younger son Jacob to claim from his dying, blind father

Isaac the birthright that rightfully belonged to his elder brother Esau. Jacob dresses in Esau's clothing and puts on skins to emulate his hairiness. Later Jacob is in turn the one deceived; he planned to marry Rachel but was instead given her older sister Leah as the bride on his wedding day. Rabbinic commentators invent a dialogue between Jacob and Leah:

> He said to her, "Deceiver, daughter of a deceiver! Did I not call you Rachel and you answered me?!" She replied, "Is there a master without students? Did your father not call you Esau and you answered him?!" (*Bereshit Rabbah* 70:17, quoted in Zornberg 1995, 144)

Some argue that the patriarchs and matriarchs are depicted as flawed but overcoming their limitations; their lies matter but the ultimate consequence matters more. Jacob had to become the one blessed, no matter how the blessing was obtained. Speech itself has consequences no matter what the speaker's intent. When Isaac discovers Jacob's deception, his anguish cannot undo the effect of his blessing having been given to Jacob rather than, as rightly belonged, to Esau (Berkun 2002). Words create worlds; words spoken cannot be unspoken. (*Words create worlds; words are dangerous and powerful.*)

Zornberg describes Jacob as fearing to appear to his father as a trickster (*ke-metateia*). Jacob's name (*Ya'akov*) derives from the Hebrew root *akov*, meaning "crooked, indirect" (Zornberg 1995, 153). Zornberg complicates the story by showing Jacob's transformation from a naïve man (*ish tam*, Exod. 25:27), which she compares to Lionel Trilling's notion of sincerity (1972), to a man ready to grapple with the complexities of the world that includes mimicry, transformations, and manipulations of appearances in order to arrive at authenticity (see appendix). Isaac affirms the blessing even though he knows it was obtained through duplicity (154–55). "The voice is the voice of Jacob, yet the hands are the hands of Esau" (Exod. 17:22). If Zornberg's reading is correct, then rather than taking it as an error, Isaac's blessing should be seen as acceptance that the dangers of language and deception are inseparable from human choice and intelligence. (*Language and deception are inseparable from human choice and intelligence.*) In this sense, Jewish ethics contrast starkly with Christian ethics, wherein Jesus, Augustine, Aquinas, and Kant all affirm the singularity and imperative of truth. It also differs from Chinese ethics because of the power of speech to cause events in the world.

When Jacob arrives at his father's deathbed, Isaac asks who he is. Jacob tells what seems like a bald-faced lie. "I [am] Esau your firstborn" (Exod. 27:19).[7] One commentator suggests that she would like to regard "Jacob's statement as representing a kind of truth, a truth of authenticity, rather than of sincerity" (Zornberg 1995, 172). Thus Jacob, taking on the appearance of Esau, does in fact become him, taking on other of his characteristics, but only in the sense that there is a mask, a distinction between appearance and reality.

While truthfulness is always valued in the abstract, the Jewish tradition includes discussion of potential alternatives. Abraham Joshua Heschel (1973) writes of a battle in Hasidism, the charismatic movement that began in the Jewish ghettoes of Poland in the seventeenth and eighteenth centuries, between those rabbis who placed "love" first and those who placed "truth" first. The exemplar of the latter, echoed (according to Heschel) by Kierkegaard, was the Kotzker rabbi, Rabbi Menachem Mendel Morgenstern (1787–1859) of Kotzk, Poland. The Kotzker rabbi's main concern was Truth (Emeth)—a virtue threatened by routine, obligation, repetition. It was attained through spontaneity and is very much akin to what Trilling described as authenticity. "Every day prayer had to have a fresh approach. One ought to search out the Truth daily, as if it had not been known before. . . . Truth . . . could be reached only by way of the utmost freedom. Such freedom meant not to give in to any outside pressures, not to conform, not to please oneself or anyone else" (Heschel 1973, 11). In many ways, this is the antithesis of a predominant Han Chinese view of the proper role of language in society, though it does resemble the Chan and Daoist non-mainstream views.

Language is spoken of as extremely powerful. A common imprecation in Jewish life is against lashon ha-ra (lashon hora), evil words or gossip. It is said that gossiping is like committing three murders: against the person being spoken of, against the person speaking, and against the person listening to the gossip. Even true comments that would be hurtful are to be avoided as ethical if not legal infractions. One who chooses to refrain from passing on gossip is considered like God. Rabbi Joseph Telushkin cites rabbis in the Talmud who refer to a passage in the Torah: When Sarah was told by three angels that she would bear a child, she said "Now that I am withered, am I to have [the] enjoyment [of having a child], with my husband so old?" and laughed. Abraham asked why she laughed, and God, repeating Sarah's words to Abraham, omitted Sarah's comment about Abraham's age, though God did repeat her words about her own age (Gen. 18; Telushkin 2000, 66). The power of words to wound is well recognized. That God is reported to have been tactful is taken as a model for human considerateness.

Though the commandment to "stay far away from falsehoods" (Exod. 23:7) is made frequently in the Torah and Talmud (one of the Ten Commandments is "You will not bear false testimony against your neighbor"), there are notable exceptions in writings on ethics. In contrast to Kant's and Augustine's absolute proscription against lying, Judaism recognizes that there are occasions in which lies are not only accepted but celebrated. Just as the Egyptian midwives who saved Israelite male babies and lied to Pharoah (Exod. 1:19) were rewarded by God, so the righteous gentiles and others who hid Jews from Germans during the Holocaust are considered heroes. Saving a life is more important than the absolute value on telling the whole truth (Telushkin 2000, 100–102).

Rabbinic sources permit lies in three situations: to save peace, to save a life, and in some social situations to save face. A debate between the schools of two famous rabbis, Shammai and Hillel, revolved around what one should say to a bride. Should one say that she is "graceful and beautiful"? What, argued Shammai, if she is lame and ugly? Surely she would know that the praise was false. No, argued Hillel, there is no harm in praising her. Amsel (1994, 294–95) reminds us that from a certain perspective—that of her husband, at least—she is surely beautiful, perhaps as a person if not physically. Thus the praise is honest and truthful. (Even while accepting what might seem to be a lie, great effort is made in still finding a way to read it as truthful.)

Religious scholars are permitted to lie in three domains: Scholars may downplay the extent of their own knowledge in order to be modest and humble, they may dissemble about their sexuality to preserve their privacy, and they may refrain from praising someone's hospitality to prevent others from abusing that person's generosity (Amsel 1994, 295–96; Telushkin 2000, 104–5). But only those scholars advanced and wise enough to know how to use a lie are permitted to do so. If they build up great enough trust and faithfulness, they are taken on faith and then, for the good, they may lie, as Moses's brother Aaron did in attempting to reconcile two people who had been feuding. Aaron told each that the other had expressed a desire to make up for their argument, and the two were restored to their previously peaceful relations. Still, commentaries point out that the two *did* want to make peace (Amsel 1994, 296). Thus Aaron's lie was also a kind of truth. (*The wise are permitted exceptions to truth telling; for ordinary people an exception to truth telling may be made when the motive is avoiding hurting others' feelings.*)

The ethical values expressed in biblical, talmudic, and rabbinic writing may have much to do with real-life dilemmas of people living at the time, but we have no access through their writings to actual behavior. In contrast, a study of contemporary Israeli speech norms by Tamar Katriel titled *Talking Straight: Dugri Speech in Israeli Sabra Culture* (1986) describes actual language use and ideas revolving around such use. Influences on Israeli culture include but are not limited to traditional religious and ethical precepts.

Katriel contrasts the premium placed on bluntness and directness with the indirectness of Arabs and others within Israel. The speech form known as *dugri* (itself a term borrowed from Arabic but with a change in meaning) involves an ideology of truthfulness and bluntness, of directness, and is evaluated positively even when it is manipulated for effect. The appearance of truthfulness may sometimes result in duplicity. Encounters with Israelis are apt to result in others' views of them as impolite and harsh, impossibly antisocial. For Sabras (Israel-born Jewish Israelis) *dugri* refers to the *form* of telling while for Arab Israelis it refers to the accuracy of a statement. Jewish Israeli *dugri* emphasizes stylistic directness while Arab Israeli *dugri* emphasizes close correspondence with the facts of the world—speaking the truth.

The maxims for Judaism are:

God knows the truth.

Words create worlds; words are dangerous and powerful.

Language and deception are inseparable from human choice and intelligence.

Appearances may be manipulated in service of a greater truth.

The wise are permitted exceptions to truth telling; for ordinary people an exception to truth telling may be made when the motive is avoiding hurting others' feelings.

The Jewish views of truth and deception contrast with Christian views in their permitting some lies and also with Chinese views in their privileging of language.

This chapter has shown how truth, deception, and lying are regarded in the context of three societies. There are circumstances in which expectations of truth are suspended, and circumstances in which truth is undesirable. There are circumstances in which lies are permitted, and circumstances in which they are deplored. Parents must teach by both precept and example, but the precepts are much simpler than the practices. Religion and philosophy attempt to guide behavior on the basis of principles, but there are many principles at work in every situation and human beings must make split-second decisions about which will prevail. Literature tends to provide complex and contradictory models of ideal action.

Thus the morality of deception and truth in China cannot be explained entirely as a universal human set of practices. It shares most with Japanese notions and contrasts in some fairly pointed ways with American and Jewish ideas about language and reality, though some commonalities are also evident. In explaining contemporary Chinese practices, I have tried to show the general overarching tendencies rather than unique disembodied cases. It is true that every example I have described in China could likely be found everywhere else in the world. Everywhere one could find people who shield relatives from the grim facts about terminal illnesses; everywhere there are some people who are extremely tactful and polite, choosing their words to make others feel good; everywhere there are people who cheat and lie and scam and con. In China there are people who are scrupulous about telling the truth; in China there are people who are inept at being gracious with others and are simply blunt; in China there are honest lawyers and businesspeople. But what I hope to have shown is that the balance and attributed meanings of such behavior differ from place to place, and differ in fairly systematic ways. That is to say, people's behavior is not purely individual and momentary, but occurs within the system of what anthropologists used to call culture. This system is not rigidly confining—it always has loopholes and leaks—but our actions are always made meaningful by the past of our own experience and the past of our larger societal milieu.

The final chapter turns to what all this means.

Notes

1. I am grateful to Penelope Brown for this reference.

2. Duranti (2001) has written a different account of greetings. He argues that they are never expected to be truthful or informational yet are not entirely phatic. They also serve to establish relationships and roles in a given interaction, and thus have a very important function as not merely indicating but performing social roles.

3. Again, I have benefited from conversations with Penelope Brown on this topic.

4. A search on Google for the phrase *Liar liar pants on fire* turned up about 6,580 websites, mostly with this phrase as the title of an article blaming someone for having lied.

5. Thanks to Janet Fair for this very helpful reference.

6. The nature of "inside" and "outside" are also elaborated on by articles in a collection titled *Situated Meaning: Inside and Outside in Japanese Self, Society, and Language* (Bachnik and Quinn 1994).

7. Zornberg points out that many commentators, including Rashi (Rabbi Solomon ben Isaac), the eleventh-century French commentator on Talmud and Torah, go to great lengths to demonstrate that this is not really what he meant. Perhaps there is a grammatical break between "I" and "Esau [is] your firstborn"; the Hebrew has no copula (verb *to be*) between subject and predicate. Deception in the patriarchs' behavior clearly leads commentators to great hair splitting to preserve morality and truthfulness.

CHAPTER NINE

Knowing How to Play
with Words and Minds

Lies are the bastard offspring of symbols.

—Roy A. Rappaport 1976

I began this book with a consideration of deception and truth in contemporary China and ended with a sampling of deception and truth in other societies. I attempted to account for the morality of public deception in China in four ways: through detailed contemporary cultural rules, through consideration of ancient Chinese beliefs and ideas of cultural essence, through looking at revolutionary Chinese behavior as evidence of a radical change, and a brief survey of middle-class U.S., Japanese, and Jewish notions of deception and truth. In this conclusion, I will consider broader questions: Why do people argue that truth is best, yet lie? Why does everyone assent to the importance of honesty, yet sometimes deceive? What are people doing with words and minds? Why do people sometimes tell the truth? What is going on in language? What prevents people from exploiting the possibilities of misrepresentation more often than they do? Why do people ever tell the truth?

A partial answer lies in the nature of humankind. Humans desire sociality, needing reputation and good name, so that ongoing relationships may be maintained. Still, only from an individual perspective may one even raise the question of motives for truth telling; from a social perspective there can be no functioning society that is not filled primarily with truth.

Lying is possible because there is a general understanding that language is used honestly. Liars are "free riders"; since most people aren't liars, those few who do lie are believed.

Yet it is so easy to lie, to cheat, to dissemble, to omit, to twist, to deceive, to ruse, that we must still inquire about the limits to such deception.

As Roy Rappaport pointed out, our very evolution, enabled by language, causes us to have a tendency to believe lies. The ability to discuss matters removed in time and space from the moment of utterance is central both to any human interaction and to all deception. Humans all have the ability to lie and deceive; some primatologists have observed instances of deception in chimpanzees as well. (For example, a chimp will utter an alarm call apparently in order to cause her or his companions to abandon desirable food which the clever one can then enjoy alone [see Quiatt 1984].)

But the general ability to deceive through ruses, shared even with the plant kingdom, does not mean that we should lump together behavior that has many distinctions and nuances. I've tried to show that matters of truth in China are connected to questions of social harmony, of achieving/attaining limited good—without saying that truth telling is not common in Chinese society. Considering particular circumstances is a sign of intellectual and moral maturity; in this context an abstract ideal of truth appears to be unfeeling, selfish, and improper. Far from arguing that people in China act without regard for truth, I hope to have shown that moral concerns intersect with concern for truth to produce actions tailored to each circumstance. These include discrimination between strangers and familiars, cases of negative and positive face, and anticipation of hearers' reactions and consequences of their reactions.

While some of this focus on the consequences of language can be harmless or positive, taken to its extreme, as we see in some of the Cultural Revolution and contemporary cons, it can yield a pathology that illuminates the hazards of divorcing language from its referents. When pronouncements have to be approved no matter what people think, and with a hearty appearance of sincerity to the point that people find it nearly unendurable (and some could not endure it and were forced to suicide), or when the clever can bilk the simple of their life savings, then the obvious need for truthfulness and sincerity is crystal clear. No society can endure if it does not have some allegiance to truthfulness.

I also suspect that things work in many places as they do in China. Some preliminary similarities suggest themselves in Mexico (Agar 1994, 154–60, 162), Japan, and Indonesia (Keane 1997). If this comparative question were pursued, my guess is that the unusual would be our practices, and that the more common would be the Chinese (cf. Mondry and Taylor 1973).[1]

How does any of this contrast with U.S. views of deception? Deception can be celebrated in various settings. The stories of Rumpelstiltskin, Robin

Hood, Br'er Rabbit, and Coyote tell of the underdog using cleverness and deception, knowledge of others' desires, to achieve a greater justice. According to Detienne and Vernant (1978), ancient Greek stories demonstrate the centrality of "cunning intelligence," *mētis*, which is more well developed than in recent trickster stories.

In nature, we find many examples and instances of deception. The beauty of many species can be explained biologically as creating diversions, camouflages, and traps for those who are unwary or greedy. Butterflies, cacti, frogs, mushrooms, and so forth present themselves in particular ways to preserve their own survival, lest they be prey to another. Observers of chimpanzees, such as Frans de Waal (1986), write frequently of their charges deceiving one another to gain something, often food. These descriptions are sometimes used in turn to bolster claims that chimpanzees have a "theory of mind," or a sketch of how others think.

Wherever one wishes to draw the line between species that have a theory of mind and those that do not—and dogs, four-year-olds, and people with Asperger syndrome are the favorite test cases (Baron-Cohen 1995; Ceci and Leicht-man 1992; Mitchell and Thompson 1986a)—it is clear that adult humans do and that this is where the possibility of deception and lying arises. One can set up an elaborate ruse if one can predict how others will react. The ability to do so demonstrates sensitivity; a person who can anticipate others' needs and wants is often considered a good friend, an ideal host, a sensitive teacher. That is to say, using this ability purely for the good of others is lauded. Yet if people take the same talents and turn them into a means to get what is not rightfully their own, they are chastised or jailed. Rather than risk such a fate, in the United States at least, parents may not explicitly draw out the likely consequences of an act. But in China conscientious parents may do just that. They may rehearse the potential unfolding of a scene, so that the proper responses can be, as it were, spontaneously produced.[2] Americans often seem naïve in their lack of preparation, the sense that they respond from the heart. As this spontaneity resonates with other aspects of their notion of self, it is valued as pure and desirable and unique—and scorned by clever Han Chinese.

Deception is glorified in some cases because it shows such an exquisite knowledge of humans and their motives. Only by intense study, connoisseurship, can one genuinely anticipate the falling for a compliment, the appearance of friendship, the merchandise that glitters like real gold. Indeed, if it glitters enough to fool buyers, why is it not in turn as valuable as the real thing? If a friendship is set up to emulate a real one, is it not also real? If social actions function as proxies for other actions, do they not too serve a social function?

The theory of mind in China, the theory of self and other, the theory of society, includes great nuance and sophistication with regard to anticipation of others' reactions. This must be taught, both defensively and offensively. Yet it is now in some cases something like sensitivity run amok, or taking perspicacity to its logical limits, as clever people, desperate people, righteous people, have little to lose and everything to gain.[3] The ordinary constraints that cause humans to shape their ordinary actions in conformity with morality have unraveled. As Durkheim might have described it, China is an anomic society now, a society in which people are becoming less tied to one another, but they still retain all the skill in guessing others' motives and responses, and so it is a place where the sophisticated theories of others' minds can serve advantageously those who can outfox, endure, or outwit the rest. One person judges whether it is possible that the other is being genuine, truthful, honest. If not, which aspects are illegitimate? If so, will the other be insulted if the first continues to probe for verification? How can someone express suspicion without appearing too suspicious? What about move number two? The game of parrying one another's feints, the fencing of verbal interaction with strangers, is complex, dangerous, and ubiquitous. One cannot just walk around hoping for the best, but constant suspicion is exhausting.

Still, it is not only politics and economics, practical matters, that account for the morality of deception in China. There are more profound notions of the person and collectivity involved. The notion that words must match inner states comes from a Western model of a self, with its own individual, unique, and contextless feelings and thoughts. In speaking, this person must produce words that transparently reveal those thoughts, no matter what the consequences or pressure to do otherwise. Anything else would make one untrue to herself. But what of a society where—not to overdraw the contrast—selves are regarded as at least in part nodes in relationships? In that case, the person speaking would be different in different contexts, and therefore the words produced by that person would shift according to the circumstances and situations, without any likelihood that there is something deceptive occurring. In fact, this is a desirable, and taught, kind of shift, easier said than done. How to act in school? How to act with Grandma? How to act with the boss? How to act with government officials? How to act with servants? All these require a different set of rules, expectations, scripts. Anyone not willing or able to learn these, or not properly coached by parents, is seen as insincere, selfish, self-centered, seeing their own views and positions as more important than those of the people around them. Any properly considerate person must do the hard work of knowing how to be deferential or solicitous or flattering.

In contrast, a model in which the self sees itself as unchanging, unyielding, invariant, and able to express itself bluntly through a burst of direct feeling straight from inside appears simple-minded, graceless, uncaring. Of course one can blurt out one's feelings—but a sensitive person will not. Ultimately those who believe themselves to be guided purely by truth yet find other forces compelling them to deceive, for reasons not acknowledged to be as powerful, will have guilty consciences and a sense of contradiction. In fact, they will feel themselves to be practicing self-deception, at best, or at worst they will have no idea why they have acted as they have. It is far better to be clear about one's reasons, even if they do not accord fully with other explicit ideals, than to believe falsely that one is moral only to find out that one is acting differently. I thus urge Americans, in order to stop acting hypocritically, to be much more fully aware of the complex forces guiding behavior, advocating truth at every turn yet practicing a subtle mix of deception and lying. We thus have much to learn from China, where pragmatic and self-conscious awareness of the full range of social practice is taught from youth.

My topic has been deception, which is not to say deceptive. There are some true observations to make about lies, and some of what is delusion is clearly known. The ruses that save, the honesty that betrays . . . much of what people do as we interact with one another is not what it seems, but sometimes it is what it seems. A first stab at this venerable subject might suggest that in the best of all possible worlds, there should be nothing but the truth. Yet a further glance has shown how much more slippery, complicated, and interesting social life is when we see with open eyes all that people can do with their mastery of language and other kinds of social action.

My material is Chinese—a broad font of material indeed, though I have also made enormously broad comparisons with entities I call "American," "Japanese," and "Jewish." With very broad brush strokes I have drawn some comparisons between an Anglo-American view favoring simplicity, honesty, and naturalness with regard to language and a Han Chinese view that acknowledges complexity, artifice, and skill. I have roamed around China's past and present, sometimes relying on my own experiences to clarify points, telling stories that may serve as exemplary cases. I showed that though moral concerns are always involved in portrayal of the truth and manipulation of appearances, they do not automatically favor truth and transparency.

Fundamentally, all humans ask whether and when rusing and deception, trickery and lying, cheating and politeness, are warranted. By what values?

What is the balance between, as Christians phrase it, your mortal and immortal souls? The momentary justification for a lie may create a slippery slope of protective or harmless lies, or it may point to sophisticated and complex moral and ethical reasoning.

At the same time, lying is a fact of life. A popular American movie from the mid-1990s, *Liar, Liar*, showed the impossibility and indeed undesirability of spending a whole life in truthfulness (Shadyac 1997). What if one could not say pleasant, if not entirely accurate, things to one's friends, coworkers, and family? The blunt truth is often too painful to bear. Lying is necessary to grease the wheels of social intercourse. Some lies bind people to one another through kindness, through reciprocity, through mutual flattery.

Every time I open the paper there is a new scandal about deception—in the United States as well as in China. In the United States we have a *New York Times* reporter, Jayson Blair, who fabricated, plagiarized, and falsified articles for several years. His undoing led to the resignation of top editors of the *Times* and led to much hand wringing in journalism circles. We have the knowing misrepresentation of George W. Bush about weapons of mass destruction in justifying a war on Iraq and the quest to find someone to blame for knowingly including in his State of the Union speech (January 2003) evidence that was known to be suspect. We have Enron executives who denied complicity in fixing prices and selling stock just in time to emerge with their fortunes intact, while employees lost their pensions and life savings. In 2006 a memoir by James Frey, *A Million Little Pieces*, was revealed as containing significant falsifications. The revelation yielded shrugs from some—such as originally Oprah Winfrey, who argued that his book still contained "emotional truths"—and horror at the casual disregard of truth (Dowd 2006a) which is now being supplanted by "truthiness" (Rich 2006). Oprah subsequently changed her mind and repudiated the book, coming out in favor of literal truth.

In China we have the SARS cover-up, the AIDS cover-up, and ongoing repression of unflattering news about the realities of life in rural China. Between them is the case of a Chinese-American FBI double agent, Katrina Leung, who misled her "handler" (who was also her lover [why is that relevant?]) even while she fed information to both China and the United States.

Deception abounds. Yet Americans in particular harbor a naïve folk philosophy with regard to such matters. A dominant strain of Euro-American thought continues to regard all non-truths knowingly uttered as sinful, immoral, and unacceptable (see, e.g., Bok 1979; Coleman and Kay 1981; Zagorin 1990). We feel bad when we are forced to lie, and we often resort to a number of forced circumlocutions in order to avoid it. I have coached my children before they open gifts at birthday parties: If you already have something that one of your friends gives, don't say so (because it will hurt your friend's feelings), but rather say "Oh, what a great-looking book" or "I love the candle" because these are truthful. Still they should not go so far as to say "Oh, I always wished I could have this" because that would be false. We attempt to walk a fine line between nurturing the relationship and maintaining integrity. The sacredness of language means that uttering non-truthful words would be a cause for guilt and avoidance. A book on deception by two American psychoanalysts (Gediman and Lieberman 1996) discusses the betrayal and difficulty the analysts experience with patients/clients who fail to be truthful. The authors appear shocked that the basic foundation of trust is lacking in far too many cases. This reflects a view that language is somehow natural, stemming without guile from the self that produces thoughts, and that anything that interferes with this process is deplorable—or at least in need of explanation.

The topics relevant here, as you have seen, are the nature of the relationship between intention and expression, different relationships among people, which sometimes require truthfulness and sometimes forbid it, the value placed on that much-maligned notion of "face," urban Han views of cleverness in contrast to peasants' and minorities' value of honesty, and ultimately the view of the person, self, and role and how they relate to language. There have been a number of recent studies of these topics in Indonesia (Keane 1997, 2002) and Samoa (Duranti 1988, 1992, 1993), and a multitude of studies in China that can be brought to bear on them. But there has been no study that has connected them all in the case of China. My ultimate purpose is to demonstrate the range of potentially human behaviors, showing that "ours"—however construed—is not the best or only way to solve the fundamental question of how to be a person in the complex humanly constituted world.

In emphasizing that my aim is *not* to say that Han Chinese are liars but to say that language use is extraordinarily complex, I have pointed out that what may at first blush appear to be deception may in fact be language used for other, perhaps noble, purposes. I have also suggested that the contrasts between a Chinese and a "white middle-class American" way to use language are in some ways more apparent than real, but that Chinese metapragmatics (ways of thinking about practice) accords more fully with practice than American metapragmatics does. Deception may indeed be a universal human practice, but the specifics vary from culture to culture. All other things being equal, it is common for value to be placed on truth—but my aim has been to figure out what all those other things are that *aren't* always equal. The maxims for China are one way to impose order on some of the reasoning that explains observations. They might apply in other places—or we might equally likely find an entirely different set of maxims.

Over the course of several years while I wrote this book, I vacillated between appreciating the constant truthfulness of most people in most contexts and noticing the frequency of small and larger lies and deceit, including my own. For a short time I became suspicious of everything everyone did and said, suspecting that people gave compliments only for ulterior motives or slyly set up contexts that would permit certain opinions to be made of them that were misleading. This period was very disturbing; it was as if a cloud of paranoia descended on me and made it impossible to enjoy the social graces that surround us all the time.

As a parent, this book grew with me and my daughters. When I first began thinking about the topic (around 1994, though I had begun to incubate questions even before that), Hannah and Elena were very young (four and one). I assumed that I had merely to exhort them to complete truthfulness and that all would be well. I expected the same of myself, though I learned quickly that this was not possible. When Hannah was two and a half and heard on National Public Radio about the daddies being forced away from their families in Bosnia in 1992, our solution was to turn off the radio whenever she could hear bad news. (Blatant censorship!) We began to realize that our view—quite unlike that of many other contemporaries—was that children did not need to know everything nor should they encounter the worst, puzzling behavior of humans throughout time and space. Since we do not watch television, this has been possible. Still, the girls read and observe. They know about the Holocaust and about the brutal crimes that we cannot possibly mask. As I finish the book, they are now sixteen and thirteen. We talk often about the subtleties of how not to hurt a friend's feelings without lying, how to be an honest person, how to deal with others' sometimes hurtful bluntness, what to do about classmates' cheating, why we might choose not to mention something to Dad that we know will upset him, and all the other ordinary things that come up.

The spontaneous eruption of feeling that was charming in toddlers is less desirable in teenagers; I sometimes wish for a bit more selection of script and would be willing to witness even false politeness. My younger daughter has a wicked sense of humor. She can imitate the polite niceties of a conversation or put on the hyper-solicitous voice she uses with young children or anyone she feels somehow superior to. Once, she found out that someone was not as young as she thought; she then knowingly shifted to her ordinary, sarcastic voice. Her more serious older sister is always disturbed by Elena's easy manipulation; sincerity and singularity are her anchor. In middle school she would not even take on a nickname, unlike her friends who called themselves "Sparkle" and "Candy" and "Monkey" and "Charley." But she believes in the notion of self as a singular essence, which should be consistent and correspond with all external expression.

All this has borne home to me how many ways language and other aspects of behavior are manipulated consciously as well as unconsciously in daily life. The metalinguistic behavior of Americans, as well as Chinese, is complex and ubiquitous. Parents decide what to say in front of their children. They coach them to say certain things and reprimand them for saying other things. They discuss what people said and attribute motives to them. When untruths are "necessary," they are grudgingly excused through appeal to a greater good. In China there is much less apology or need to excuse.

I also began the book expecting to excuse most of the behavior I witnessed in China, once I understood it and the principles on which it was based. This was partially an antidote to my own sometimes intense anger over instances of being lied to (some of which are described in various chapters). The inquiry was motivated by the dual motives of understanding why my own expectations about truthfulness were so often violated and of grasping why so often urban Han scorned the honesty of rural minorities. The intermediate position was to understand the principles, but my final position is that there are some social tendencies in some societies that cannot be embraced. American inequalities are unacceptable. Jewish smugness is unacceptable. Chinese manipulation of the innocent is unacceptable. So I end not accepting all that I describe, but with appreciation for the dangers and possibilities of human life.

In the introduction I promised that I would end with some observations about the strangeness of American practices. Many anthropologists find that the "culture shock" they experience at going to a new place and learning about its lifeways pales by comparison with what they experience at "returning home." If the cliché about not returning home again holds, then it is no wonder one cannot step unchanged back into the world one left. Yet the profundity of the shock at what some call "re-entry" goes beyond the mere fact that all experiences change us. Once we begin to see the world through the patterns we so painstakingly take on in order to grasp the consistencies of life elsewhere, they become a third nature (following the second nature of our own original culture patterns). (The idea of "second nature" gets at the sense that all culture begins to feel natural but is not.) Then it seems obvious, say, that daughters marry out and live with their husbands, or that shoes should be removed upon entering domestic or sacred spaces, or that strangers bumping into one another in crowded public spaces need not waste energy apologizing. The square thresholds that stick up and require a step to cross, the gauze masks that people wear to prevent inhalation of dust, the thick green glass bottles of yogurt that are returned to the vendors, all this begins to feel right in the body. And upon returning "home" they are missed. Why are huge slabs of meat served in the middle of a plate? Where are all the people who are usually outside? Why are homes and streets so big and empty? Supermarkets feel unnecessarily overwhelming and the vegetables in packages look like tasteless plastic. Choices of beverages at friends' houses seem designed to create the stress of too many decisions. Everything feels wrong and unnatural. The second nature of one's home culture is unmade.

So what have I learned about the strangeness of white middle-class northern American culture with regard to deception and truth?

My first and most overwhelming discovery lies in the contradictory beliefs held about truthfulness. There is a first-level approximation of morality that holds that one should always be truthful. As I have stated so often, though, this is mitigated by the grudging recognition that sometimes we have to bend the truth in order to protect people's feelings. Yet we do so with the discomfort that accompanies lack of honesty.

We are also quite hurt when we discover any sort of dishonesty. Our general expectation in going out into the world is that people will be truthful and honest and that deviation from that is shocking, wrong, and hurtful. Our naïveté strikes many people elsewhere as possibly sweet and childlike but also unbelievable and unrealistic.

Americans also see language as stemming from within bounded individuals without regard to other speakers and listeners. Our ideal model is a person of "integrity," which means refusal to be influenced, refusal to bend or compromise just for the opinion of others. In all circumstances we are to be the same because any change is seen as wishy-washy behavior and a sign of weak identity. Adolescents who change their manner depending on which group of friends is around are pitied; I don't know anyone who would willingly repeat that stage of life.

❧

The issue of lies is connected to the nature of language, in turn to questions of language origins. Language origins are usually approached from four dimensions: from study of cranial morphology (which parts of the brain were developed at what time; Bickerton 1990) or of the vocal tract (at what point could hominids have produced enough sounds to differentiate a minimal number of phonemes; Lieberman 1984); from study of art and tools and other symbolic behavior; and recently as an extension of grooming behavior in non-human primates (Byrne and Whiten 1988; Dunbar 1996; Goody 1995; Whiten and Byrne 1997). All these types of studies rely on their identification of a particular feature as central to human language:

Syntax (brain power for locus of deciphering)
Phonetics (brain and vocal tract)
Semantics (symbolic behavior)
Pragmatics (social meaning)

Yet all of them also assume that language is essentially a sequence of meaningful utterances created by individuals.

If one regards language as essentially interactive, then what matters are the relationships it creates among people. It is increasingly clear that human sociality is part of our nature. Not only do humans, like other mammals, need to interact in order to reproduce, but we need to live together, gossip together, and have some kind of meaningful, lasting bonds with others.

Dyadic relationships are not necessarily primary; humans may have needed group complexity to develop the tools to convey the subtlety of dominance and submission, of secrets and lies, of deceiving one set of people in deference to another. How to detect this in the fossil record is unclear; but it seems to me that the questions should precede the methods.

Given the power of humans to invent, and the pleasure of listening to stories, of hearing about the past and of dreaming about the future, of inventing gods and describing spiritual worlds, it could look as if most of what we do with language has little to do with telling the truth. Still, what compels us to do so, ever?

Psychoanalysts describe the development of the superego; developmental psychologists and psychological ethicists or specialists in morality tell us that an independent moral sense develops by approximately age ten or twelve. Many argue that it is impossible for children to detect or carry out lies until approximately five. This involves both the moral valence connected with truthfulness and the self-conscious manipulation of words for effect on an audience. In many ways this cannot be divorced from the other accomplishments of humans with language. Evolutionary biologists describe the changes in species between humans and our closest primate relatives as centering on human use of the symbol. If we can create meaning through connection between symbol and its referent, we can also dissociate them and use the symbols in different ways, so they point elsewhere (as the contemporary artist Xu Bing uses Chinese character-like images to convey a sense of meaninglessness). They can be directed primarily as a way of expressing an intention or as a way of accomplishing something completely different.

While information exchange is one effect of the use of language, there is also the willing suspension of disbelief that accompanies story telling, promises, and even things that are too good to be true. Eighteenth-century writer J. B. Mencke described how "the world wants to be deceived" (*mundus vult decipi*) as a way of explaining the easy audience for forgeries. None of this would be possible without the existence of symbols and the separability of symbols and their referents. The multilayered enterprise of forging a document involves taking words and representing them, then representing the representation, then the receiving public analyzes both the object and the way it was represented, imagining how it might have been produced, hidden, and found. The fact that forgers could be punished by severe sentences—in the past by hanging—shows that symbols are the very stuff of life for humans.

Taking China and the United States as in some ways opposed to each other in the ideology of language, we can see that misunderstandings could easily arise. If Americans enter an interaction with the assumption that speaking about themselves is the mark of a satisfying event, while Chinese expect that the interplay will require a certain amount of strenuous planning to respond, then it will be rare for such interactions to satisfy both parties.

In no way am I suggesting that truth does not matter. I am not saying that there is no such thing as truth; I do not advocate deception. But I am urging that we have a more truthful understanding of truth and deception, that we be less self-deceptive about how frequently we deceive and about its consequences. Truth and deception matter as much as the vows of marriage and as the love between parent and child. These are the very stuff of humanity, and these are what make us members of society. But just as kindness is sometimes more important than bluntness (Yes, you look terrible!), so many things must

be weighed at all times. A simple morality that says "Do not lie" does violence to the subtlety of human understanding; self-righteous injury of others
in the name of truth can be justified in one way but not in another.

But just as marriage and love are purely in the human realm, there are aspects of the world that are in the physical realm and thus unaffected by notions of identity, kindness, desire. While all science involves judgment and
models, some things really happen. Some actions are indeed real and true;
even in human terms there are incontrovertible facts. These are not usually
debatable. What *is* debatable is all the other stuff, the stuff that involves
weighing people's reactions, that takes power into account, that may be right
for one situation but wrong for another.

Beyond all that, our human capacity to play, to pun, to wiggle around with
truth-but-not-the-whole-truth, to anticipate and to entertain . . . whether
one's view is religious or biological, these are all part of our human nature.
All humans make these choices; surely it is better to know what we do rather
than to believe we do it for pure reasons. The greater self-consciousness of
the people I've studied in southwest China has shown me that a social complexity with regard to deception and truth may have positive results (in making people comfortable) or may have negative results (in forcing an entire society to play with the mask of agreement). Lies may bind us together, or lies
may oblige us to fail or to lose. We can find examples of both, and more, in
all societies.

Though some readers might, on first reflection, suggest that many Chinese
practices in the present are a consequence of fifty years of socialism, I have
shown that this claim requires investigation. I have demonstrated both continuities and discontinuities in the Chinese record. In the end, it adds up to
a view that suggests some peculiarities in Chinese practices, many peculiarities in Anglo-American practices, and many commonalities across all the
cultures mentioned. This should of course be the case. This anthropological
voyage between the United States and China and back again could serve as
a case study for any kind of human inquiry, and results in the same kind of
finding: in some ways we are all the same, and in intriguing ways we differ.
Humans are all entirely biological and entirely cultural. The balance between these facets can never be entirely ascertained. All humans lie, all humans deceive, and all humans require a kind of anchoring to physical and social reality. Where and how they do all those things is quite a story.

And that's the truth.

Notes

1. In fact I also believe that an American ideology of language that focuses on truth is also similarly misguided—but that is a topic for another time.

2. See Fingarette 1972 for an accessible discussion of how spontaneity may be produced through practice.

3. David Callahan argues the same thing about the United States in his book *The Cheating Culture: Why More Americans are Doing Wrong to Get Ahead* (2004).

APPENDIX

Theoretical Foundations
and Implications

Truth isn't outside power, or lacking in power: contrary to a myth whose history and functions would repay further study, truth isn't the reward of free spirits, the child of protracted solitude, nor the privilege of those who have succeeded in liberating themselves. Truth is a thing of this world: it is produced only by virtue of multiple forms of constraint. And it induces regular effects of power. Each society has its régime of truth, its "general politics" of truth: that is, the types of discourse which it accepts and makes function as true; the mechanisms and instances which enable one to distinguish true and false statements, the means by which each is sanctioned; the techniques and procedures accorded value in the acquisition of truth; the status of those who are charged with saying what counts as true.

—Michel Foucault 1980

All grammars leak.

—Edward Sapir 1921

This book is one of a number of anti-Gricean critiques of universal pragmatics (see, e.g., Wierzbicka 2003) but is more anthropological than linguistic. While I share Wierzbicka's lament over Grice's superficial claims about human needs, it is important to consider whether at another level there are in fact shared communicative goals. Understanding how and why humans deceive must be situated within the largest understanding of what it is to be human—a framework that necessitates recalling humans' nature as biological beings related to other beings.

This book essentially takes a pragmatic look at language, but it also looks at "language ideology" or what I consider more appropriate, "the ontology of language." There are countless approaches to the study of truth, deception, and lies, but because the real insight here comes from observing and interacting with people, listening to their jokes and hearing about their fears, the theories matched up only after the experience. My ultimate target is my own starting point—the U.S. view of language as an optimally pure and context-free vehicle for truth that Michael Silverstein terms the "semantico-referential" language ideology.

In this appendix, I present semantic approaches to truth and lying, focusing on meaning and intention, the relations of language to the world, and pragmatic approaches to deception and truth, focusing on power and efficacy, relations of language to its context. A short consideration of human nature and the nature of language is followed by discussion of politeness, sincerity, authenticity, and intention. My final thoughts are concerned with the ontology of language.

Truth and Lying: Semantic Approaches

Semantic approaches to the question of truth and lying ask, essentially, what things *mean*. Truth is at the core of most of Western philosophy and is in many ways central to Christian theology. Aristotle's *correspondence theory of truth* defines truth as when the words spoken correspond to the reality that they describe. Plato's *social theory of truth*, and one that is very current now in the (postmodern) social scientific studies of the connection of knowledge to power, suggests that those with superior social positions have the right to determine truth. The correspondence theory of truth is sometimes attacked because it presupposes a single, objective reality that stands outside and prior to any expression or interaction.

"Truth" has been discredited from many directions. Postmodernists, feminists, and Foucaultians all critique claims to objectivity, master narratives, and regimes of truth. If knowledge is power, then claims to have knowledge of the truth—transcendent, objective, universal, panchronic, biological, scientific—obscures others' rights to their own truths. Powerful social sectors often claim to possess the truth (the "social theory of truth"); how truth claims serve power, often in religion, economy, politics, and science, is a central question for some anthropologists, but these are pragmatic concerns.

Philosophy

A structuralist perspective builds higher units on lower ones; in issues of truth, structuralists focus primarily on word and sentence meaning. Word meaning is often said to derive from a correspondence between word and thing. Most commonly invoked examples are of tangible "things," such as nouns or verbs, but the meanings of some abstractions are much discussed and often translated into "logical operators," the quasi-mathematical symbols used in symbolic logic.

Sentence meaning is focused on the truth conditions that would make it correspond with the facts of the world.[1] In strictest logical terms, the meaning of sentences was taken to equal their "truth value" in philosophy's effort to emulate mathematics, as in the work of Bertrand Russell and others. Then the truth conditions could be explored. One starting point for analytic philosophers is Tarski's definition of truth, which is as follows: For a sentence p, where X is the name of the sentence, X is true if, and only if, p (Tarski 1956). Such a model of language regards meaning as a one-to-one correspondence between the elements of speech and logical operators, and its use in context as entirely irrelevant.

If truth is equated with meaning, and in turn with reference, then words that have no referent present problems. It is impossible to determine the truth conditions of a sentence like "The king of France is bald" if there is no king of France. Yet it is also counterintuitive to claim that it is meaningless. Questions, similarly, pose a problem: If meaning is truth conditions, are questions true or false? Davis (1991, 5) describes "answer conditions" as the possible answers to questions and the equivalent of truth conditions for statements.

Other philosophical arguments revolve around the so-called liar's paradox and evaluation of the statement "I am lying." Either the statement is false, in the sense that the speaker is not lying (but then misstating), or it is true, which would lead to a judgment of lying (see, e.g., Barwise and Etchemendy 1987; Yaqūb 1993). This inherently self-contradictory utterance has occupied thinkers for some time.

Law

Life in society is filled with non-truth, whether economic deception or medical practice or words among friends. One source of protection against such dangers is legal. All societies have mechanisms for managing conflict, whether or not through an independent institution of law. The American legal system attempts, overall, to ascertain the facts of a case and, ultimately, to achieve justice. We have contracts, implicit guidelines for behavior, and, if all else fails, a system of civil and criminal courts. This may require repayment or punishment, with several, sometimes incompatible goals (deterrence, rehabilitation, retribution). The relationship between the law and truth is complex. Perjury itself is punishable. Witnesses "swear" or "affirm" their allegiance to the truth. In the evolution of Anglo-American legal thought, "pathology replaces evil" (Kaplan 1995, 120). It is no longer merely behavior that matters but the "mental promptings that lie behind a crime." The "intentions" (*mens rea*) of those who commit crimes are considered in assigning appropriate punishment.

In the 1980s, legal theorists were inspired by literary and other critics to acknowledge the socially constructed nature of human action. In this view, many concepts are neither true nor false, but merely believed in by society. A book criticizing critical legal studies called *Beyond All Reason: The Radical Assault on Truth in American Law* (Farber and Sherry 1997) portrays the battle as one between those who hold a belief in singular reason, as in the Enlightenment, and those who see all truth claims as multiple and therefore as all equally valid (postmodern). These authors despair at what they see as conflation of three types of truth, involving recall of events:

1. "If you had been watching, this is what you would have seen."
2. "The situation might not have looked this way to you, but this is how it felt to me."
3. "The situation didn't feel this way to me at the time, but this is how it seems to me now." (Farber and Sherry 1997, 97)

Thus they accept only the first, semantic, notion of truth. They criticize "radicals" for their "casual attitude toward truth," citing the well-publicized case of a young African American woman, Tawana Brawley, who eventually admitted having fabricated an accusation of brutal rape by a group of white men. Farber and Sherry quote from several writers who claim that the actual facts did not matter; she *could* have been the victim of such a crime. Akin to the Freudian debates about the seduction theory (see below), analysts differ greatly in terms of how they judge the truth of the case. The law, however, retains a hard-line view of fact. The accused were acquitted.

Lying

Lying is usually considered from ethical and moral vantages rather than analytically. All theologians address it. Augustine's first essay on lying, *De Mendacio* (Lying), from around the year 395, was actually a letter addressing a dispute with Jerome about the interpretation of an event in Galatians 2, concerning whether lying for a good purpose was ever justified (Deferrari 1952, 47–49). His second essay, *Contra Mendacium* (Against Lying), from around 420 (again originally a letter) was written when Catholics were posing as the heretical sect of Priscillianists who masked all evidence of their heresy—thus using lies to catch liars. Augustine viewed all lying as a mortal sin; rather than risk one's eternal life, one must be willing to sacrifice one's mortal soul. "Since . . . eternal life is lost by lying, a lie may never be told for the preservation of the temporal life of another" (Augustine 1952b, 67). Further, "by truth must we guard against lies, by truth catch them, and by truth wipe them out" (Augustine 1952a, 139). Augustine's view is that language is given by God and any misuse of one of God's gifts is an extreme sin. Augustine discusses lying with admirable subtlety, taking the clearest case of lying to be "a false statement made with the desire to deceive" (Augustine 1952b, 60) but acknowledging other kinds of lies as well.

"The heart of a liar is said to be double, that is, two-fold in its thinking; one part consisting of that knowledge which he knows or thinks to be true, yet does not so express it; the other part consisting of that knowledge which he knows or thinks to be false, yet expresses as true" (Augustine 1952b, 55). He discusses all the typical hard cases with great subtlety: saving a life, easing the psychological burden of a terminally ill person, scriptural lies in the Hebrew Bible, and polite lies. The last type is rejected as harmful to the teller of the lie, "because they prefer to please their auditors rather than to reverence truth" (Augustine 1952b, 79). "There are many kinds of lies, all of which, indeed, we should detest uniformly" (Augustine 1952a, 129).

Following Augustine closely, Kant gives the famous apparently obvious example: If a murderer coming to murder one's family asks if there is anyone in the house, it would be simple to lie and save them. But Kant argues that this would save only their mortal, not immortal, souls, so the good person must answer truthfully. Kant opposed any nonce justifications for using lying "just this time." Despite good intentions and desirable consequences, the lies are denounced.

Psychoanalysis

Seeking illumination about deception from psychoanalysis, we need to recall two of its most basic assumptions: that nothing is ever completely forgotten, and that events or feelings must be processed. Failure to come to terms with trauma, often stemming from repression, leads to various afflictions, from tics to anxiety to sexual misfortunes, to dreams and slips of the tongue (Freud 1999 [1901]), to psychosis. In this sense, truth will out, no matter how much effort is expended in avoiding or suppressing it. Much of the evidence for repression is verbal, though some is also physical. A primary goal of therapeutic treatment is to uncover the past and its truth and to make sense of it. Freud said that his "single motive was the love of truth" (Thompson 1994, 1)—though he never explicitly discussed truth in his own writings. The traditional Freudian view is that truth will be recovered. Further, there are aspects of the real that are fantastic, and there are ways that people sometimes lie to themselves even while they desire the truth.

If the central question in psychoanalysis is that of truth, and if analysts are supposed to guide patients toward truth through their own greater insight, an event that occurred several decades ago shows some of the irony of assuming this can be done.

In 1983, a scandal erupted in psychoanalytic circles. Janet Malcolm of the *New Yorker* claimed that Jeffrey Moussaieff Masson, at that time the keeper of the Freud archives, had lied about his actions. The crux of the matter was a key element of psychoanalysis and of Freud's, the master's, method—the idea that dreadful, traumatic events were repressed but could be retrieved through careful guidance. Freud's earliest writings, evident in material contained in the archives, show that he believed that the sexual assault had occurred; his later writings, which formed the basis of psychoanalysis, renounced that view and claimed that most women only fantasized about the incest, as symptoms of their own sexual urges and conflicted emotions regarding sexuality and their fathers (Malcolm 1984 [1983]).

In *The Assault on Truth* (1984), Masson claimed that Freud's seduction theory, the idea that real sexual abuse lay at the core of many patients' neuroses, had not only been abandoned by Freud in favor of the idea that these were fantasies, but also was covered up by the keepers of the Freud archives, who sought to maintain a certain image of Freud. Masson believed that Anna Freud, the daughter and disciple of Sigmund Freud, covered it up on the grounds that "since her father eventually abandoned the seduction theory, she felt it would only prove confusing to readers to be exposed to his early hesitations and doubts." Masson, in contrast, "felt that these passages not only were of great historical importance, they might well represent the truth" (Masson 1984, xvii). Masson's book demonstrates case after case of apparent cover-up of truth.

Masson demonstrated that Freud was troubled by the seduction theory all his life. When Masson made this public, he was dismissed from his position in the Freud archives for showing bad judgment—but not for falsification. His disgust with psychoanalysis grew to the point that he abandoned it and now writes (very successful) books about the emotional life of animals.

In her account of this series of events, *In the Freud Archives* (1984), Malcolm portrays Masson as an arrogant, manipulative self-promoter who deceived many, including Anna Freud, about his motives. Malcolm's dismissive treatment of Masson provides details that suggest he is a flake and a liar, and soon after Malcolm's account, Masson was essentially excommunicated from the psychoanalytic world.

Masson sued Malcolm for libel. Though she had much evidence, she was unable to produce tapes of every quotation she had used in her book. Ultimately she won the suit, but as Seligman (2000) points out, she has earned a reputation for ruthlessness. At the same time, Malcolm shows how disappointed and embarrassed the analysts were at their own failure to detect, if not literal deception, then possible imposture, in their own midst. Both Masson and Malcolm argue that their version is the truth and that the other holds a deliberately erroneous position.

I recount this controversy at some length—and examples could be multiplied endlessly, though this one has some nice ironies—because it shows how bloody arguments about truth can be; notwithstanding claims that our world is mired in relativism, disputes about truth and deception can ruin people's lives. A decade-later meditation on the libel suit brought against Malcolm by Masson has the enticing leading line: "In her relentless pursuit of the truth she's left a few bodies in her wake, but isn't that part of a journalist's job?" (Seligman 2000).

In the 1990s a trend arose in which some practitioners of psychotherapy claimed to be able to retrieve suppressed memories of trauma, usually sexual abuse. Thousands of people reported discoveries about betrayal from loved ones. Opponents of "retrieved memory" argue that the memories claimed are only apparent and that they are false introductions by interested, partisan therapists who stand to gain from the trauma (Crews 1990). In 2002 the scandals of the Catholic Church in the United States, in which hundreds of priests were accused of sexual harassment (making unwanted sexual advances on children, mostly boys), had similar features. One psychiatrist appointed to the lay board to investigate was a frequent debunker of retrieved memory— a fact that led some to accuse the Church of stacking the deck against the accusers. In any case, the matter of truth lies at the heart of the case.

Psychology

More mainstream psychological views of lying suggest that there are physical costs to lying; such things can be measured, it is assumed, by stress and its signs: sweating, changes in heart rate, and so forth. The polygraph, or lie detector, assumes that there is truth and there are lies and that the difference between them is measurable. Though most courts do not permit the use of polygraph evidence and a study released in October 2002 by the National Research Council (National Academy of Sciences) demonstrated its non-effectiveness, its use is widely urged. When JonBenet Ramsey was murdered in Boulder in December 1996, in conversations in Colorado people frequently mentioned that her parents refused to take lie detector tests, which was taken as a sure sign of their guilt. (Sullivan [2001, 189–210] has a delightful spoof of lie detectors, which she presents as a patented item, "The APEX Truth Meter®.")

Academic psychologists often share the assumptions of their society. One study demonstrated researchers' astonishment that people not only lie when asked to perform self-introductions but deny that they do so (Feldman, Forrest, and Happ 2002). The disappointed expectations about the truthfulness of self-presentations must be explained here because the assumption is that they will not occur, and that utter truthfulness is usually found.

The prominent expert on the psychology of lying, Paul Ekman, pioneered an approach to the study of lying and other actions with emotional components, the Facial Action Coding System (FACS), that is now studied and employed around the world (Ekman and Rosenberg 1997). The basic premise is that facial expressions reveal inner emotion, and that all these can be considered universal and incontrovertible.[2]

Ekman has claimed that he is able to detect lies from looking at a speaker's face (2001). He also admits in an earnest personal book, *Why Kids Lie*, that in his own family he was totally oblivious to his son's surreptitious convening of a party when Ekman and his wife were away (1989). (Here the lie was one of omission or deception, rather than the outright telling of a bald-faced lie.) Still, the basic claim is that (1) lies are identifiable without too much difficulty and (2) lies must be detected one way or another.

Certain expressions on faces reveal tension, which is caused by knowing that there is a mismatch between one's true intention and one's words. The strain of feeling one thing and saying another, according to this view, is evident in physical signs such as asymmetrical facial expressions, pupil dilation, and blushing or blanching.

The research is painstaking and very creative, relying on innovative methods such as asking volunteers to watch films either with the belief that they are alone or that they are being videotaped, and comparing their expressions with their reported emotion; some are asked to express and others to repress their true feelings. Still, as all philosophers of science know, basic concepts are often born from the cultural soil in which they are cultivated; scientists such as Paul Ekman assume that there are "genuine smiles," "phony smiles," and "masking smiles" (Ekman, Friesen, and O'Sullivan 1997 [1988]), among other types.

In a strikingly more subtle view, the sociologist Arlie Hochschild has shown in her brilliant research on flight attendants, *The Managed Heart* (1983), that smiles may be genuine yet caused by a great deal of what might look like propagandistic influence on the part of airlines. In the 1970s and 1980s, flight attendants, mostly women, attended training seminars where they were given tools to rethink how they regarded belligerent passengers; they were taught that "smiles" that are "genuine" were their greatest asset, and huge amounts of time and money were invested to persuade these work-ers to *mean* it when they smiled.[3]

The question of the "genuineness" and the individuality of emotion has been a fertile subject for psychological anthropologists since the 1980s. Dif-ferent societies conceptualize emotion differently; sometimes they see emo-tion as arising from the body (Rosaldo 1984) and sometimes as arising from interaction and situation (Lutz 1988), not necessarily as individual and spon-taneous. When a widow cries at a funeral, are all her tears genuine, or are some expected by the guests? Ritual wailing is commonly found in many so-cieties, in which a specific contour of the voice is common to all mourning (Urban 1991); is this genuine, even if it has a cultural and social shape?

This question about the real or true underlies much of the psychological research on lying. I believe that much of it is culturally bounded by assump-tions that researchers have never thought to examine, no matter how thoughtful they are. And the very concept of *culture* or social variation is never raised.

The semantic approaches to truth and lying are essentially the position with which I began this study, and the one against which I argue. In contrast, I end with a pragmatic understanding. Pragmatic approaches come largely from Speech Act Theory, politics and business, and from studies of ethology and human development that place humans in a broad biological context. These approaches ask what language *does*, in contrast to semantic approaches that ask what language *means*.

Deception and Truth: Pragmatic Approaches

Speech Act Theory
Speech Act Theory comes from the work of so-called ordinary language philosophers such as J. L. Austin, John Searle, Paul Grice, and the later Wittgenstein. They pointed out some of the peculiar ways language behaves, in which truth is either irrelevant or apparently flouted. J. L. Austin's series

of lectures on what he called "performatives" (1975 [1962]) pointed out first that there was a class of declarative sentences in English that are neither true nor false because they do not describe a set of facts about the world. Rather they enact those facts; by uttering them, the speaker brings about such a state of affairs. These are sentences such as "I christen the ship the *Queen Elizabeth*" or "I promise I'll take out the trash." These sentences are evaluated on the basis of their "felicity conditions" or whether the antecedent conditions that make such events occur are adhered to. If a person without the standing to christen a ship were to utter the first sentence, she would not thereby christen the ship; if the promiser did not sincerely intend to carry out the promise, then the promise would not in fact have been made.

In the end, Austin's analysis leads to the conclusion that all sentences are in some way performatives and the kinds of sentences that constitute the core of most philosophical analysis—those that describe a state of affairs—are a special subset of all possible sentences (constatives).

John Searle then attempted to classify all sentences into a number of categories (this varies in his several treatments of this topic), usually on the basis of their intention (Searle 1969). It was clear that the intended force (illocutionary force) and actual effect (perlocutionary force) of sentences did not always resemble their grammatical form (locutionary form), so that questions could function as commands and statements could function as questions, etc. This body of literature demonstrates powerfully that language *does* things and is not primarily descriptive of the world. This pragmatic view of language attends to the practical accomplishments of language in a real social world and context.

Paul Grice also made some striking observations about the way language functions in actual human interactions. He pointed out that we often draw conclusions about speakers' meaning (intention) from a set of interactions between context and utterance. He called these conclusions "conversational implicature" since they are like "implication" but require a kind of inferential work to uncover them. In trying to figure out how speakers did this, he argued that speakers began with a *cooperative principle*, which says basically that all other things being equal, speakers are inclined to cooperate with one another. (I do not think this holds in public life in China.) Below this big principle are four maxims:

Quantity
1. Make your contribution as informative as is required (for the current purposes of the exchange).
2. Do not make your contribution more informative than is required.

Quality
(supermaxim:) Try to make your contribution one that is true.

1. Do not say what you believe to be false.
2. Do not say that for which you lack adequate evidence.

Relation
1. Be relevant.

Manner
(supermaxim:) Be perspicuous.

1. Avoid obscurity of expression.
2. Avoid ambiguity.
3. Be brief (avoid unnecessary prolixity).
4. Be orderly. (Grice 1989, 26–27)

These were intended by Grice to mimic the assumptions hearers brought to interactions, where sometimes there were apparent violations of the maxims. If Allison says, "When did you come home last night?" and Brittany answers, "I really like the movie version of *Harry Potter*," it is an apparent breach of the maxim of relevance. But wait! Allison assumes that Brittany was still being cooperative, so that Brittany is trying to be informative about something that Allison did not know about. Perhaps it was a warning that Allison's husband, whom Allison was attempting to deceive, had just appeared behind Allison's back and Brittany was trying to convey a message that the subject should be changed. Grice's maxims have led to very subtle analyses of linguistic pragmatics and have led beyond a consideration of truth as the core of linguistic meaning. Grice's maxims also reveal a number of assumptions about Anglo-American society that do not necessarily hold for other communicative systems (see, e.g., Keenan 1976). Grice's work has led to work on politeness of Penelope Brown and Stephen Levinson, and to critiques of that work as blind to effects of culture by Elinor Ochs Keenan, Emily Martin Ahern, Michelle Rosaldo, Alessandro Duranti, and Anna Wierzbicka, among many others.

Linguistic Anthropology
The claims of philosophical and psychological approaches to truth and deception are usually universalistic. They tend to rely on introspection, case studies in laboratories and clinics, and anecdotal evidence from Western

cultures. In contrast to these perspectives—or perhaps, better, supplementing them—linguistic anthropologists use observations from field sites often located elsewhere and begin with the assumption that common-sense understandings of how language works might not be accurate. One of the earliest anthropological observations of language in use was made by Bronislaw Malinowski, who pointed out that an informational perspective on language did not account for the uses he observed in the Trobriand Islands. In his important paper "The Problem of Meaning in Primitive Languages" (1923), he coined the term *phatic communion* to account for the informationally empty talk that appeared to dominate daily life. Examples of phatic communion are greetings and talking about the weather. A number of linguistic anthropologists and sociologists such as Erving Goffman, Michael Silverstein, Duranti, and more take a pragmatic, practice-oriented, or performative approach. It is this approach that animates the present work.

Politics and Business

The abstract and absolute nature of many theological and philosophical treatments of truth contrasts dramatically with most of the political literature on lying and deception. The classic case is that of Niccolò Machiavelli, author of *The Prince*, who wrote what is considered a sort of tutorial for those who would rule. Scruples about such fastidious matters as truth were obstacles in the pursuit of power. Similarly, many more recent accounts of political life admit that lying and deception are part and parcel of the nature of public life in the modern world (see Anderson 1994; Barnes 1994; Bowyer 1982; Bailey 1991; Chu 1991; Nyberg 1993; *Success* 1994; *Time* 1992; *Utne Reader* 1992; Weaver 1994). Accounts of lying in business, in journalism, in politics, and in war show that despite a more general view of the immorality of lying and deception, these are expected in certain domains.

Ekman, for example, recalls President Jimmy Carter's categorical denial of any rescue mission in Iran precisely at the moment this mission was being carried out in 1980 (2001, 304–6). Ekman considers this lie justified because of its goals. At the same time, cynicism has its limits. There is often widespread distaste for such practices. In early 2002 the government of George W. Bush attempted to intervene with governments elsewhere by establishing essentially an office of disinformation ("Office of Strategic Influence" at the Pentagon), modeled on World War II and Vietnam experiences, through which they would plant false, misleading stories in the foreign press in order to influence foreign opinion in ways beneficial to U.S. interests. The outcry from the public and politicians of the opposing party forced this office to be shut down—at least as far as anyone knows!

Lying in politics is expected, yet if it happens in a certain way it can become a public issue and can lead to serious consequences. Richard Nixon and Bill Clinton are two American presidents who are often charged with lying excessively, the former about matters of international policy and the latter about his personal life. George W. Bush is about to join them. One writer claims that we now live in a "post-truth era" (Keyes 2004). The role of journalists is, in theory, to seek the truth, knowing that many politicians lie (see, e.g., Schechter 2004). The United States appeared briefly to have grown weary of such accounts; for a time people scarcely seem appalled when it was evident that public figures and writers lied (Dowd 2006a). Then a barrage of attacks on the idea of "truthiness" defended truth (Dowd 2006b; Kakutani 2006; Karr 2006; New York Times 2006; Rich 2006; Wyatt 2006a, 2006b).

Business is another domain in which certain expectations about truthfulness hold. Used cars are known as a typical enterprise of potential cheating, though of course buyers always hope to outsmart sellers. Folklorist/linguistic anthropologist Richard Bauman (1996) shows that everybody going to buy or sell dogs at certain kinds of markets in Texas knows that the exchanges between seller and buyer are filled with hyperbole and feint. The fun—and this is one of the goals of these events—comes in the cleverness with which such exchanges are constructed.

Savvy consumers do not regard advertising as truthful (Lutz 1989). When a company alleges that its products can improve one's appearance and lead to happiness, or solve one's laundry problems and gain admiration, most consumers take it with a grain of salt. We rely on watchdog agencies, such as Consumers Union, to protect consumers, understood to require and deserve such protection from the temptation of false claims by those who sell or advertise. This debate about truthfulness in advertising goes back quite a long time. Lionel Trilling points out that the first meaning of *sincere* was pure, clean, and unadulterated, as in wine (1972, 12–13). Similarly, the first advertisements for produced foods (rather than fruits and vegetables) such as canned foods and spices in the late eighteenth and early nineteenth centuries were careful to proclaim their purity—because it was so difficult for consumers to know what the products consisted of (Goody 1997).

These more pragmatic considerations of truth and deception revolve around an implicit understanding that those who come to such interactions must beware. *Caveat emptor* declares the ancient Roman bromide. Buyers *are* wary; economic life involves a competitive game with producers attempting to give as little as possible, consumers attempting to gain as much as possible, and each walking a fine line between truthfulness and duplicity. Yet this too could vary across cultures. Small-scale, face-to-face societies bring knowledge of individuals' histories to each encounter. People known to cheat can scarcely succeed in relying on others' trust, as they can in contemporary fraud-filled China (see chapter 4).

Truth and Power

Totalitarian, authoritarian, autocratic, and often religious regimes in the Western world have staked their claims on the basis of possession of the truth, even while they have enormous apparatuses devoted to keeping the truth from ordinary people. Garry Wills's book *Papal Sin: Structures of Deceit* (2000) laments the deliberate maintenance of hypocritical or actually duplicitous positions of Catholic popes in the domains of saints, history, and doctrine. All popes have had massive entourages devoted to shaping public consumption of the image that is conveyed—often reminiscent of the Chinese Communist Party's concern with propaganda, and more recently of the Bush administration's lock on public statements about the war on Iraq. Speeches are shaped to package the truth as it is to be received by the innocent flock. This chasm, Wills argues, accounts for the trouble in the American Catholic church and can only be narrowed if the popes are more honest about their own actions and positions.

In South Africa, Argentina, East Timor, Sierra Leone, and elsewhere, "Truth and Reconciliation" inquiries attempt to redress wrongs committed by earlier regimes, in which the aim is to air the deeds and to allow public hearing and consequently healing. "Truth" here means several different things, not all of which are always differentiated. Merely naming such bodies thus has rhetorical force. The sophisticated musings on "truth" in the South African commission's report acknowledge how difficult it is to be certain of truth yet how crucial it is to try to approach it (see Truth and Reconciliation Commission 2002). They demonstrate awareness of the paradoxical danger in opening up facts and ardently hoping nonetheless for reconciliation, in part by admitting that there are four kinds of truth that they must consider:

> factual or forensic truth
> personal and narrative truth
> social truth
> healing and restorative truth

Quite in contrast to the first level of truth, which resembles the semantic approaches discussed earlier, the three subsequent aspects of truth are all contextual and social, requiring attention to the process of procuring the truths. In sharp contrast to Western legal, philosophical, and theological notions of truth, but also disputing an entirely subjective view of truth, these commissions attend to the pragmatic consequences of the truth.[4]

Battles over truthfulness in public and religious life are often quite interesting. The Inquisition provides an exemplary case: there were some truths that were going to be uncovered, no matter what the alleged perpetrators claimed. Those in power were said to know, and it was a matter of the confessors confessing to their sins and crimes. Torture might be required to obtain the final willingness to extract those confessions, perhaps because of a devilish insistence on unsupportable innocence. The inquisitors knew better; for the immortal good of their interrogatees, they had to urge them to the final moment of confession, so that they could be punished and therefore absolved (Le Roy Ladurie 1978). So knowledge of truth accompanies power. The innocent humble individuals did not know their own sins and had to be led to find them.

Much the same thing can be observed in China's Cultural Revolution, where "truth" was at the center of many battles. Memoirs of this period, especially written by intellectuals (Cheng 1986; Gao 1987, etc.), show the suffering of those forced to confess to thoughts and deeds that they either had not had or that should have produced no such punishment. At the same time, the Party and its leaders claimed to know what was really true; it was only a matter of time and willingness before the people followed.

Ethology and Evolution

To put human deception into its evolutionary context and to understand its role in human nature, scientists study deception in non-humans.

Animal and even plant behavior includes a number of forms that students of human behavior might never consider: camouflage, mimicry ("Batesian mimicry"), decoying, birds' dive-bombing, singing two or more different songs to give the impression that more birds are present, fireflies' mimicry of other species' signals in order to eat them, fish adoption of stripes of other fish, puffing up to appear bigger. These all have the effect of confusing or misleading predators, and are in some sense deceptive, if not lying.

Analysts distinguish levels of deceptive behavior on the basis of control, intention, and awareness (Mitchell 1986). First-level deception is entirely involuntary (as when fish develop camouflaging stripes to match the background); second-level deception is not voluntary but responds to the presence of other beings; third-level deception is learned (as when dogs feign limping in order to receive solicitude from their owners) but does not require a theory on the actor's part of observers' mental reactions; fourth-level deception is intentional and requires a strategy dependent on views of receivers' likely reactions and responses (a "theory of mind"). Chimpanzees have been observed to practice this level of deception, as when one leads a group to a site as if a supply of food were there, only to run to the actual food source and enjoy it alone (Cheney and Seyfarth 1990; de Waal 1986; Quiatt 1984).

De Waal classifies five types of deceptive behavior in captive chimpanzees, in natural communication: (1) camouflage, (2) feigning interest, (3) feigning a mood, (4) signal correction, and (5) falsification (1986, 226). Certainly these are all familiar in human behavior, though camouflage shares more with other animals. What is evident in the behaviors he describes is the significant degree of control the chimps exercise over their behavior and physical actions. Though primatologists have been reluctant to posit deliberate, premeditated, planned actions, de Waal argues that the existence of such deliberate thinking may be required for accurate scientific accounts of ape behavior. (All this tentativeness is a corrective to the sentimental anthropomorphizing that preceded the current wave of primate studies.)[5]

One of the goals of much of the literature on primates and deception is to demonstrate that they "think" and have the ability to plan, predict, and "outfox" others, ultimately to demonstrate intentionality, which means manipulation of mental states, not just behavior (Mitchell and Thompson 1986a, 203).

Human Development

Ethological and evolutionary perspectives are sometimes combined with developmental psychological treatments of when children move from third- to fourth-level deception, when they are able to master lying themselves, and when they are able to predict others' responses (Chandler and Hala 1991; Chevalier-Skolnikoff 1986; Eck 1970; Feldman and Philippot 1991; Peterson 1991). Children younger than approximately five often accuse others of "lying" when in fact they have made a mistake. Only at around ten years can children differentiate between "authentic" and "polite" smiles (Bugental, Kopeikin, and Lazowski 1991) or produce convincing but false facial expressions (Feldman and Philippot 1991).

The ability to lie demonstrates sophisticated skill: "[T]o lie successfully, one must have knowledge of another's knowledge and beliefs, recognize the information required to sway the beliefs of the listener, and communicate such that this information, rather than information which suggests one's intent to deceive, is passed on" (Vasek 1986, 287). This requires the ability to take the perspective of another person ("theory of mind"). Motives for deceiving are myriad, from the instrumental wish to avoid punishment or obtain desired ends to the fun of deceiving (pretending) in games and play.

Human Nature and the Nature of Language

Evolutionary psychologists and others who wish to explain human behavior as having evolved to meet the goals of physical and genetic survival often point to the advantage gained when proto-humans gained the ability to use language. One of the principal aspects of human language that sets it apart from the communicative systems of other species is its ability to fabricate and to persuade by means of a decontextualized set of symbols (Hockett 1960). Linguist Charles Hockett wrote originally of "displacement" as a key feature of human language and later added "prevarication" as one of the essential aspects of our linguistic system (Hockett 1966, 12–13). Along with our ability to use sets of symbols comes the development of attentiveness to others around us and an understanding of their understanding (Dunbar 1996). "Theory of mind" is the term given to this ability; humans above the age of four or five possess it, as do the great apes, but it appears that monkeys lack this quality. Hence, something about "theory of mind" is crucial in the development of the ability to deceive and lie.

Research on "Machiavellian intelligence," the concept that human and other primates are motivated primarily by social interactions and manipulations of others, emphasizes social complexity and interaction rather than individual capacity. Any theory of language origins must go beyond the semantic understanding of the role of language to the pragmatic. A deep understanding of how and why people deceive and lie must occupy a central place in any discussion of the nature of human language (Byrne and Whiten 1988; Goody 1995; Whiten and Byrne 1997)—and the nature of humans.

Pragmatic approaches to truth frequently address the issue of intention, as meaning is sometimes assumed to come from a speaker's intention as well as from social context. Many factors are involved in discerning a match between intention and expression. Questions of politeness and other manifestations of genuine or false respect have occupied a number of scholars.

Politeness, Sincerity, Authenticity: Intention

In studies of language, the term "politeness" has a particular meaning, partially overlapping with the common-sense, ordinary meanings of the term. It involves expressions or intonation or vocabulary that indicate deference to the hearer or diminution of the speaker. Examples of this include titles used for superiors ("Professor Brown"), euphemisms used with elders in contrast to the stark terms used with peers ("I have to use the restroom" versus "I'm going to pee"), the couching of requests in refusable questions ("Could I please have some help?"), and other ways of permitting a hearer to refuse things. Since Penelope Brown and Steven Levinson's groundbreaking study of this phenomenon in 1978, there have been many studies of the linguistic correlates of politeness.

Striking similarities across societies are evident; for example, polite ways of speaking are often longer than direct or less polite expressions. "Excuse me, could you please tell me what time it is?" is more polite than "Tell me the time!" and many languages/societies exhibit similar phenomena. Some languages, such as Japanese and Javanese, institutionalize politeness with what is called a "politeness register"; Japanese *keigo* includes prefixes for nouns, particular nouns used only when being deferential, verb endings, pronouns, and ways of being indirect. The three levels of speech in Javanese (*krama*, "high"; *madya*, "middle"; and *ngoko* "low") differentiate status primarily through vocabulary differences (Romaine 2000, 21).

The primary measure of politeness in European languages comes from pronouns and the verbs corresponding to them, such as distinguishing between the polite (and plural) second-person *vous* or *Usted* or *Sie* (in French, Spanish, and German, respectively) and the familiar (and singular) *tu*, *tu*, and *du*. English formerly had such a distinction as well, retained in vestiges of old English such as *thee* and *thou* and *ye* and *you*. (See Brown and Gilman 1960 for the authoritative account of the prevalence of *you*.) Chinese pronouns do not include such distinctions; the pronoun *nin*, which is considered the polite second-person pronoun, is available but little used. Pronoun use is much less ubiquitous in Chinese in general than in Indo-European languages; for the greatest politeness, as in Japanese, pronouns are avoided (Blum 1997). A sentence addressed to a teacher uses the noun/title *Laoshi*, instead of the second-person pronoun. *Laoshi de shijian yiding youxian ba.* "The teacher's time is undoubtedly limited" or "You [teacher] undoubtedly have very little time."

In Chinese the term *keqihua*, polite talk, is used to indicate the sometimes "insincere" phrases used prototypically by guests (literally *keqihua* means "talking in the manner of a guest"), whose role is to flatter, demur, and praise the host's efforts. (Guests are in a position of debt once they have accepted hospitality, which makes them to some extent the inferiors in relationships. See Yan 1996; Yang 1994.)

Politeness in the United States is regarded with ambivalence. When I teach students to analyze conversations by looking at turn taking, they are amazed and sometimes offended by what they consider "interruptions" but which Tannen (1981, 1989) and other conversation analysts term "overlap." In white middle-class midwestern politeness norms, "good listening" requires one speaker to finish before the next begins. When speakers overlap too much, they are considered offensive and self-centered. At the same time, expression of interest requires some overlap and participation in the conversation. A conversation consisting entirely of "polite" phrases is seen as unsatisfying, as if the speakers are unwilling to give anything of themselves.

The politeness of educated urban people in China acting with people they do not know intimately—but not strangers—requires at minimum the attempt to give face to the other by diminishing oneself ("How's business?" "Oh, business is fair.") and elevating the other ("You have been to so many places and I've been to so few."). In the African American verbal play genres known as the dozens, signifying, and marking, turn taking similarly requires attention to the other, and is not merely a stage for sincere self-expression and confession—but the goal is to be more clever than the others and to come up with an unanswerable retort (see, e.g., Mitchell-Kernan 1972; Rickford and Rickford 2000; Smitherman 1977). In polite conversation in China the goal is to keep offering opportunities for the other's elevation. Social psychologists Gao, Ting-Toomey, and Gudykunst call this "listening-centeredness" (1996, 285).

In Europe and America, there is a significant tradition of rejecting society's expectations as false. The Calvinists, for instance, valued plain speaking, speaking one's mind even to the highest figures (as long as one was assured of one's divine authority). Social expectations were insignificant in contrast to the mandate to give witness to godly truths. For them, social expectations were the quintessential false promises that led people astray from the stark truths of their religion. Quakers regarded politeness phenomena, including greetings, salutations, titles, and honorific pronouns as lies and refused to use them (Bauman 1983, 43, 46).

In his much-cited book *Sincerity and Authenticity*, Lionel Trilling (1972) defines sincerity as "a congruence between avowal and actual feeling" (2). Sincerity rose in importance with the rise of theatricality and social roles in Western Europe over the past 400 years; it became desirable to know the difference between a person's role and her or his self. Sincerity includes "telling the offensive truth to those who [have] no wish to hear it" (Trilling 1972, 22).

In contrast to sincerity, authenticity is a matter of genuineness, unalienated original self. The theatrical nature of human behavior, as portrayed by Shakespeare (Greenblatt 1980) and Goffman, among many others, suggests a role-playing aspect of human life that does not necessarily reveal a unitary, single essence (see also Geertz 1966; Keeler 1987; Mauss 1938). In societies such as Bali and Java, we find a notion of the person that is in essence determined by a person's place within the social order. Roles, which changed over a person's lifetime and are often indexed by names, are visible through the use of masks. Societies with these imperatives, such as ancient Rome or the Pueblo groups in southwestern Native America, regard masks not as hiding a person's real identity but rather as providing the necessary identity for the occasion. People do not say what is in their heart, but recite the appropriate lines. In the West this would be considered "just going through the motions" in contrast to a more genuine expression of our spontaneously produced feelings (which come out in words).[6]

Authenticity does not appear much in Chinese discussions except in the sense of the real, *zhen*. (This is the word used to discuss truthfulness; it has also become a coded word for the illegal religious group Falun Gong.)[7] As Trilling points out, however, this value is a fairly new one even in Western aesthetics; why not value the playful and obviously fake? Preservation of genuinely old architecture, display of only original art works, sale of only old pots (see Feng 1994)—all these are obviously desirable to Westerners and genuinely perplexing to Chinese.

"Authenticity" in historic representations such as the New Salem Historic Site in Illinois where Abraham Lincoln lived from 1831 to 1837, according to Bruner, has four meanings: verisimilitude, genuineness, originality, and authority (1994, 401). Considerations include the experience of visitors (tourists) to the site as well as the behind-the-scenes discussions about how best to represent the genuine experience of the 1830s to people living in the 1990s.

Like "truth," "authenticity" as a commodity is a powerful marketing device. For example, the Abercrombie and Fitch website portrays "authentic quality gear," slightly rumpled and preworn, to contrast with the new, shiny, polished clothing that other manufacturers offer. The idea is that concern with surface and appearance is inauthentic, other-directed, whereas wearing such consciously unself-conscious simple clothing demonstrates purity of purpose and genuine reflection of the person's inner nature. Of course in today's America, that is demonstrated through the purchase of expensive clothing that has been manufactured to look old.

Trilling saw the best literature as expressing truth, antithetical to politeness. "The literature to which we give our admiration and gratitude fulfills its function exactly by rending the false veil of politeness" (1972, 61). This literature sees politeness as neither welcome nor always possible. A strong antisocial view privileging authenticity, free of the entanglements of social relations and roles, may be seen in *Walden* or *Catcher in the Rye*.

Trilling argues that "we" in the twentieth century[8] are most concerned about those who deceive themselves, in contrast, say, to Shakespeare's time when people were most interested in those who deceived others. "The hyp-ocrite-villain, the conscious dissembler, has become marginal, even alien, to the modern imagination of the moral life. The situation in which a person systematically misrepresents himself in order to practise upon the good faith of another does not readily command our interest, scarcely our credence. The deception we best understand and most willingly give our attention to is that which a person works upon himself" (Trilling 1972, 16).[9] Thus self-delusion is the grave danger.

At all times and in all places we might observe the obligations that pull between being true to ourselves and pleasing others, between speaking plainly and speaking politically, between the solitary honest individual and the nested member of society, between the id and the ego. While Trilling, in some ways giving voice to European views, sees opposition between polite-ness, authenticity, and sincerity, in China's elite circles, by contrast, polite-ness is a requisite of sincerity.

Sincerity is a much-valued trait among familiars in China. For millennia, writers have discussed *cheng* (sometimes translated "integrity" or "trustwor-thiness" [interchangeable with *xin*], represented in writing with a speech rad-ical and a phonetic element pronounced *cheng*). Traditional Chinese ety-mology analyzes the word *cheng* as including a component of the phonetic element's meaning, which is "completeness." The meaning appears to have changed; in the *Shuowen jiezi*, an etymological dictionary from around 100 CE, the meaning is given as "trustworthy, *xin*, from *yan* [words]" (Xu 100, 92). In turn, *xin* is glossed as "when there is nothing untrustworthy about a per-son's words" (92).[10] According to Chen Chun, a thirteenth-century scholar-official, "[p]erfect *cheng* means being real and true to the highest degree with-out the slightest deficiency. Only a sage can measure up to this. How can it be easily expected of ordinary people?" (quoted in Chan 1986, 97).

The sincerity that is valued as *cheng* in China requires training, fore-thought, and consideration of the context of expression. It includes a kind of humility and knowing about one's social position; of course one could not ut-ter the same words at home and on the street. Only the most simple-minded could do that.

In everyday contemporary contexts, *cheng* ('sincerity') and *chengshi* (also 'sincere') signify not necessarily honesty and truthfulness, but rather a moral stance that suggests willingness to be taught by the appropriate authorities, and a kind of humility, a stance toward one's expected role. It can mean a sense of reasonableness, purity, loyalty, respectfulness, selflessness. It can mean *sounding* sincere and heartfelt—which is not to say the performance has to belie a match with real thoughts and feelings, nor does it require such a match. What is crucial is the performance; a match with internal states is incidental. (*Performance counts.*)

Intention is irrelevant in judging the value of speech in some societies (Du Bois 1992 in Africa; Duranti 1988, 1993 on Samoa; Fajans 1985 on Baining; and Paul 1995 on Sherpa). In some societies a focus on others' intention is non-existent; in some societies there are great sanctions against considering another person's intention. Michelle Rosaldo showed how this was the case for the Ilongot in the Philippines: "Concerned less with 'motivation' than with action, Ilongots are interested in feelings because affective life has consequences for health, cooperation, daily labor, and political debate" (1980, 43). Robert Paul (1995, 17–21) describes Sherpa (Nepal) society and the knowledge drawn upon to explain others' actions: Peasants have substantial common knowledge of each other's lives and contexts, which they draw on to explain what others are doing for what purpose, on most occasions. It is unnecessary and undesirable to infer others' intentions, but their goals may be guessed—not as idiosyncratic but as would apply to anyone with such a personality in such circumstances. Focus on individual self is irrelevant.

Ontology of Language

This book illustrates that language *does* things. Some societies view language as standing apart from other behavior, but others do not. Language, by its very nature, as it has evolved, can be independent of reality. This provides dangers and opportunities. The theory of mind is thus connected to love, to fiction, and to deception. American ideas of language as sacred, individual, connected to reality, and moral stem from the Puritans, who saw language as "pure," unadorned, sincere. Many ideas about truth and lying—even in psychology—rely on this referential view. A more widespread view cross-culturally is pragmatic. Language is contextual, focused on consequences, unified with other aspects of behavior.

Whenever we speak we are simultaneously using semantic and pragmatic aspects of language (just as we are simultaneously chemical and biological), but the values of different societies focus sometimes on one and sometimes on another. The dominant moral aspects of language can be analyzed for every society. At root all humans share the same predicament—we can deceive and lie just as the accompaniment of our sophisticated minds and our recognition of other minds—but we have different evaluations of that predicament.

This appendix and this book present some ways to think about truth and lying, using both scholars' ideas and ordinary people's actions and words, in China and elsewhere. The differences among them demonstrate the range of human possibility. The similarities show the ways we are all connected. We can celebrate both aspects; all I ask is that we do so honestly.

Notes

1. Many of these preoccupations are unique to "Western" notions of language, some arguing that this in turn stems from the structure of Western languages (Benveniste 1971 [1958]; Hansen 1983), especially its grammatical features such as articles, obligatory plurals, and relatively isolating grammar (compared to the polysynthetic grammar of, say, many Native American languages such as Mohawk [Bonvillain 2000, 254–56]).

2. Some of this work derives from his well-known if overinterpreted study of facial expressions, inspired by Darwin's questions about the continuity or discontinuity between non-human and human facial expressions (Ekman 1973). Ekman studied the interpretation of emotion from facial expression in Papua New Guinea as a way of avoiding the obvious possibility that shared interpretation comes from shared causes. Still, this work is methodologically suspect, using actors and translating from English to Tok Pisin. There are seven facial expressions that Ekman believed to be basic, which means that they occur universally with essentially the same meaning. (Ekman acknowledges in his 1993 book that the existence of basic emotions is far from settled.)

3. Psychology inevitably locates emotion within individuals; some anthropologists and sociologists might be more likely to locate it between individuals, as a co-created atmosphere. Thus, the questions of any particular emotion being genuine or not smuggles in assumptions, especially that of methodological individualism.

4. At Notre Dame, a large component of the Catholic mission is that of social justice. The Joan B. Kroc Institute for International Peace Studies brings fellows to campus each year to write, think, and talk about how to bring about greater peace in a war-filled world. At a campus lecture on November 6, 2002, anthropologist E. Valentine Daniel spoke of violence in Sri Lanka. During the question-and-answer period following the talk, one of the Kroc fellows asked about the possibility of a Truth and Reconciliation Commission in Sri Lanka now that there is a truce between the two parties that had fought one another for two decades. He dismissed this as "too Christian." A set of rituals, on the other hand, might have some effect. As in China, mere statement and belief, even of seriously benevolent intention, is insufficient; action is what is required.

5. Much has been made of the language-trained gorilla Koko's lying and humor, though there has also been controversy about methods used to identify these acts (Miles 1986, 251).

6. The concept of "role" has been central at various times in anthropology and sociology, especially in Great Britain, often indicating a kind of nexus of expectation, a node in an intersecting set of grids. Cohen (1994) challenges this idea, while Bock (1999, 299–32) discusses its recent eclipse in favor of "self." See also Banton 1965 on roles.

7. Americans who study ethnic minorities often feel that the tourist sites, theme parks, and song-and-dance performances are inauthentic (but see Rees 2000).

8. From an informal study of twenty-first-century values in the United States, one overriding popular cultural ethos—as on television—is to mock authenticity. A postmodern flippancy sees clinging to singularity as quaint; fluidity is the mark of the cool. A new generation in China is playing with this as well. See Blum n.d.; Wang 2000; Wei 2001; Moore on *ku* ('cool') in China (in press).

9. There is a large literature on self-deception supporting Trilling's point. It also bolsters mine, since it presupposes knowing not only what "self" and "deception" are, but that one can discern honesty and deception. A few examples include Ames and Dissanayake 1996; Demos 1960; and Fingarette 1969.

10. The literature of so-called "Neo-Confucianism" is very much concerned with the matter of "sincerity" or "integrity," but this kind of philosophical examination takes us far from the topic. For some examples, see de Bary 1991; de Bary & Bloom 1979.

References

Abrahams, Roger D. 1983. *The Man-of-Words in the West Indies: Performance and the Emergence of Creole Culture.* Baltimore: The Johns Hopkins University Press.

Agar, Michael. 1994. *Language Shock: Understanding the Culture of Conversation.* New York: William Morrow.

Alai. 2002. *Red Poppies.* Translated by Howard Goldblatt and Sylvia Li-chun Lin. Boston: Houghton Mifflin.

Altman, Lawrence K., and Keith Bradsher. 2003. China Bars W.H.O. Experts From Origin Site of Illness [electronic document]. *New York Times*, March 26 [cited March 26, 2003]. Available from www.nytimes.com.

Ames, Roger T., and Wimal Dissanayake, eds. 1996. *Self and Deception: A Cross-Cultural Philosophical Enquiry.* Albany: State University of New York Press.

Amnesty International. 2002. Deadly Web—China's Internet Users at Risk of Arbitrary Detention, Torture and Execution [electronic document]. November 26 [cited March 18, 2003]. Available from http://www.amnestyusa.org/news/2002/china11262002.html.

Amsel, Nachum. 1994. *The Jewish Encyclopedia of Moral and Ethical Issues.* Northvale, N.J.: Jason Aronson.

An, Yanming. 1997. The Idea of *Cheng* (Integrity): Its Formation in the History of Chinese Philosophy. Ph.D. dissertation, Department of Asian Languages and Cultures: Chinese, University of Michigan, Ann Arbor.

Anagnost, Ann. 1997. *National Past-Times: Narrative, Representation, and Power in Modern China.* Durham, N.C.: Duke University Press.

Anderson, Duncan Maxwell. 1994. The Art of Business War: From China, Principles of Strategy and Deception for Entrepreneurs. *Success*, March: 46–51.

Apter, David E., and Tony Saich. 1994. *Revolutionary Discourse in Mao's Republic.* Cambridge, Mass.: Harvard University Press.

Augustine. 1952a. Against Lying. Translated by Harold B. Jaffee. In *Saint Augustine: Treatises on Various Subjects,* edited by Roy J. Deferrari, pp. 111–79. New York: Fathers of the Church.

———. 1952b. Lying. Translated by Mary Sarah Muldowney, SSJ. In *Saint Augustine: Treatises on Various Subjects,* edited by Roy J. Deferrari, pp. 45–110. New York: Fathers of the Church.

Austin, J. L. 1975 [1962]. *How to Do Things With Words.* 2d ed. Cambridge, Mass.: Harvard University Press.

Bachnik, Jane M., and Charles J. Quinn, Jr., eds. 1994. *Situated Meaning: Inside and Outside in Japanese Self, Society, and Language.* Princeton, N.J.: Princeton University Press.

Bai Hua. 1994 [1988]. *The Remote Country of Women.* Translated by Qingyun Wu and Thomas O. Beebee. Honolulu: University of Hawai`i Press.

Bailey, F. G. 1991. *The Prevalence of Deceit.* Ithaca, N.Y., and London: Cornell University Press.

Bakhurst, David. 1992. On Lying and Deceiving. *Journal of Medical Ethics* 18: 63-66.

Banton, Michael P. 1965. *Roles: An Introduction to the Study of Social Relations.* New York: Basic Books.

Barnes, J. A. 1994. *A Pack of Lies: Towards a Sociology of Lying.* Cambridge: Cambridge University Press.

Baron-Cohen, Simon. 1995. *Mindblindness: An Essay on Autism and Theory of Mind.* Cambridge, Mass.: MIT Press.

Barwise, Jon, and John Etchemendy. 1987. *The Liar: An Essay on Truth and Circularity.* New York: Oxford University Press.

Basso, Ellen B. 1987. *In Favor of Deceit: A Study of Tricksters in an Amazonian Society.* Tucson: University of Arizona Press.

Bateson, Gregory. 1972. *Steps to an Ecology of Mind.* New York: Ballantine.

Bauman, Richard. 1983. *Let Your Words be Few: Symbolism of Speaking and Silence Among Seventeenth-Century Quakers.* Cambridge: Cambridge University Press.

———. 1996. "Any Man Who Keeps More'n One Hound'll Lie to You": A Contextual Study of Expressive Lying. In *The Matrix of Language: Contemporary Linguistic Anthropology,* edited by Donald Brenneis and Ronald H. S. Macaulay, pp. 160–81. Boulder, Colo.: Westview Press.

Becker, Jasper. 1996. *Hungry Ghosts: Mao's Secret Famine.* New York: Free Press.

Befu, Harumi. 1986 [1974]. An Ethnography of Dinner Entertainment in Japan. In *Japanese Culture and Behavior,* edited by Takie Sugiyama Lebra and William P. Lebra, pp. 108–20. Honolulu: University of Hawai`i Press.

Beijing Review. 2006. Growing Income Disparity. Vol. 49 Issue 21 (May 25): 7.

Benveniste, Emile. 1971 [1958]. Categories of Thought and Language. In *Problems in General Linguistics,* pp. 55–64. Coral Gables, Fla.: University of Miami Press.

Berkun, Lauren Eichler. 2002. Parasha Commentary: Toledot 5763, Genesis 25:19–28:9. November 9, 2002 4 Kislev 5763 [E-mail list]. Jewish Theological Seminary [cited November 9, 2002].

Bernstein, Thomas P. 1977. *Up to the Mountains and Down to the Villages: The Transfer of Youth from Urban to Rural China*. New Haven, Conn., and London: Yale University Press.

Best, Joel. 2001. *Damned Lies and Statistics: Untangling Numbers from the Media, Politicians, and Activists*. Berkeley and Los Angeles: University of California Press.

Bickerton, Derek. 1990. *Language and Species*. Chicago: University of Chicago Press.

Bloodworth, Dennis, and Ching Ping Bloodworth. 1976. *The Chinese Machiavelli: 3,000 Years of Chinese Statecraft*. New York: Farrar, Straus and Giroux.

Blum, Susan D. 1986. Of Metaphor and Motion: The Theme of Kinesis in *Chuang Tzu*. M.A. Thesis. The University of Michigan, Ann Arbor, Department of Asian Languages and Cultures.

———. 1997. Naming Practices and the Power of Words in China. *Language in Society* 26 (3): 357–79.

———. 2000. China's Many Faces: Ethnic, Cultural, and Religious Pluralism. In *China Beyond the Headlines*, edited by Timothy B. Weston and Lionel M. Jensen, pp. 69–95. Lanham, Md.: Rowman & Littlefield.

———. 2001. *Portraits of "Primitives": Ordering Human Kinds in the Chinese Nation*. Lanham, Md.: Rowman & Littlefield.

———. 2005. Five Approaches to Explaining "Truth" and "Deception" in Human Communication. *Journal of Anthropological Research* 61 (3). Autumn: 289–315.

———. n.d. Plagiarism, Intentionality, and the Performance Self: Undergraduates Writing in the Academy. Unpublished manuscript.

Blum, Susan D., and Lionel M. Jensen, eds. 2002. *China Off Center: Mapping the Margins of the Middle Kingdom*. Honolulu: University of Hawai`i Press.

Bock, Philip K. 1999. *Rethinking Psychological Anthropology: Continuity and Change in the Study of Human Action*. 2d ed. Prospect Heights, Ill.: Waveland Press.

Bok, Sissela. 1979. *Lying: Moral Choice in Public and Private Life*. New York: Pantheon Books.

Bonvillain, Nancy. 2000. *Language, Culture, and Communication: The Meaning of Messages*. 3d ed. Upper Saddle River, N.J.: Prentice Hall.

Bower, Anne R. 1998. The Sincere Self in the African-American Christian Prayer Tradition. Paper presented at the annual meeting of the American Anthropological Association. Philadelphia.

Bowyer, J. Barton. 1982. *Cheating: Deception in War & Magic, Games & Sports, Sex & Religion, Business & Con Games, Politics & Espionage, Art & Science*. New York: St. Martin's Press.

Briggs, Charles L. 1986. *Learning How to Ask: A Sociolinguistic Appraisal of the Role of the Interview in Social Science Research*. Cambridge: Cambridge University Press.

Bright, William. 1993. *A Coyote Reader*. Berkeley and Los Angeles: University of California Press.

Brown, Joshua Samuel. 2003. *Disdain and Doubt over Shock and Awe* [electronic document]. H-ASIA list for Asian History and Culture, March 22 [cited March 24, 2003].

Brown, Penelope, and Stephen C. Levinson. 1978. Universals in Language Usage: Politeness Phenomena. In *Questions and Politeness: Strategies in Social Interaction*, edited by Esther N. Goody, pp. 56–311. Cambridge: Cambridge University Press.

Brown, Roger, and Albert Gilman. 1960. The Pronouns of Power and Solidarity. In *Style in Language*, edited by Thomas A. Sebeok, pp. 253–76. Cambridge, Mass.: MIT Press.

Bruner, Edward M. 1994. Abraham Lincoln as Authentic Reproduction: A Critique of Postmodernism. *American Anthropologist* 96 (2): 397–415.

Bugental, Daphne Blunt, Hal Kopeikin, and Linda Lazowski. 1991. Children's Responses to Authentic Versus Polite Smiles. In *Children's Interpersonal Trust: Sensitivity to Lying, Deception, and Promise Violations*, edited by Ken J. Rotenberg, pp. 58–79. New York: Springer-Verlag.

Byrne, Richard, and Andrew Whiten, eds. 1988. *Machiavellian Intelligence: Social Expertise and the Evolution of Intellect in Monkeys, Apes, and Humans*. Oxford: Clarendon Press.

Callahan, David. 2004. *The Cheating Culture: Why More Americans are Doing Wrong to Get Ahead*. San Diego: Harcourt.

Campbell, Jeremy. 2001. *The Liar's Tale: A History of Falsehood*. New York: W.W. Norton.

Cao Zhengyan and Ma Wanli. 1988. *Pianzi Xianxingji: Wuhua Bamen de Pianju Jiemi [Contemporary swindlers: Uncovering the secrets of all sorts of hoaxes]*. Shenyang: Zhongguo zhengfa daxue chubanshe.

Ceci, Stephen J., and Michelle DeSimone Leichtman. 1992. "I Know That You Know That I Know That You Broke the Toy": A Brief Report of Recursive Awareness Among 3-Year-Olds. In *Cognitive and Social Factors in Early Deception*, edited by Michelle DeSimone Leichtman, Stephen J. Ceci, and Maribeth Putnick, pp. 1–10. Hillsdale, N.J.: Lawrence Erlbaum.

Central News Agency. 2003. Widespread Corruption among Chinese Officials. [electronic document] September 1 [cited February 7, 2006]. Available from www.falunnews.org.il/ch_ec/cna_001-2.shtml.

Chai, Winston. 2003. China: Catching Crooks with Phone Spam [electronic document]. March 24 [cited March 24, 2003] CNETAsia.

Chan, Wing-tsit, trans. and ed. 1986. *Neo-Confucian Terms Explained (The Pei-hsitzu-i) by Ch'en Chun, 1159–1223*. New York: Columbia University Press.

Chan-Kuo Ts'e [Zhan'guo Ce]. 1970. Translated by J. I. Crump, Jr. Oxford: Clarendon Press.

Chandler, Michael, and Suzanne Hala. 1991. Trust and Children's Developing Theories of Mind. In *Children's Interpersonal Trust: Sensitivity to Lying, Deception, and*

Promise Violations, edited by Ken J. Rotenberg, pp. 135–59. New York and Berlin: Springer-Verlag.

Chang, Chung-yuan. 1969. *Original Teachings of Ch'an Buddhism*. New York: Vintage.

Chang, Jung. 1991. *Wild Swans: Three Daughters of China*. New York: Simon and Schuster.

Chen Kaige, dir. 1984. *Yellow Earth* (film).

Chen, Xing, Lei Ye, and Yanyin Zhang. 1995. Refusing in Chinese. In *Pragmatics of Chinese as Native and Target Language*, edited by Gabriele Kasper. Honolulu: Second Language Teaching and Curriculum Center, University of Hawai`i at Manoa (distributed by University of Hawai`i Press).

Cheney, Dorothy L., and Robert M. Seyfarth. 1990. *How Monkeys See the World: Inside the Mind of Another Species*. Chicago: University of Chicago Press.

Cheng, Nien. 1986. *Life and Death in Shanghai*. New York: Grove Press.

Chevalier-Skolnikoff, Suzanne. 1986. An Exploration of the Ontogeny of Deception in Human Beings and Nonhuman Primates. In *Deception: Perspectives on Human and Nonhuman Deceit*, edited by Robert W. Mitchell and Nicholas S. Thompson, pp. 205–20. Albany: State University of New York Press.

Chu, Chin-ning (Zhu Jinning). 1991. *The Asian Mind Game: Unlocking the Hidden Agenda of the Asian Business Culture—A Westerner's Survival Manual*. New York: Rawson Associates.

———. 1992. *Thick Face Black Heart: The Path to Thriving, Winning, and Succeeding: A Timeless Wisdom—Vital to the 90's*. Beaverton, Ore.: AMC Publishing.

———. 1993. *Meiguo Hou-Hei Xue [The American Art of Thick Face, Black Heart]*. Beijing: Zhongguo youyi chuban gongsi.

Chu, Godwin C. 1977. *Radical Change through Communication in Mao's China*. Honolulu: University of Hawai`i Press.

Clifford, James, and George E. Marcus, eds. 1986. *Writing Culture: The Poetics and Politics of Ethnography*. Berkeley and Los Angeles: University of California Press.

Cohen, Adam. 2003. Editorial Observer; The McNugget of Truth in the Lawsuits Against Fast-Food Restaurants. *New York Times*, February 3, p. A24.

Cohen, Anthony P. 1994. *Self Consciousness: An Alternative Anthropology of Identity*. London: Routledge.

Cohen, Monique. 2002. Genuine or Fake? In *Dunhuang Manuscript Forgeries*, edited by Susan Whitfield, pp. 22–32. London: British Library.

Coleman, Linda, and Paul Kay. 1981. Prototype Semantics: The English Word "Lie." *Language* 57: 26–44.

Conover, Ted. 2006. Capitalist Roaders. *New York Times Magazine*. July 2.

Crews, Frederick C. 1995. *The Memory Wars: Freud's Legacy in Dispute*. New York: New York Review of Books.

Crump, J. I., Jr. 1964. *Intrigues: Studies of the Chan-kuo Ts'e*. Ann Arbor: University of Michigan Press.

Dalla-Vorgia, P., K. Katsouyanni, T. N. Garanis, G. Touloumi, P. Drogari, and A. Koutselinis. 1992. Attitudes of a Mediterranean Population to the Truth-Telling Issue. *Journal of Medical Ethics* 18: 67–74.

Daniel, E. Valentine. 1984. *Fluid Signs: Being a Person the Tamil Way*. Berkeley: University of California Press.

Davis, Steven. 1991. Introduction. In *Pragmatics: A Reader*, edited by Steven Davis, pp. 3–13. New York: Oxford University Press.

de Bary, Wm. Theodore. 1991. *Learning for One's Self: Essays on the Individual in Neo-Confucian Thought*. New York: Columbia University Press.

de Bary, Wm. Theodore, and Irene Bloom, eds. 1979. *Principle and Practicality: Essays in Neo-Confucianism and Practical Learning*. New York: Columbia University Press.

de Waal, Frans. 1986. Deception in the Natural Communication of Chimpanzees. In *Deception: Perspectives on Human and Nonhuman Deceit*, edited by Robert W. Mitchell and Nicholas S. Thompson, pp. 221–44. Albany: State University of New York Press.

Deferrari, Roy J. 1952. Introduction. In *Saint Augustine: Treatises on Various Subjects*, edited by Roy J. Deferrari, pp. 47–50, 113–20. New York: Fathers of the Church.

Demiéville, Paul. 1970. *Récents travaux sur Touen-houang [Dunhuang]; aperçu bibliographique et notes critiques*. Leiden: E.J. Brill.

Demos, Raphael. 1960. On Lying to Oneself. *Journal of Philosophy* 57: 588–95.

Detienne, Marcel, and Jean-Pierre Vernant. 1978 [1974]. *Cunning Intelligence in Greek Culture and Society*. Translated by Janet Lloyd. Sussex: The Harvester Press.

Dickinson, Emily. 1993. Tell all the Truth but tell it slant. In *Dickinson*. Everyman's Library Pocket Poets, p. 18. New York: Alfred A. Knopf.

Dobson, W. A. C. H. 1968. Some Legal Instruments of Ancient China: The Ming and the Meng. In *Wen-lin: Studies in the Chinese Humanities*, edited by Chow Tse-tsung, pp. 269–82. Madison: University of Wisconsin Press.

Doi, Takeo. 1985, 1986. *The Anatomy of Self: The Individual Versus Society*. Translated by Mark A. Harbison. Tokyo: Kodansha.

Dowd, Maureen. 2006a. Oprah! How Could Ya? *New York Times*. Jan. 14, p. A31.

———. 2006b. Oprah's Bunk Club. *New York Times*. Jan. 28, p. A27.

Du Bois, John W. 1992. Meaning Without Intention: Lessons From Divination. In *Responsibility and Evidence in Oral Discourse*, edited by Jane H. Hill and Judith T. Irvine, pp. 48–71. Cambridge: Cambridge University Press.

Dunbar, Robin. 1996. *Grooming, Gossip, and the Evolution of Language*. Cambridge, Mass.: Harvard University Press.

Duranti, Alessandro. 1988. Intentions, Language and Social Action in a Samoan Context. *Journal of Pragmatics* 12: 13–33.

———. 1992. Intentions, Self, and Responsibility: An Essay in Samoan Ethnopragmatics. In *Responsibility and Evidence in Oral Discourse*, edited by Jane H. Hill and Judith T. Irvine, pp. 24–47. Cambridge: Cambridge University Press.

———. 1993. Intentionality and Truth: An Ethnographic Critique. *Cultural Anthropology* 8: 214–45.

———. 2001. Universal and Culture-Specific Properties of Greetings. In *Linguistic Anthropology: A Reader*, edited by Alessandro Duranti, pp. 208–38. Malden, Mass.: Blackwell.

Eberhard, Wolfram. 1971 [1965]. Chinese Regional Stereotypes. In *Moral and Social Values of the Chinese: Collected Essays*, pp. 305–17. Taipei: Ch'eng-wen.

Eck, Marcel. 1970 [1965]. *Lies and Truth*. Translated by Bernard Murchland. London: Macmillan.

Eckholm, Erik. 2003a. China Admits Underreporting Its SARS Cases [electronic document]. *New York Times*, April 21 [cited April 21, 2003]. Available from wysiwyg://2/http://www.nytimes.com/2003...1?tntemail1=&pagewanted=print& position=.

———. 2003b. W.H.O. Team Visits Hospital in Beijing to Investigate Disease [electronic document]. *New York Times*, April 13 [cited April 14, 2003]. Available from wysiwyg://26/http://www.nytimes.com/200...CHIN.html?pagewanted=print& position=top.

Ekman, Paul. 1973. *Darwin and Facial Expression: A Century of Research in Review*. New York: Academic Press.

———. 2001. *Telling Lies: Clues to Deceit in the Marketplace, Politics, and Marriage*. 3d ed. New York: W.W. Norton.

Ekman, Paul, with Mary Ann Mason Ekman and Tom Ekman. 1989. *Why Kids Lie: How Parents Can Encourage Truthfulness*. New York: Charles Scribner's Sons.

Ekman, Paul, Wallace V. Friesen, and Maureen O'Sullivan. 1997 [1988]. Smiles When Lying. In *What the Face Reveals: Basic and Applied Studies of Spontaneous Expression Using the Facial Action Coding System (FACS)*, edited by Paul Ekman and Erika L. Rosenberg. New York and Oxford: Oxford University Press.

Ekman, Paul, and Erika L. Rosenberg, eds. 1997. *What the Face Reveals: Basic and Applied Studies of Spontaneous Expression Using the Facial Action Coding System (FACS)*. New York and Oxford: Oxford University Press.

Fajans, Jane. 1985. The Person in Social Context: The Social Character of Baining "Psychology." In *Exploring Pacific Ethnopsychologies*, edited by Geoffrey M. White and John Kirkpatrick, pp. 367–97. Berkeley: University of California Press.

———. 1997. *They Make Themselves: Work and Play Among the Baining of Papua New Guinea*. Chicago: University of Chicago Press.

Farber, Daniel A., and Suzanna Sherry. 1997. *Beyond All Reason: The Radical Assault on Truth in American Law*. New York and Oxford: Oxford University Press.

Farquhar, Michael. 2005. *A Treasury of Deception: Liars, Misleaders, Hoodwinkers, and the Extraordinary True Stories of History's Greatest Hoaxes, Fakes and Frauds*. New York: Penguin.

Feldman, Robert S., James A. Forrest, and Benjamin R. Happ. 2002. Self-Presentation and Verbal Deception: Do Self-Presenters Lie More? *Basic and Applied Social Psychology* 24 (2): 163–70.

Feldman, Robert S., and Pierre Philippot. 1991. Children's Deception Skills and Social Competence. In *Children's Interpersonal Trust: Sensitivity to Lying, Deception, and Promise Violations*, edited by Ken J. Rotenberg, pp. 80–99. New York: Springer-Verlag.

Feng Jicai. 1994. *The Three-Inch Golden Lotus*. Translated by David Wakefield. Honolulu: University of Hawai`i Press.

———. 1996. *Ten Years of Madness: Oral Histories of China's Cultural Revolution*. San Francisco: China Books and Periodicals.

Fields, John A., and Kenneth R. Seddon. 2002. Scientific Detection of Fakes and Forgeries? In *Dunhuang Manuscript Forgeries*, edited by Susan Whitfield, pp. 33–40. London: British Library.

Fingarette, Herbert. 1969. *Self-Deception*. London: Routledge and Kegan Paul.

———. 1972. *Confucius: The Secular as Sacred*. New York: Harper & Row.

Foucault, Michel. 1980 [1977]. Truth and Power. Translated by Colin Gordon, Leo Marshall, John Mepham, and Kate Soper. In *Power/Knowledge: Selected Interviews & Other Writings 1972-1977*, edited by Colin Gordon, pp. 109–133. New York: Pantheon.

Frake, Charles O. 1964. How to Ask for a Drink in Subanun. *American Anthropologist* 66 (6 no. suppl. 3): 127–32.

Franken, Al. 2003. *Lies: And the Lying Liars who Tell Them: A Fair and Balanced Look at the Right*. New York: Dutton.

———. 2005. *The Truth (with Jokes)*. New York: Penguin.

French, Howard W. 2006a. China Covers up Violent Suppression of Village Protest. *New York Times*. June 27, p. A3.

———. 2006b. Chinese Discuss Plan to Tighten Restrictions on Cyberspace. *New York Times*. July 4.

Freud, Sigmund. 1999 [1901]. *The Interpretation of Dreams*. Translated by Joyce Crick. Oxford: Oxford University Press.

Frey, James. 2003. *A Million Little Pieces*. USA: Doubleday.

Gao Fayuan, ed. 1990. *Zhongguo Xinan Shaoshuminzu Daode Yanjiu [Morality among China's southwest nationalities]*. Kunming: Yunnan minzu chubanshe.

Gao, Ge, Stella Ting-Toomey, and William Gudykunst. 1996. Chinese Communication Processes. In *The Handbook of Chinese Psychology*, edited by Michael Harris Bond, pp. 280–93. Hong Kong: Oxford University Press.

Gao Xiaosheng. 1987 [1979]. Li Shunda Builds a House. In *The Broken Betrothal*, translated by Madelyn Ross, pp. 25–57. Beijing: Panda Books.

Gao, Yuan. 1987. *Born Red: A Chronicle of the Cultural Revolution*. Stanford, Calif.: Stanford University Press.

Gediman, Helen K., and Janice S. Lieberman. 1996. *The Many Faces of Deceit: Omissions, Lies, and Disguise in Psychotherapy*. North Vale, N.J.: J. Aronson.

Geertz, Clifford. 1966. Person, Time, and Conduct in Bali. In *The Interpretation of Cultures*, pp. 360–411. New York: Basic Books.

Goffman, Erving. 1981 [1979]. Footing. In *Forms of Talk*, pp. 124–59. Philadelphia: University of Pennsylvania Press.

Gong, Ting. 1994. *The Politics of Corruption in Contemporary China: An Analysis of Policy Outcomes*. Westport, Conn.: Praeger.

Goody, Esther N., ed. 1995. *Social Intelligence and Interaction: Expressions and Implications of the Social Bias in Human Intelligence*. Cambridge: Cambridge University Press.

Goody, Jack. 1997. Industrial Food: Towards the Development of a World Cuisine. In *Food and Culture: A Reader*, edited by Carole Counihan and Penny van Esterik, pp. 338–56. New York and London: Routledge.

Grafton, Anthony. 1990. *Forgers and Critics: Creativity and Duplicity in Western Scholarship*. Princeton, N.J.: Princeton University Press.

Graham, A. C. 1958. *Two Chinese Philosophers: Ch'eng Ming-tao and Ch'eng Yi-ch'uan*. London: Lund Humphries.

———. 1981. *Chuang Tzu: The Seven Inner Chapters and Other Writings from the Book Chuang-tzu*. Translated by A. C. Graham. London: George Allen & Unwin.

Greenblatt, Stephen. 1980. *Renaissance Self-Fashioning: From More to Shakespeare*. Chicago: University of Chicago Press.

Grice, H. P. 1989. *Studies in the Ways of Words*. Cambridge, Mass.: Harvard University Press.

Gu Cheng. 1983 [1980]. One Generation. Translated by William Tay. In *Stubborn Weeds: Popular and Controversial Chinese Literature after the Cultural Revolution*, edited by Perry Link, p. 185. Bloomington: Indiana University Press.

Guangming Ribao. 1978. Special editorial. Shijian shi jianyan zhenli de weiyi biaozhun [Practice is the sole criterion of establishing truth]. May 11, pp. 1–3.

Hansen, Chad. 1983. *Language and Logic in Ancient China*. Ann Arbor: University of Michigan Press.

———. 1992. *A Daoist Theory of Chinese Thought: A Philosophical Interpretation*. New York and Oxford: Oxford University Press.

Harrell, Stevan. 2001. *Ways of Being Ethnic in Southwest China*. Seattle: University of Washington Press.

Hauptman, Robert. 2002. Dishonesty in the Academy. *Academe* (November–December): 39–44.

Heath, Shirley Brice. 1983. *Ways With Words: Language, Life, and Work in Communities and Classrooms*. Cambridge: Cambridge University Press.

Henricks, Robert G. 2000. *Lao Tzu's Tao Te Ching: A Translation of the Startling New Documents Found at Guodian*. New York: Columbia University Press.

———, trans. 1989. *Lao-tzu Te-Tao Ching: A New Translation Based on the Recently Discovered Ma-wang-tui Texts*. New York: Ballantine Books.

Heschel, Abraham Joshua. 1973. *A Passion for Truth*. New York: Farrar Straus and Giroux.

Hill, George Roy, dir. 1973. *The Sting* (film).

Hinton, William. 1966. *Fanshen: A Documentary of Revolution in a Chinese Village*. New York: Vintage.

Hochschild, Arlie Russell. 1983. *The Managed Heart: Commercialization of Human Feeling*. Berkeley: University of California Press.

Hockett, Charles. 1960. The Origin of Speech. *Scientific American* 203 (3): 88–96.

———. 1966. The Problem of Universals in Language. In *Universals of Language*. 2d ed., edited by Joseph H. Greenberg, pp. 1–29. Cambridge, Mass.: MIT Press.

Holmes, Janet. 1998. Complimenting—A Positive Politeness Strategy. In *Language and Gender: A Reader*, edited by Jennifer Coates, pp. 100–120. Oxford: Blackwell.

Hope, Tony. 1995. Deception and Lying. *Journal of Medical Ethics* 21: 67–68.

Huff, Darrell. 1954. *How to Lie with Statistics*. New York: Norton.

Hyde, Lewis. 1998. *Trickster Makes this World: Mischief, Myth, and Art*. New York: North Point Press.

Ibn Khaldun. 1967 [1377]. *The Muqaddimah: An Introduction to History*. Translated by Franz Rosenthal. Princeton, N.J.: Bollingen Series, Princeton University Press.

Irvine, Judith T. 1996. Shadow Conversations: The Indeterminacy of Participant Roles. In *Natural Histories of Discourse*, edited by Michael Silverstein and Greg Urban, pp. 131–59. Chicago: University of Chicago Press.

Jackson, Jennifer. 1991. Telling the Truth. *Journal of Medical Ethics* 17: 5–9.

Jen-Siu, Michael. 2003. Relief and Anger after Officials Finally Come Clean on Real Figures [electronic document]. *South China Morning Post*, April 21 [cited April 21, 2003]. Available from wysiwyg://13/http://china.scmp.com/cgi-...agename=SCMP/ Printacopy &aid=ZZZKYQ45PEI.

Jensen, Lionel M. 1997. *Manufacturing Confucianism: Chinese Traditions and Universal Civilization*. Durham, N.C.: Duke University Press.

Johnson, Samuel. 1969 [1751]. *Works of Samuel Johnson*, edited by W. J. Bate and Albrecht B. Strauss. Vol. 5.

Kahn, Joseph. 2003. Mystery Illness on Wane in City of Outbreak, Chinese Say [electronic document]. *New York Times*, April 8 [cited April 14, 2003]. Available from wysiwyg://42/http://www.nytimes.com/200...HINA.html?pagewanted=print&position=top.

———. 2006a. Beijing Official Says Curbs Apply to Foreign Journalists. *New York Times*. July 4.

———. 2006b. China May Fine News Media to Limit Coverage. *New York Times*. June 27, p. A3.

———. 2006c. A Sharp Debate Erupts in China over Ideologies. *New York Times*. March 12.

Kakutani, Michiko. 2006. Bending the Truth in a Million Little Ways. *New York Times*. January 17.

Kalathil, Shanthi, and Taylor C. Boas. 2003. *Open Networks, Closed Regimes: The Impact of the Internet on Authoritarian Rule*. Washington, D.C.: Carnegie Endowment for International Peace.

Kaplan, Leonard V. 1995. Intention and Responsibility: The Attenuation of Evil, the Unfairness of Justice. In *Other Intentions: Cultural Contexts and the Attribution of Inner States*, edited by Lawrence Rosen, pp. 119–40. Santa Fe, N.M.: School of American Research.

Karr, Mary. 2006. His So-Called Life. *New York Times*. January 15.

Katriel, Tamar. 1986. *Talking Straight: Dugri Speech in Israeli Sabra Culture*. Cambridge: Cambridge University Press.

Keane, Webb. 1997. From Fetishism to Sincerity: On Agency, the Speaking Subject, and their Historicity in the Context of Religious Conversion. *Comparative Studies in Society and History* 39 (4): 674–93.

———. 2002. Sincerity, "Modernity," and the Protestants. *Cultural Anthropology* 17 (1): 65–92.

Keeler, Ward. 1987. *Javanese Shadow Plays, Javanese Selves*. Princeton, N.J.: Princeton University Press.

Keenan, Elinor Ochs. 1976. On the Universality of Conversational Implicature. *Language in Society* 5 (1): 67–80.

Keightley, David N. 2002. Epistemology in Cultural Context: Disguise and Deception in Early China and Early Greece. In *Early China, Ancient Greece: Thinking Through Comparisons*, edited by Steven Shankman and Stephen Durrant, pp. 119–53. Albany: State University of New York Press.

Kerr, Philip, ed. 1990. *The Penguin Book of Lies: An Anthology*. London: Viking.

Keyes, Ralph. 2004. *The Post-Truth Era: Dishonesty and Deception in Contemporary Life*. New York: St. Martin's.

Kingston, Maxine Hong. 1989. *Tripmaster Monkey: His Fake Book*. New York: Knopf.

Kipnis, Andrew B. 1997. *Producing Guanxi: Sentiment, Self, and Subculture in a North China Village*. Durham, N.C.: Duke University Press.

Kluver, Alan R. 1996. *Legitimating the Chinese Economic Reforms: A Rhetoric of Myth and Orthodoxy*. Albany: State University of New York Press.

Kolker, Andrew, and Louis Alvarez, dirs. 1986. *American Tongues* (film). New York: CNAM.

Kowallis, Jon, trans. 1984. *Wit and Humor from Old Cathay*. Beijing: Panda Books.

Kristoff, Nicholas D. 2006. In China It's ******* vs. Netizens. *New York Times*. June 20.

Kwong, Julia. 1997. *The Political Economy of Corruption in China*. Armonk, N.Y.: M.E. Sharpe.

Laozi. 1989. *Laozi: Dedao Jing: A New Translation Based on the Recently Discovered Mawang-dui Texts*. Translated by Robert G. Henricks. New York: Ballantine Books.

Latham, Kevin. 2000. Nothing But the Truth: News Media, Power and Hegemony in South China. *China Quarterly* (163): 633–54.

Lau, D. C., trans. 1963. *Lao Tzu: Tao Te Ching*. Middlesex: Penguin Books.

Le Roy Ladurie, Emmanuel. 1978. *Montaillou: Cathars and Catholics in a French Village, 1294–1324*. Translated by Barbara Bray. London: Scolar.

Lebra, Takie Sugiyama. 1992. Self in Japanese Culture. In *Japanese Sense of Self*, edited by Nancy R. Rosenberger, pp. 105–20. Cambridge: Cambridge University Press.

Leech, Geoffrey. 1983. *Principles of Pragmatics*. London: Longman.

Lester, Julius, and Jerry Pinkney. 1988. *More Tales of Uncle Remus: Further Adventures of Brer Rabbit, His Friends, Enemies, and Others*. New York: Dial Books.

Levinson, Stephen C. 2001. Maxim. In *Key Terms in Language and Culture*, edited by Alessandro Duranti, pp. 139–42. Malden, Mass.: Blackwell.

Levy, Richard. 2002. Corruption in Popular Culture. In *Popular China: Unofficial Culture in a Globalizing Society*, edited by Richard P. Madsen, Perry Link, and Paul G. Pickowicz. Lanham, Md.: Rowman & Littlefield.

Lewis, Mark Edward. 1990. *Sanctioned Violence in Early China*. Albany: State University of New York Press.

Leys, Simon [Pierre Ryckmans]. 1977 [1974]. *Chinese Shadows*. New York: Viking.

Li Zhisui, with the editorial assistance of Anne F. Thurston. 1994. *The Private Life of Chairman Mao: The Memoirs of Mao's Personal Physician*. Translated by Professor Tai Hung-chao. New York: Random House.

Liang Heng and Judith Shapiro. 1983. *Son of the Revolution*. New York: Knopf.

Lieberman, P. 1984. *The Biology and Evolution of Language*. Cambridge, Mass.: Harvard University Press.

Lieberthal, Kenneth. 1993. The Great Leap Forward and the Split in the Yan'an Leadership 1958–1965. In *The Politics of China 1949–1989*, edited by Roderick MacFarquhar, pp. 87–147. Cambridge: Cambridge University Press.

Lifton, Robert Jay. 1989 [1961]. *Thought Reform and the Psychology of Totalism: A Study of "Brainwashing" in China*. Chapel Hill and London: University of North Carolina Press.

Link, Perry. 1992. *Evening Chats in Beijing: Probing China's Predicament*. New York: Norton.

Lipman, Jonathan N. 1990. Ethnic Violence in Modern China: Hans and Huis in Gansu, 1781–1929. In *Violence in China: Essays in Culture and Counterculture*, edited by Jonathan N. Lipman and Stevan Harrell, pp. 65–86. Albany: State University of New York Press.

Liu Binyan. 1983a [1979]. Listen Carefully to the Voice of the People. Translated by Kyna Rubin and Perry Link. In *People or Monsters? And Other Stories and Reportage from China after Mao*, edited by Perry Link, pp. 1–10. Bloomington: Indiana University Press.

———. 1983b [1981]. Sound Is Better than Silence. Translated by Michael S. Duke. In *People or Monsters? And Other Stories and Reportage from China after Mao*, edited by Perry Link, pp. 98–137. Bloomington: Indiana University Press.

———. 1989. *Tell the World! What Happened in China and Why*. With Ruan Ming and Xu Gang, translated by Henry L. Epstein. New York: Pantheon Books.

———. 1990. *A Higher Kind of Loyalty: A Memoir by China's Foremost Journalist*. Translated by Zhu Hong. New York: Pantheon Books.

Liu Shaoqi. 1964 [1939]. *How to be a Good Communist: Lectures Delivered at the Institute of Marxism-Leninism in Yan'an, July 1939 [Lun Gongchandangyuan de xiuyang]*. Translated by Foreign Languages Press. Beijing: Foreign Languages Press.

Lloyd, Geoffrey, and Nathan Sivin. 2002. *The Way and the Word: Science and Medicine in Early China and Greece*. New Haven, Conn.: Yale University Press.

Lu Xun. 1960 [1921]. The True Story of Ah Q. In *Selected Stories of Lu Hsun*, translated by Yang Xianyi and Gladys Yang, pp. 65–112. Beijing: Foreign Languages Press.

———. 1973 [1925]. On Expressing an Opinion. In *Silent China: Selected Writings of Lu Xun*, edited and translated by Gladys Yang, p. 126. London: Oxford University Press.

Lubman, Stanley B. 1999. *Bird in a Cage: Legal Reform in China After Mao*. Stanford, Calif.: Stanford University Press.

Luo Guanzhong (attrib.) 1991 [14th century]. *Three Kingdoms: A Historical Novel*. Translated by Moss Roberts. Berkeley and Los Angeles: University of California Press.

Lutz, Catherine A. 1988. *Unnatural Emotions: Everyday Sentiments on a Micronesian Atoll and Their Challenge to Western Theory*. Chicago: University of Chicago Press.

Lutz, Catherine A., and Jane L. Collins. 1993. *Reading National Geographic*. Chicago: University of Chicago Press.

Lutz, William. 1989. *Doublespeak: From "Revenue Enhancement" to "Terminal Living": How Government, Business, Advertisers, and Others Use Language to Deceive You*. New York: Harper & Row.

Lynch, Daniel C. 1999. *After the Propaganda State: Media, Politics, and "Thought Work" in Reformed China*. Stanford, Calif.: Stanford University Press.

MacFarquhar, Roderick. 1974. *The Origins of the Cultural Revolution, I: Contradictions Among the People, 1956–1957*. London: Oxford University Press; New York: Columbia University Press; both for Royal Institute of International Affairs.

————. 1983. *The Origins of the Cultural Revolution, II: The Great Leap Forward, 1958–1960*. London: Oxford University Press; New York: Columbia University Press; both for Royal Institute of International Affairs.

————. 1997. *The Origins of the Cultural Revolution, III: The Coming of the Cataclysm, 1961–1966*. London: Oxford University Press; New York: Columbia University Press; both for Royal Institute of International Affairs.

MacFarquhar, Roderick, Timothy Cheek, and Eugene Wu, eds. 1989. *The Secret Speeches of Chairman Mao: From the Hundred Flowers to the Great Leap Forward*. Cambridge, Mass.: Council on East Asian Studies, Harvard University.

Malcolm, Janet. 1984 [1983]. *In the Freud Archives*. New York: Knopf.

Malinowski, Bronislaw. 1923. The Problem of Meaning in Primitive Languages. In *The Meaning of Meaning*, edited by C. K. Ogden and I. A. Richards, pp. 296–336. New York: Harcourt, Brace.

Mangan, Katherine S. 2002. UCLA Heightens Scrutiny of Foreign Applicants. *Chronicle of Higher Education* 49 (5): A58.

Mao Zedong [Mao Tse-tung]. 1967a [1937]. On Practice. In *Selected Readings From the Works of Mao Tse-tung [Mao Zedong]*, edited by Editorial Committee for Selected Readings from the Works of Mao Tse-tung, pp. 54–69. Beijing: Foreign Languages Press.

————. 1967b [1941]. Reform our Study. In *Selected Readings From the Works of Mao Tse-tung [Mao Zedong]*, edited by Editorial Committee for Selected Readings from the Works of Mao Tse-tung, pp. 162–70. Beijing: Foreign Languages Press.

Masson, Jeffrey Moussaieff. 1984. *The Assault on Truth: Freud's Suppression of the Seduction Theory*. New York: Farrar, Straus and Giroux.

Mauss, Marcel. 1938. Une Catégorie de l'esprit humain: la Notion de personne, celle de "Moi." *Journal of the Royal Anthropological Institute*.

Mawby, Ronald, and Robert W. Mitchell. 1986. Feints and Ruses: An Analysis of Deception in Sports. In *Deception: Perspectives on Human and Nonhuman Deceit*, edited by Robert W. Mitchell and Nicholas S. Thompson, pp. 313–22. Albany: State University of New York Press.

McDougall, Bonnie S. 1980. *Mao Zedong's "Talks at the Yan'an Conference on Literature and Art": A Translation of the 1943 Text with Commentary*. Ann Arbor: Center for Chinese Studies, University of Michigan.

Miles, H. Lyn. 1986. How Can I Tell a Lie? Apes, Language, and the Problem of Deception. In *Deception: Perspectives on Human and Nonhuman Deceit*, edited by Robert W. Mitchell and Nicholas S. Thompson, pp. 245–66. Albany: State University of New York Press.

Miller, Gerald R., and James B. Stiff. 1993. *Deceptive Communication*. Newbury Park, Calif.: Sage.

Miller, Lucien, ed. 1994. *South of the Clouds: Tales from Yunnan*. Translated by Guo Xu, Lucien Miller, and Xu Kun. Seattle: University of Washington Press.

Misra, Kalpana. 1998. *From Post-Maoism to Post-Marxism: The Erosion of Official Ideology in Deng's China*. New York and London: Routledge.

Mitchell, Robert W. 1986. A Framework for Discussing Deception. In *Deception: Perspectives on Human and Nonhuman Deceit*, edited by Robert W. Mitchell and Nicholas S. Thompson, pp. 3–40. Albany: State University of New York Press.

Mitchell, Robert W., and Nicholas S. Thompson. 1986a. Deception in Play Between Dogs and People. In *Deception: Perspectives on Human and Nonhuman Deceit*, edited by Robert W. Mitchell and Nicholas S. Thompson, pp. 193–204. Albany: State University of New York Press.

———, eds. 1986b. *Deception: Perspectives on Human and Nonhuman Deceit*. Albany: State University of New York Press.

Mitchell-Kernan, Claudia. 1972. Signifying and Marking: Two Afro-American Speech Acts. In *Directions in Sociolinguistics: The Ethnography of Communication*, edited by John J. Gumperz and Dell Hymes, pp. 161–79. Oxford: Basil Blackwell.

Mondry, Henrietta, and John R. Taylor. 1973. On Lying in Russian. *Language and Communication* 12 (2): 133–43.

Moore, Robert L. In press. Generation "Ku": Individualism and China's Millennial Youth. *Ethnology*.

Mori, Kyoko. 1997. *Polite Lies: On Being a Woman Caught Between Cultures*. New York: Henry Holt & Co.

Mueggler, Erik. 2001. *The Age of Wild Ghosts: Memory, Violence, and Place in Southwest China*. Berkeley and Los Angeles: University of California Press.

Munro, Donald J. 1969. *The Concept of Man in Early China*. Stanford, Calif.: Stanford University Press.

Murphy, Robert F. 1990. *The Body Silent*. New York: Norton.

New York Times. 2002. World Briefing: Asia: China: Finance Official Sentenced [electronic document]. October 10. [cited February 7, 2006]. Available from http://query.nytimes.com/gst/fullpage.html?res=9F00E6D7163AF933A25753C1A 9649C8B63.

New York Times. 2003. Governor Freeing 13 in Drug Case. June 3, p. A22.

New York Times. 2006. Call It Fiction. Editorial. January 13.

Nunberg, Geoffrey. 2003. Computers in Libraries Make Moral Judgments, Selectively. *New York Times,* March 9.

Nyberg, David. 1993. *The Varnished Truth: Truth Telling and Deceiving in Ordinary Life.* Chicago: University of Chicago Press.

Opie, Iona Archibald. 1960. *The Lore and Language of Schoolchildren.* Oxford: Clarendon Press.

Oprah. 2002. Truth: Embracing it, Denying it, Spinning it, and (Brave Move) Telling it Like It Is, and How to Spot a Lie. January.

Oxford English Dictionary. 1989. 2d ed. Oxford: Oxford University Press.

Paul, Robert A. 1995. Act and Intention in Sherpa Culture and Society. In *Other Intentions: Cultural Contexts and the Attribution of Inner States,* edited by Lawrence Rosen, pp. 15–45. Santa Fe, N.M.: School of American Research Press.

Pear, Robert. 2002. Investigators Find Repeated Deception in Ads for Drugs. *New York Times* [electronic document]. December 4 [cited December 4, 2002]. Available from wysiwyg://129/http://www.nytimes.com/20…eadlines=&pagewanted =print&position=top.

People's Daily (China). 2003a. China Holds Press Conference on SARS (Full Text) [electronic document]. *China Daily,* April 21, 2003 [cited April 21, 2003]. Available from http://english.peopledaily.com.cn/200304/21/print20030421_115534 .htm.

———. 2003b. Cover-up of SARS Cases not Found: Official [electronic document]. *People's Daily,* April 20, 2003 [cited April 21, 2003]. Available from http://english.peopledaily.com.cn/200304/21/print20030420_115497.html.

People's Daily Online. 2005a. China's Floating Population Tops 140 Mln [electronic document]. July 27 [cited July 9, 2006]. Available from http://english.people.com .cn/200507/27/eng20050727_198605.html.

———. 2005b. Peng Dehuai [electronic document]. [cited November 29, 2005] Available from http://english.people.com.cn/data/people/pengdehuai.shtml.

Perry, Elizabeth J., and Li Xun. 1999. Revolutionary Rudeness: The Language of Red Guards and Rebel Workers in China's Cultural Revolution [electronic document]. Working papers—Indiana University, 1999 [cited March 25, 1999]. Available from http://www.easc.indiana.edu/Pages/Easc/working_papers/NOFRAME_2a-revol .htm.

Peterson, Candida C. 1991. What is a Lie? Children's Use of Intentions and Consequences in Lexical Definitions and Moral Evaluations of Lying. In *Children's Interpersonal Trust: Sensitivity to Lying, Deception, and Promise Violations,* edited by Ken J. Rotenberg, pp. 5–19. New York: Springer-Verlag.

Pu Songling. 1989. *Strange Tales from Make-Do Studio.* Translated by Denis C. and Victor H. Mair. Beijing: Foreign Languages Press.

Quiatt, Duane. 1984. Devious Intentions of Monkeys and Apes? In *The Meaning of Primate Signals,* edited by Rom Harré and Vernon Reynolds, pp. 9–40. Cambridge: Cambridge University Press.

Rabinow, Paul. 1977. *Reflections on Fieldwork in Morocco.* Berkeley: University of California Press.

Radio Australia News. 2003. China Declares Thousands Guilty of Corruption [electronic document]. *Radio Australia News,* March 12 [cited March 11, 2003]. Available from wysiwyg://1.26/http://abc.net.au/ra/newstories/RANewsStories_804424 .htm.

Rahman Khan, Azizur, and Carl Riskin. 2005. China's Household Income and Its Distribution, 1995 and 2002. *China Quarterly* 182 (June): 356–84.

Raphals, Lisa. 1992. *Knowing Words: Wisdom and Cunning in the Classical Traditions of China and Greece.* Ithaca, N.Y., and London: Cornell University Press.

Rappaport, Roy A. 1976. Liturgies and Lies. *International Yearbook for the Sociology of Knowledge and Religion* 10: 75–104.

Reddy, Michael J. 1993 [1979]. The Conduit Metaphor: A Case of Frame Conflict in Our Language about Language. In *Metaphor and Thought,* edited by Anthony Ortony, pp. 164–201. Cambridge: Cambridge University Press.

Rees, Helen. 2000. *Echoes of History: Naxi Music in Modern China.* Oxford: Oxford University Press.

Rich, Frank. 2006. Truthiness 101: From Frey to Alito. *New York Times.* January 22. Week in Review, p. 16.

Rickett, Allyn and Adele. 1973 [1957]. *Prisoners of Liberation: Four Years in a Chinese Communist Prison.* Garden City, N.Y.: Anchor Doubleday.

Rickford, John Russell, and Russell John Rickford. 2000. *Spoken Soul: The Story of Black English.* New York: John Wiley & Sons.

Roberts, John W. 1989. *From Trickster to Badman: The Black Folk Hero in Slavery and Freedom.* Philadelphia: University of Pennsylvania Press.

Romaine, Suzanne. 2000. *Language in Society: An Introduction to Sociolinguistics.* 2d ed. Oxford: Oxford University Press.

Rosaldo, Michelle Z. 1980. *Knowledge and Passion: Ilongot Notions of Self and Social Life.* Cambridge: Cambridge University Press.

———. 1982. The Things We Do with Words: Ilongot Speech Acts and Speech Act Theory in Philosophy. *Language in Society* 11: 203–37.

———. 1984. Toward an Anthropology of Self and Feeling. In *Culture Theory: Essays on Mind, Self, and Emotion,* edited by Richard A. Shweder and Robert A. LeVine, pp. 137–57. Cambridge: Cambridge University Press.

Rosen, Lawrence, ed. 1995. *Other Intentions: Cultural Contexts and the Attribution of Inner States.* Santa Fe, N.M.: School of American Research Press.

Rosenthal, Elisabeth. 2003a. A Beijing Doctor Questions Data on Illness [electronic document]. *New York Times,* April 10 [cited April 14, 2003]. Available from wysiwyg: //31/http://www.nytimes.com/200...SARS.html?pagewanted=print&position=top.

———. 2003b. Doctors Say China Minimizes Pneumonia Outbreak's Extent [electronic document]. *New York Times,* March 20 [cited March 20, 2003]. Available from http://www.nytimes.com/2003/03/20/international/asia/20CHIN.html.

——— . 2003c. More New Cases Question Beijing's Candor on New Pneumonia [electronic document]. *New York Times*, March 19 [cited March 19, 2003]. Available from http://www.nytimes.com/2003/03/19/international/asia/19CND-CHINA .html.

Ryan, Christopher James, Greg de Moore, and Martyn Patfield. 1995. Becoming None but Tradesmen: Lies, Deception and Psychotic Patients. *Journal of Medical Ethics* 21: 72–76.

Sacks, Harvey. 1975. Everyone has to Lie. In *Sociocultural Dimensions of Language Use*, edited by M. Sanches and B. G. Blount, pp. 57–80. New York: Academic Press.

Sakai, Kazuo, M.D., and Nakana Ide. 1998. *The Art of Lying*. Translated by Sara Aoyama. New York: Red Brick Press.

Sang Ye. 2006. *Candid China: The People on the People's Republic*. Edited by Geremie R. Barmé, with Miriam Lang. Berkeley and Los Angeles: University of California Press.

Sapir, Edward. 1921. *Language: An Introduction to the Study of Speech*. New York and London: Harcourt, Brace, Jovanovich.

Schechter, Danny, dir. 2004. *WMD: Weapons of Mass Deception* (film).

Schieffelin, Bambi B., Kathryn A. Woolard, and Paul V. Kroskrity, eds. 1998. *Language Ideologies: Practice and Theory*. New York and Oxford: Oxford University Press.

Schoenhals, Martin. 1993. *The Paradox of Power in a People's Republic of China Middle School*. Armonk, N.Y.: M.E. Sharpe.

Schoenhals, Michael. 1991. The 1978 Truth Criterion Controversy. *The China Quarterly* 126: 243–69.

——— . 1992. *Doing Things with Words in Chinese Politics: Five Studies*. Berkeley: Institute of East Asian Studies, University of California, Berkeley, Center for Chinese Studies.

——— , ed. 1996. *China's Cultural Revolution, 1966–1969: Not a Dinner Party*. Armonk, N.Y.: M.E. Sharpe.

Schwartz, Benjamin I. 1996. Review of *Knowing Words: Wisdom and Cunning in the Classical Traditions of China* by Lisa Raphals. *Harvard Journal of Asiatic Studies* 56 (1): 227–44.

Scollon, Ron. 1995. Plagiarism and Ideology: Identity in Intercultural Discourse. *Language in Society* 24 (1): 1–28.

——— . 2001. Plagiarism. In *Key Terms in Language and Culture*, edited by Alessandro Duranti, pp. 184–86. Malden, Mass: Blackwell.

Scott, James C. 1985. *Weapons of the Weak: Everyday Forms of Peasant Resistance*. New Haven, Conn.: Yale University Press.

Searle, John. 1969. *Speech Acts: An Essay in the Philosophy of Language*. London: Cambridge University Press.

Seligman, Craig. 2000. Janet Malcolm: In Her Relentless Pursuit of the Truth She's Left a Few Bodies in Her Wake, But Isn't That Part of a Journalist's Job? [electronic document]. Salon.com, February 29 [cited October 18, 2002]. Available from http://cobrand.salon.com/people/bc/2000/02/29/malcolm/print.html.

Sha Yexin, Li Shoucheng, and Yao Mingde. 1983 [1979]. What If I Really Were? [Jiaru wo shi zhende]. Translated by Edward M. Gunn. In *Stubborn Weeds: Popular and Controversial Chinese Literature after the Cultural Revolution*, edited by Perry Link, pp. 198–250. Bloomington: Indiana University Press.

Shadyac, Tom, dir. 1997. *Liar, Liar* (film).

Shapin, Steven. 1994. *A Social History of Truth: Civility and Science in Seventeenth-Century England*. Chicago: University of Chicago Press.

Shen Rong. 1983. *Zhen zhen jia jia [True or false]*. Shanghai: Shanghai wenyi chuban-she. Translated as "Snakes and Ladders—Or Three Days in the Life of a Chinese Intellectual" by Geremie Barmé and Linda Jaivin, in *At Middle Age*, pp. 119–236, Beijing: Panda Books, 1987.

Shi Nai'an, and Luo Guanzhong. 1981 [14th century]. *Shuihu Zhuan [Outlaws of the marsh]*. Translated by Sidney Shapiro. 2 vols. Bloomington: Indiana University Press.

Silverstein, Michael. 1998. The Uses and Utility of Ideology: A Commentary. In *Language Ideologies: Practice and Theory*, edited by Kathryn A. Woolard, Bambi B. Schieffelin, and Paul V. Kroskrity, pp. 123–45. New York and Oxford: Oxford University Press.

Smitherman, Geneva. 1977. *Talkin and Testifyin: The Language of Black America*. Boston: Houghton Mifflin.

———. 1994. *Black Talk: Words and Phrases from the Hood to the Amen Corner*. Boston: Houghton Mifflin.

Solinger, Dorothy J. 1999. *Contesting Citizenship in Urban China: Peasant Migrants, the State, and the Logic of the Market*. Berkeley and Los Angeles: University of California Press.

South China Morning Post. 2001. China and the WTO [electronic document]. Available from http://special.scmp.com/reports/chinajoinswto/bground/ZZZJTHQWJRC .html.

Spence, Jonathan D. 1990. *The Search for Modern China*. New York: Norton.

Spiro, Melford E. 1996. Postmodernist Anthropology, Subjectivity, and Science: A Modernist Critique. *Comparative Studies in Society and History* 38 (4 (October)): 759–80.

Straits Times (Singapore). 2003. Beijing Hospitals "Hid Patients from WHO" [electronic document]. Straits Times Interactive, April 21 [cited April 21, 2003]. Available from http://straitstimes.asia1.com.sg/storyprintfriendly/0,1887,184416,00 .html?

Stranahan, Patricia. 1999. The Politics of Persuasion: Communist Rhetoric and the Revolution [electronic document]. Working Papers—Indiana University, 1999 [cited March 25 1999]. Available from http://www.easc.indiana.edu/Pages/Easc/ working_papers/NOFRAME_4B_POLIT.htm.

Success. 1994. The Art of Deceit: Outsmart the Competition. March.

Sullivan, Evelin. 2001. *The Concise Book of Lying*. New York: Farrar, Straus and Giroux.

Sun-Tzu [Sunzi]. 1993. *The Art of Warfare: The First English Translation Incorporating The Recently Discovered Yin-Ch'ueh-Shan Texts*. Translated by Roger T. Ames. New York: Ballantine Books.

———. 2002. *The Art of War: The Essential Translation of the Classic Book of Life*. Translated by John Minford. New York: Viking.

Sweetser, Eve V. 1987. The Definition of "Lie": An Examination of the Folk Models Underlying a Semantic Prototype. In *Cultural Models in Language and Thought*, edited by Dorothy Holland and Naomi Quinn, pp. 43–66. Cambridge: Cambridge University Press.

Tannen, Deborah. 1981. New York Jewish Conversational Style. *International Journal of the Sociology of Language* 30: 133–49.

———. 1989. *Talking Voices: Repetition, Dialogue, and Imagery in Conversational Discourse*. Cambridge: Cambridge University Press.

Tarski, Alfred. 1944. The Semantic Conception of Truth and the Foundations of Semantics. *Philosophy and Phenomenological Research* 4.

Teasdale, Kevin, and Gerry Kent. 1995. The Use of Deception in Nursing. *Journal of Medical Ethics* 21: 77–81.

Telushkin, Rabbi Joseph. 2000. *The Book of Jewish Values: A Day-by-Day Guide to Ethical Living*. New York: Bell Tower.

Thompson, M. Guy. 1994. *The Truth About Freud's Technique: The Encounter with the Real*. New York: New York University Press.

Time. 1992. Lying: Everybody's Doin' It (Honestly). October 5.

Transparency International. 2003 [electronic document]. Transparency International, 2003 [cited March 18, 2003]. Available from http://www.transparency.org/faqs/faq~corruption.html.

———. 2005. International Corruption Perceptions Index [electronic document]. Transparency International and Goettingen University [cited January 13, 2006]. Available from http://www.transparency.org/policy_and_research/surveys_indices/cpi/2005.

Trilling, Lionel. 1972. *Sincerity and Authenticity*. Cambridge, Mass.: Harvard University Press.

Truth and Reconciliation Commission. 2002. *Concepts and Principles* [electronic document]. Truth and Reconciliation Commission, January 28 [cited September 27, 2002]. Available from http://www.polity.org.za/govdocs/commissions/1998/trc/1chap5.htm.

U.S. Department of State. 2002. *International Information Programs: China* [electronic document]. U.S. Department of State, n.d. [cited December 4, 2002]. Available from http://usinfo.state.gov/regional/ea/uschina/chinahr2k.htm.

Urban, Greg. 1991. *A Discourse-Centered Approach to Culture: Native South American Myths and Rituals*. Austin: University of Texas Press.

Utne Reader. 1992. The Whole Truth about Lying (Trust Us). November/December.

Vasek, Marie E. 1986. Lying as a Skill: The Development of Deception in Children. In *Deception: Perspectives on Human and Nonhuman Deceit*, edited by Robert W. Mitchell and Nicholas S. Thompson, pp. 271–92. Albany: State University of New York Press.

Verstappen, Stefan H. 1999. *The Thirty-Six Strategies of Ancient China*. San Francisco: China Books and Periodicals.

Wald, Jonathan. 2003a. Lawyers Revise Obesity Lawsuit Against McDonald's. *CNN.Com*, February 21.

———. 2003b. McDonald's Obesity Suit Tossed: U.S. Judge Says Complaint Fails to Prove Chain is Responsible for Kids' Weight Gain. *CNNMoney*, February 17.

Walder, Andrew G. 1986. *Communist Neo-Traditionalism: Work and Authority in Chinese Industry*. Berkeley and Los Angeles: University of California Press.

Waley, Arthur. 1939. *Three Ways of Thought in Ancient China*. New York: Doubleday.

———, trans. 1938. *The Analects of Confucius*. New York: Vintage.

Walfish, Daniel. 2001. Chinese Applicants to U.S. Universities Often Resort to Shortcuts or Dishonesty: Students can Buy Essays, Stand-ins for Exams, and Improper Access to Standardized Tests. *Chronicle of Higher Education* (January 5, 2001): A52.

Wang Shuo. 1993. *Wan Zhu*. Hong Kong: Tiandi tushu youxian gongsi.

———. 2000. *Please Don't Call Me Human*. Translated by Howard Goldblatt. New York: Hyperion East.

Wang Youlin et al. 2000. *Dangdai Pian Shu Jing Shilu [Cautions about the contemporary art of swindling]*. Beijing: Zhonghua gongshang lianhe chubanshe.

Watson, Burton, trans. 1963. *Hsün Tzu [Xunzi]: Basic Writings*. New York: Columbia University Press.

Weaver, Paul H. 1994. *News and the Culture of Lying*. New York: The Free Press.

Weems, Mason Locke. 1814 [1806]. *The Life of George Washington: With Curious Anecdotes, Equally Honourable to Himself and Exemplary to his Young Countrymen*. Philadelphia: Mathew Carey.

———. 1918 [1800]. *A History of the Life and Death, Virtues and Exploits of General George Washington: With Curious Anecdotes, Equally Honourable to Himself and Exemplary to his Young Countrymen*. Philadelphia and London: Lippincott.

Wei Hui. 2001 [1999]. *Shanghai Baby*. Translated by Bruce Humes. New York: Pocket Books.

Weiser, Benjamin. 2003. Word for Word/Fast-Food Fracas; Your Honor, We Call Our Next Witness: McFrankenstein. *New York Times*, January 26, p. A5.

Wen, Fong. 1962. The Problem of Forgeries in Chinese Painting. *Artibus Asiae* 15: 95–119.

Weston, Timothy B. 2000. China's Labor Woes: Will the Workers Crash the Party? In *China Beyond the Headlines*, edited by Timothy B. Weston and Lionel M. Jensen, pp. 245–71. Lanham, Md.: Rowman & Littlefield.

Wheeler, David L. 2002. Testing Service Says GRE Scores From China, South Korea, and Taiwan Are Suspect. *Chronicle of Higher Education* (August 16, 2002): A41.

Whiten, Andrew, and Richard W. Byrne, eds. 1997. *Machiavellian Intelligence II: Extensions and Evaluations*. Cambridge: Cambridge University Press.

Whitfield, Susan, and Frances Wood. 1996. *Dunhuang and Turfan: Contents and Conservation of Ancient Documents from Central Asia*. London: British Library.

Whyte, Martin King. 1974. *Small Groups and Political Rituals in China*. Berkeley: University of California Press.

Wierzbicka, Anna. 1996. Contrastive Sociolinguistics and the Theory of "Cultural Scripts": Chinese vs English. In *Contrastive Sociolinguistics*, edited by Marlis Hellinger and Ulrich Ammon, pp. 313–44. Berlin: Mouton de Gruyter.

———. 2003. *Cross-Cultural Pragmatics: The Semantics of Human Interaction*. 2d ed. Berlin and New York: Mouton de Gruyter.

Wills, Garry. 2000. *Papal Sin: Structures of Deceit*. New York: Doubleday.

Witke, Roxane. 1977. *Comrade Chiang Ch'ing*. Boston: Little, Brown.

Woolard, Kathryn, and Bambi B. Schieffelin. 1994. Language Ideology. *Annual Review of Anthropology* 23: 55–82.

Wu, Vivien. 2006. China: Axe Falls on Influential Weekly that Fired Debate [electronic document]. *South China Morning Post*. January 25 [cited February 2, 2006]. Available from http://www.asiamedia.ucla.edu/print.asp?parentid=37799.

Wyatt, Edward. 2006a. Live on "Oprah," a Memoirist Is Kicked Out of the Book Club. *New York Times*. January 27.

———. 2006b. Oprah Calls Defense of Author a Mistake. *New York Times*. January 26.

Xu Shen. 1983. [100 CE] *Shuo-wen Jie-zi [Analysis of Words]*. Duan Yucai, ed. Sibu kanyao ed. Taipei: Hanjing wenhua shiye.

Yan, Yunxiang. 1995. Everyday Power Relations: Changes in a North China Village. In *The Waning of the Communist State: Economic Origins of Political Decline in China and Hungary*, edited by Andrew G. Walder, pp. 215–41. Berkeley and Los Angeles: University of California Press.

———. 1996. *The Flow of Gifts: Reciprocity and Social Networks in a Chinese Village*. Stanford, Calif.: Stanford University Press.

———. 2003. *Private Life Under Socialism: Love, Intimacy, and Family Change in a Chinese Village 1949–1999*. Stanford, Calif.: Stanford University Press.

Yang, Mayfair Mei-hui. 1994. *Gifts, Favors, and Banquets: The Art of Social Relationships in China*. Ithaca, N.Y.: Cornell University Press.

Yaqūb, Aladdin M. 1993. *The Liar Speaks the Truth: A Defense of the Revision Theory of Truth*. New York: Oxford University Press.

Yu Jie. 2005. Who tells the truth? Mourning Mr. Liu Binyan [electronic document]. December 5 [cited December 14, 2005]. Available from http://www.liubinyan.com/lifejourney/condolence/concolence.person/YuJie.htm.

Yue, Daiyun, and Carolyn Wakeman. 1985. *To The Storm: The Odyssey of a Revolutionary Chinese Woman*. Berkeley and Los Angeles: University of California Press.

Zagorin, Perez. 1990. *Ways of Lying: Dissimulation, Persecution, and Conformity in Early Modern Europe*. Cambridge, Mass.: Harvard University Press.

Zhang, Li. 2001. *Strangers in the City: Reconfigurations of Space, Power, and Social Networks within China's Floating Population.* Stanford, Calif.: Stanford University Press.

Zittrain, Jonathan, and Benjamin Edelman. 2002. Empirical Analysis of Internet Filtering in China [electronic document]. Berkman Center for Internet and Society, Harvard Law School, 2002 [cited December 4, 2002]. Available from http://cyber.law.harvard.edu/filtering/china/.

Zornberg, Avivah Gottlieb. 1995. *The Beginning of Desire: Reflections on Genesis.* New York: Doubleday.

Index

About the Author

Susan D. Blum is associate professor of anthropology and director of the Center for Asian Studies at the University of Notre Dame. Her previous books include *Portraits of "Primitives": Ordering Human Kinds in the Chinese Nation* and *China Off Center: Mapping the Margins of the Middle Kingdom* (coedited with Lionel M. Jensen). She has also written articles about ethnicity and nationalism, truth, multilingualism, food, naming practices, and other aspects of contemporary China. Her newest work concerns language, morality, and selfhood among American college students.